Transitional Justice and Memory in Cambodia

Memories of violence, suffering and atrocities in Cambodia are today being pulled in different directions. A range of transitional justice practices have been put to work in the name of redressing, restoring and renewing memory. At the centre of this stage is the Extraordinary Chambers in the Courts of Cambodia (ECCC), a hybrid tribunal established to prosecute the leaders of the Khmer Rouge regime, under which 1.6 million Cambodians died of hunger or disease or were executed.

This book unpicks the way memory is reconstructed through appeals to a national memory, the legal reframing and coding of memories as crimes, and bids to locate personal memories within collective biographies. Analysing the techniques and interventions of the ECCC, as well as exploring the role of non-governmental organisations (NGOs), the book explores the relationships in which Cambodian communities navigate memories of political violence. This book is essential for understanding transitional justice in Cambodia in, and beyond, the courtroom. *Transitional Justice and Memory in Cambodia* shows that the governing logic of transitional justice interventions – that societies are unable to 'deal with' memories of atrocity and violence without some form of transitional justice mechanism – neglects the complexity of memory and remembering in post-atrocity contexts and the agency of the subjects to which such mechanisms are addressed.

Drawing on documentary sources, legal transcripts, interviews and participant observation data, the book situates transitional justice processes in Cambodia within a wider context of social and cultural memory politics, examining (old and new) conflicts of memory that have emerged between the varied accounts and uses of the past that exist in Cambodia now. As such, it will appeal to students and scholars in sociology, human rights, law and criminology.

Peter Manning is Lecturer in Sociology at the University of Bath. Peter has previously lectured in sociology at Liverpool Hope University and at the Centre for the Study of Human Rights at the London School of Economics, where he was awarded a PhD in 2014.

Memory Studies: Global Constellations

Series Editor: Henri Lustiger-Thaler

Ramapo College of New Jersey, USA and Ecole des Hautes Etudes en Sciences Sociales, France.

The 'past in the present' has returned in the early twenty-first century with a vengeance, and with it the expansion of categories of experience. These experiences have largely been lost in the advance of rationalist and constructivist understandings of subjectivity and their collective representations. The cultural stakes around forgetting, 'useful forgetting' and remembering, locally, regionally, nationally and globally, have risen exponentially. It is therefore not unusual that 'migrant memories'; micro-histories; personal and individual memories in their interwoven relation to cultural, political and social narratives; the mnemonic past and present of emotions, embodiment and ritual; and finally, the mnemonic spatiality of geography and territories are receiving more pronounced hearings.

This transpires as the social sciences themselves are consciously globalising their knowledge bases. In addition to the above, the reconstructive logic of memory in the juggernaut of galloping informationalization is rendering it more and more publicly accessible, and therefore part of a new global public constellation around the coding of meaning and experience. Memory studies as an academic field of social and cultural inquiry emerges at a time when global public debate – buttressed by the fragmentation of national narratives – has accelerated. Societies today, in late globalized conditions, are pregnant with newly unmediated and unfrozen memories once sequestered in wide collective representations. We welcome manuscripts that examine and analyze these profound cultural traces

Titles in this series

1. The Slave Ship, Memory and the Origin of Modernity
Martyn Hudson

2. War Memory and Commemoration
Edited by Brad West

3. Memory and Forgetting in the Post-Holocaust Era
The Ethics of Never Again
Alejandro Baer and Natan Sznaider

4. Memory and Genocide
On What Remains and the Possibility of Representation
Edited by Fazil Moradi, Ralph Buchenhorst, and Maria Six-Hohenbalken

5. Transitional Justice and Memory in Cambodia
Beyond the Extraordinary Chambers
Peter Manning

Transitional Justice and Memory in Cambodia

Beyond the Extraordinary Chambers

Peter Manning

Routledge
Taylor & Francis Group
LONDON AND NEW YORK

First published 2017 by Routledge

2 Park Square, Milton Park, Abingdon, Oxfordshire OX14 4RN
52 Vanderbilt Avenue, New York, NY 10017

Routledge is an imprint of the Taylor & Francis Group, an informa business

First issued in paperback 2018

British Library Cataloguing in Publication Data
A catalogue record for this book is available from the British Library

Library of Congress Cataloging in Publication Data
A catalog record for this book has been requested

ISBN: 978-1-4724-5937-4 (hbk)
ISBN: 978-0-367-08548-3 (pbk)

Typeset in Times New Roman
by Deanta Global Publishing Services, Chennai, India

Contents

Acknowledgements

This book is the product of a broad and frankly unhealthy ledger of debts. I owe thanks to the editorial staff at Routledge, Shannon Kneis and Clare Jarvis, for their patience while I worked on the draft of the manuscript, as well as the generous support of Henri Lustiger Thaler, the Global Constellations Series Editor. The book emerged from questions presented in my doctoral research at the Department of Sociology at the London School of Economics and I owe an enormous debt of thanks to Claire Moon, who supervised my thesis. Claire is a courageous and inspiring academic who has mastered the art of asking the most important and difficult questions of human rights and transitional justice. Claire was a patient and constructive advisor but also, more importantly, a hugely supportive and generous friend throughout my years working on the thesis and since.

I owe further thanks to staff and former peers who were at the LSE during my time as a research student. The Department of Sociology helped to fund key periods of early fieldwork. Claire Alexander and Fran Tonkiss offered constructive and positive comments on early arguments that I have developed in the book. I was lucky to work with the late Stan Cohen for a period, whose wisdom I benefitted from enormously. Margo Picken was a valuable source of insight into Cambodian political life, as well as a generous sponsor for key introductions in the field. My peers on the PhD programme helped to develop my research and thinking, but I reserve special gratitude for Javier Trevino Rangel for his support, humour and insights. I also owe a substantial debt of thanks for the generous input, advice and encouragement of Kirsten Ainley at LSE and Phil Clark at SOAS, who examined the thesis.

I wrote early drafts of the book while lecturing at Liverpool Hope University, and I benefited from the friendship and support of colleagues in the Department of Social Science who helped me to carve out time for writing and research. Emily Hart, Ian Mahoney and George Mair deserve special mentions and great thanks.

Within Cambodia, I am indebted to the help and support of friends and colleagues that are too many to list here. I owe thanks to Yout, who was a brilliant ad hoc interpreter. I am especially thankful to the staff who worked at the Center for Social Development during fieldwork in 2008 and 2009. Theary Seng, Im Sophea and Yim Sotheary all helped to support my research at key points, especially around the public forum initiatives. I owe special thanks to Sok Leang, Om Chariya and Keo Duong, who have all helped to shape my thinking and approach over subsequent years.

I owe special thanks to Dan Kilburn, who remains a source of inspiration and a great friend.

This book would not have been possible without the love and support of my family. I owe an enormous debt of thanks to my brothers, Dan and Michael, and especially to my parents, Paul and Winnie, who are tirelessly patient and generous. Lastly, I must offer thanks that invariably cannot do justice to the love, wit, and support of Amanda and Dahlia, who, together, make everything worthwhile.

1 Introduction

This book is concerned with the different relationships that Cambodian communities are invited into with memories of political violence under the aegis of transitional justice and beyond. It has been nearly 4 decades since the Khmer Rouge were in power in Cambodia, when, in 3 years, 8 months and 20 days between 1975 and 1979, 1.6 million people died from hunger or disease or were executed (Kiernan 2001). Today, the Extraordinary Chambers in the Courts of Cambodia (ECCC) are working to prosecute "senior leaders" and "those most responsible" for the crimes perpetrated during the 'Democratic Kampuchea' regime.[1] The ECCC, commonly also referred to as the Khmer Rouge Tribunal or Khmer Rouge Trials, is tasked with the challenge of redressing one of the most serious episodes of political violence of the twentieth century. Moreover, while the ECCC has been a palimpsest onto which different (often nebulously framed) aims have been authored over its 10 years of work – ranging from justice, truth, reconciliation and deterrence to enhancing the rule of law and challenging impunity – the ECCC has been situated as *the* key site that today lays claim over memories of past political violence in Cambodia, promising to "set the record straight" and inaugurate a process of "moving forward through justice."[2]

The ECCC is a unique institution within the wider landscape of international tribunals and transitional justice. Established in 2006, the ECCC is an 'internationalized' court that is situated within a national judicial system. It includes international judicial personnel and enjoys financial support provided from the United Nations (UN) and international benefactors. It is a principally 'retributive' mechanism, focused on the punishment of perpetrators of atrocities, but it also includes a novel reparative mechanism as well as affording roles for victim participation within the courtroom. To date, the ECCC has delivered three verdicts against former Khmer Rouge figures, finding each guilty of crimes against humanity and sentencing each to a life term in prison. Yet the court has also attracted fierce criticism from scholars, human-rights groups and journalists. Critics contend that the ECCC is a politically compromised and flawed institution – *Time* magazine, for example, has branded the ECCC a "shocking failure"[3] – pointing to objections from the Cambodian government to judicial attempts to instigate the prosecution of a wider set of Khmer Rouge figures than those currently indicted, as well as to accusations of corruption.

The ECCC, of course, did not just appear out of thin air. The ECCC emerged from a protracted, complex and often fraught series of negotiations between the Royal Government of Cambodia (RGC), the UN, other interested states and non-governmental stakeholders. The shape and scope of the prosecutions ongoing at the ECCC emerge from this history. The ECCC focuses on only a handful of Khmer Rouge leaders, a condition for establishing the court for the RGC in the name of promoting peace and "national reconciliation." Yet in only examining violence perpetrated between 1975 and 1979, the ECCC also forecloses and mutes legal and public scrutiny of a long and complex history of warfare, violence and atrocities that were commissioned and perpetrated before and after the Khmer Rouge were in power, by actors within and beyond Cambodia. In other words, the ECCC works to draw a line under a wider history than it has actually been mandated to investigate. Moreover, as much as the ECCC elides a more complex history than *any* legal mechanism could attend to, a narrow analytic and empirical focus on the ECCC only also neglects the more complex and differentiated forms that transitional justice has taken within Cambodia, past and present. Non-governmental organisations (NGOs), in particular, were active in precipitating, advocating for and now monitoring the ECCC, and NGOs today deliver a wide raft of initiatives within Cambodia that seek to transform, ameliorate and enable redress with legacies of atrocity. These exercises often invoke memory as an object of transformation as well as prescribing specific techniques and practices of memory that will enable individual, social and political renewal.

Memory is then visible as an object and optic of analysis here in several respects. Criminal trials do not simply and narrowly dispense judgements. Trials are key socio-political crucibles for the resolution of competing histories, and they are deployed to renew and redress shared experiences of violence and atrocity. Techniques of memory are invoked within the courtroom, for example, to verify facts about past violence or to hear testimonies to ascertain the weight of suffering. And a wider raft of interventions is at work, operating alongside or in the background of the ECCC, that seeks out and provides Cambodian communities with new ways of thinking about memories of atrocity that equally also have specific political consequences. Moreover, the wider language through which the ECCC has been deployed and *thought* through is inflected with images and language that imply specific states of memory: Cambodia, conceptualised as a homogenous and singular body that has not, to now, "moved on," is a "broken society,"[4] is "traumatized" and in need of "healing" and "closure."[5] These representations powerfully validate the need for 'transitional justice', as such. But they also have effects in the way they locate Cambodians in a passive and uniform relationship to past experiences of atrocities. One aim of this book is to illustrate how Cambodian communities actively renegotiate a more varied set of relationships to memories of atrocity – and the techniques of memory transitional justice relies on to shape them – than such representations seem to accommodate.

Transitional justice and Cambodia

Transitional justice is a rapidly expanding field of scholarship and practice that has grown around a proliferation of institutions and initiatives that seek to remedy and reckon with experiences of conflict, political violence and suffering. The term 'transitional justice' was first coined in the context of processes of political change that unfolded across Latin America and Eastern Europe in the 1980s and early 1990s. Shifts from authoritarian rule, in these early debates, were conceptualised through a series of finite and exceptional political trade-offs over how to secure redress and accountability for abuses of previous regimes while maintaining peace, stability and civic renewal (Kritz 1996; Orentlicher 1991; see Teitel 2015, for a historical overview of the emergence of the field). Since then, galvanised by key formative 'moments' including the International Criminal Tribunals for Yugoslavia and Rwanda, the South African Truth and Reconciliation Commission and the establishment of the International Criminal Court, transitional justice has expanded and become entrenched as a set of assumptions, expectations, institutions and practices that lay claim over the question of how to deal with experiences of violence, suffering and conflict. Indeed, two pillars of transitional justice – the normative authority of human rights and international criminal law, and the presence of globally mobile institutions and groups that offer optimising 'best practice' techniques for the remedy and renewal of societies that have experienced violence – promise a field of now continuous (rather than exceptional) governance of conflicted, post-conflict and 'democratising' societies.

As much as all cases are unique, Cambodia presents several features and questions that are illuminating and important for wider debates in transitional justice and memory studies. In the first instance, it is not self-evident how or if the interventions and programmes at work in Cambodia today can be categorised as a 'case' within transitional justice. Decades have elapsed since the 1975–1979 period when the Khmer Rouge held power, presenting a troubling question of whether and if efforts today are redressing a case of 'historical injustice' as much as transitional justice. Indeed, the lived realities of Cambodia today – a demographically young and rapidly transforming society – now seem to poorly correspond to the language of peace-making and conflict resolution that attend to *immediate* transitions, even as stakeholders within and beyond Cambodia still mobilise and appropriate arguments that rely on thorny oppositions such as 'peace versus justice' or 'reconciliation versus accountability'.

The *transitions* that Cambodia has undergone are also historically multiple and uneven in form (C. Hughes 2003: 1–4): from civil war to genocide, to civil war, to peace, variously inaugurated or imposed by foreign intervention; from absolute authoritarianism, through democratic elections, to a now purportedly 'free' polity that is still marked by repressive abuses of dissenting and opposition voices; and from the absence of markets as such, through a period of planned economy, to a now neoliberal, nominally free-market system that is characterised by the (kleptocratic) concentration of land and natural resources in the hands of state-backed clients (Springer 2011). Throughout these periods and episodes, Cambodians have negotiated and been invited into varied and uneven relationships with their experiences of war and genocide. The ECCC itself – the centrepiece of transitional justice interventions in Cambodia today – emerged from a specific political history that included various antecedent attempts to redress communities for the violence they suffered. My intention here is to prefigure an argument that does not see transitional justice in Cambodia, as it is variously manifest today, as an inevitable outcome of these histories – there is more going on than the narrowly focused prosecutions at the ECCC – nor to read present problems in social orders as singularly determined by them. Transitional justice interventions do not always or inevitably happen. Rather, they are a contingent product of transnational and proximate influences and demands.

The core tools, techniques and mechanisms that are at work in Cambodia today, anchored around the ECCC, are, however, absolutely indigenous to – and more broadly constitutive of – transitional justice. The fact that a principally retributive mechanism has been mobilised to include and sponsor, for example, reparations programs, wider memorialisation drives and 'restorative' truth-seeking initiatives, is indicative of proliferating and potentially convergent domains: questions of historical injury, the proper application of international criminal law and an institutionalised field of non-governmental groups that prescribe strategies for optimising post-conflict outcomes are all present and at work in Cambodia today. These approaches and tools powerfully coalesced around the 'wax' of the ECCC life cycle, authoring transitional justice around the ECCC in Cambodia as something of a palimpsest. A series of outcomes have been used to justify and were thought to follow from transitional justice techniques in Cambodia. These include (but are not limited to) justice, reconciliation, truth, deterrence, challenging impunity and increasing local judicial capacity. On the one hand, the breadth of outcomes that were expected of Cambodia show how the case – anchored around the ECCC – is both heavily dominated by a prevailing international legalism and inflected with wider holistic assumptions about transformative and ameliorative effects of transitional justice. On the other, more cautiously, we can see that the breadth of language employed to justify transitional justice techniques, in Cambodia and beyond, means we must be cautious about the extent to which any intervention can deliver what it promises.

Memory

The ascendance of memory as an academic and popular concern is now well documented. The memory 'boom' of the past three decades has broadly tracked and reflected dramatic changes in (Western) societies. These are thought to have, on the one hand, accelerated our experience of the world to a degree that obliges a form of 'anchoring' retrospection (Huyssen 1995), while, on the other, it has foregrounded questions of identity, marginality and injustice that obviate the past as a site of socio-political correction (Olick, Vinitzky-Seroussi and Levy 2011), converging with questions of both transitional and historical injustice in important ways. The memory boom is not only visible in the growth of conservation and heritage industries, the global proliferation of museum and memorial sites, but it also coincides with the entrenchment of transitional justice in the way that it is predicated on assumptions about the value, benefits and outcomes furnished through *knowing* the past. The birth of memory studies, a space carved out between and across disciplines, has attended this arc. Memory studies has, in some respects, been defined and constituted by repositioned debates that were present within its cognate fields: to caricature, 'are memories purely individual, or socially constituted?' or 'are shared memories fabricated impositions to legitimate elites, or do they reflect authentic experiences of the world?' A consensus, of sorts, has now emerged around the idea that memory is mediated, 'dynamic', interpersonally reproduced and always unfinished, opening promising avenues for a rich landscape of empirical research that can consider the reproduction of memory in different contexts and through different techniques. As Olick notes, even neuroscientists today observe that memories are not immutably located in the psyche but remain highly cue and context dependent (Olick 2007: 26–27).

One strand of recent 'dynamic' approaches to understanding memory is that memory can be explained and examined 'discursively' (Radstone and Hodgkin 2005), which promises lenses for thinking through the relationship between memory and transitional justice further. While I develop a more sustained review of key themes and thinking in memory studies in the next chapter, it is worth pausing here to parse the concept of discourse a little more closely. The value of the concept of discourse is indebted to the work of Michel Foucault, whose thinking informs much of the analysis presented in this book. According to Foucault (2002), a discourse is a body of knowledge and statements that shape the way we think about the world, and that discourse is constitutive of its subjects. In other words, discourse makes us who we are. For Foucault, discourse is not a neutral concept; it always implicates power, inclusions and exclusions, and a hierarchy of entitlements over who is able to speak to and about the social world and how they are able to do so. In the first instance, we might observe, in the case at hand, how discourses of 'nation', 'justice' or 'healing' make it possible – or even oblige us – to *think* about memory in specific ways. Moreover, we can treat memories as discursively reproduced. In the way they are knowledge claims over past events, memories are discursively shaped, mapping the contours and content of what may and may not be remembered.

A second thread within Foucault's thinking underpins my intentions in this book. Foucault's interest in power and discourse is ineluctably scaled from the level of the population to the individual body or psyche. For Foucault, power is diffuse, enabling and constraining, productive of how we see the world rather than simply mystifying it. Power can be exercised in the name of specific *discursive* bodies of disciplinary knowledge, that is, medicine, psychology, psychiatry, penology, demography, economics and so on, which prescribe ideas of 'optimal' and 'deficient', 'normal' and 'abnormal' social order. Two further delineations are pertinent then here. Firstly, memory tends to be implicitly coded within the vocabulary of transitional justice. Memory has been a silent shibboleth of the field, a register that organises its most taken-for-granted principles that demand confrontations with the past in order to renew the present, affording 'corrected', 'redressed' or 'optimal' states of social, political and civic order. Indeed, it is difficult to write about transitional justice while avoiding a language of why *we must* 'confront', 'deal with' or 'come to terms with' the past. Such assumptions, which follow from the way psycho-therapeutic knowledge has bled into other areas of public life (Hacking 1995), including law, tend to be coded implicitly at the level of the population, whereby (principally national) collective stories are considered, confronted, redressed and purportedly renewed (Hamber and Wilson 2002; Moon 2007). Secondly, if we focus our attention more closely across scales, from the level of the population to the level of the individual body or psyche, memories are explicitly (or implicitly) located as targets and objects in their own right, especially within and adjacent to work in the 'psy' sciences. Disciplinary knowledge about memory – forms of memory expertise – obviate specific techniques for the transformation or correction of memories as a target and object of intervention, as well the authorities who are entitled to mandate such processes. This book attempts to sketch the way such interventions – in their broadest reach and in their detail – invite Cambodian communities into specific relationships with memories of atrocity, foreclosing different ways of remembering violence just as others are enabled.

Researching transitional justice and memory in Cambodia

There is a strong body of work on Cambodia that is concerned with governance, democratisation, and development (see, for example, C. Hughes 2003, 2009). The history of Cambodia – and the Khmer Rouge in particular – has been documented in a detailed and forensic corpus of works (Kiernan 2001, 2004; Chandler 1991, 1999; Vickery 1984). Much scholarship on the ECCC – and transitional justice in general – emerges from law (Ciorciari and Heindel 2014, 2016). Recent anthropological writing and work based on deeper empirical engagements have begun to yield a richer understanding of the relationships and lenses through which Cambodian communities have established relationships to memories of the Khmer Rouge (Kent 2007; Norén-Nilsson 2011; Zucker 2013). And several more critical accounts of the ECCC have been offered that seek to both historicise the work of the court as well as situating it within wider social, geographical and political contexts (Ainley 2013; Bernath 2016; Elander 2013; R. Hughes 2015).

This book echoes and draws on many of these important contributions, providing an analysis that necessarily both converges with and diverges from existing work on Cambodia and the ECCC. More importantly, my intention in staking out these disciplinary brackets is to serve the purposes of my own 'expectation management'. This book does not offer a 'black letter' legal analysis, though it does examine a legal phenomenon and borrows from arguments in critical legal studies. History and memory are thought to have a fraught interrelationship and, while I seek to better *historicise* transitional justice in Cambodia, this is not a work of history. Anthropologists are likely better equipped to explain the wider cultural politics of memory, especially as it is reproduced in vernacular forums, and there are sociologists or political scientists who would better map the variously present attitudes towards redress efforts through scaled survey work. Moreover, on normative terms, transitional justice and human rights are fields of scholarship that are mutually constituted by their relationship to advocacy work; my aims, here, do not include an executive summary of policy prescription. Instead, my argument rests on the importance of scrutinising how intertwined proximate and transnational histories, knowledge claims and forces have shaped the different transitional justice interventions that are at work in Cambodia. These make memory *possible* in specific ways and are generative of a range of responses among their constituents that we are obliged to pay closer attention to. This is an analytical exercise that is not at odds with the normative 'ideals' of transitional justice. Rather, I hope to show, firstly, that transitional justice in Cambodia did not have to look the way it does and remains empirically unfolding, and that the range of transitional justice interventions in Cambodia carries wider political effects than tend to be acknowledged. Secondly, I hope to show that Cambodians actively negotiate a varied set of relationships with techniques of transitional justice that they encounter and the memories of political violence that those techniques call attention to and attempt to animate and shape.

I have been following the ECCC since its establishment, watching its crises, successes, disappointments, impasses and breakthroughs over a long cycle, both from within Cambodia and remotely from the United Kingdom (UK). This book develops arguments and thinking that principally started life as a PhD thesis at the London School of Economics in 2007, though in some respects, my interest in developing a more 'sociological' account of memory and redress in Cambodia started earlier than this. In prior visits, writing and thinking about Cambodia, I was struck by the discordance between prevailing claims of Cambodia's 'culture of amnesia', the willingness of Khmer friends to talk about their experiences of past violence, and the ambivalence among some towards the history of the Khmer Rouge. These anecdotal insights certainly shaped my interests in conducting further research on the topic and starting a PhD. The thesis obliged a period of fieldwork in 2008 and 2009, which I use still for key insights, though I also draw on interviews and conversations conducted for and around complementary projects and visits to Cambodia variously from 2010 to 2016.

This book, then, is made up from something of a bricolage account of the ECCC, drawn together from quite disparate sources across different time frames. Much of the data is drawn from court transcripts, press releases, public statements and coverage of the ECCC gathered before, during and after fieldwork in 2008 and 2009, as well as from the developing corpus of academic analysis and commentary on the court. One significant tranche of data was developed from a period hosted at the (then) Center for Social Development (CSD) in 2008, where I assisted on the "Public Forum on Justice and Reconciliation" outreach program that was running at the time. In many respects, that year marked the start of an upswing in interest in the ECCC. As a visiting staff member, I was embedded within and afforded an 'insider' position through my role associated with practice and advocacy, though this positioning was itself contingent and relationally realised. My role at CSD was normatively freighted within the wider ambit of the ECCC and jarred with my (already) developing critical appraisal of the ECCC process. Indeed, then colleagues, who are now spread across different NGO organisations in various roles, tended to find it funny that I wanted to work on a justice project that I seemed to hold critical reservations towards. Nonetheless, those colleagues offered valuable time and help, offering interviews, discussing proceedings and their views of public outreach events, helping secure interviews with other staff at other relevant organisations and obliging follow-up meetings in subsequent years.

From January 2009, I spent time in Cambodia's northwest, keen to look beyond the immediate orbit of the ECCC in Phnom Penh and attempting to explore the role of memorial and museum sites for the communities around them. The lessons I yielded from these stretches were very different in content and form and it is worth noting how and why, because they are instructive of the wider contexts through which memory is reproduced in Cambodia. Without the anchoring position that CSD offered, grounding a sense of purpose of why and how I was present within specific milieus and legitimate in *talking* about memory, informants invariably assumed other things of me. Some were reluctant to talk to an 'outsider', while others were ambivalent about the idea of both transitional justice and research on it. Others were forthcoming and eager to talk about the issues I raised. I present these variations without meaning to characterise the research process as extractive, yielding – rather than co-producing – data. Indeed, memory does not 'work like that', as any act of remembering itself occurs within a social context. Many informants simply assumed I was a long-term tourist or interested ex-patriot, despite often lengthy explanations of research aims and the production of my then London School of Economics ID card which, I likely should have guessed, carried less weight in provincial Cambodia than on the conference circuit. In many cases, people were simply baffled by why I would want to 'hang out' around a genocide memorial or other memorial and museum sites, which, in retrospect, makes perfect sense given the complex and varied roles such sites play within Cambodia. Indeed, establishing clear relationships and expectations was 'messier' beyond institutional settings that were contextually *framed* around the purposes, aims and normative benefits of remembering and the ECCC. Beyond these contexts, a more diverse and sometimes conflicted set of contextual dynamics for how and why memories are obliged – or elided – was presented, including religious and commercial imperatives, and a wariness of overtly 'political' (i.e. partisan) claims over memory.

It remains important to reflect on the role of language within my research. Conducting cross-language research poses a problem for qualitative fieldwork because the interplay between languages is a critical part of the way data is constructed as meaningful. It is also recognised that the presumed availability of equivalent terms with equivalent meanings across languages does not necessarily exist; there may not be a single correct translation of a text across languages, and translators/interpreters must actively choose the words used from a potential variety of options to reconstruct meaning transfer (Temple and Edwards 2002). These challenges were complicated by the fact that my own K'mai language skills were, throughout the research, quite limited (despite lessons). Moreover, these problems mean that interview data has to be read with care and analysed thematically, rather than, say, for its rhetorical organisation. Different settings allowed different means of accommodating these challenges and the data will appear to readers more or less 'messy' as it arises from these contexts. In Phnom Penh, my interviews with

NGO staff were conducted in English, the ease of which is in part a reflection of the dependence of Cambodian civil society on English-speaking donors and groups. At CSD public forums, I was specifically handed the role of transcribing the English language translation of forum proceedings and was encouraged to 'tidy up' transcripts for conventions of spelling and grammar. Beyond these contexts, around memorial sites, I was able to develop informal conversations and some interviews through a mix of English and my own (broken) K'mai, and I have deliberately presented these exchanges in their 'messier' form unless drawn from fieldnotes. Lastly, I sought assistance from a paid interpreter for several key interviews with officials and senior monks, whereby more formal tone and vocabulary was requisite, which are presented in Chapter eight.

Argument

The central arguments at work in this book develop around three interrelated themes: the politics of the ECCC and memory; the wider assemblage of techniques through which transitional justice is being delivered in Cambodia; and the varied meanings and relationships Cambodian communities have negotiated with memories of political violence, in the context of the ECCC and beyond.

The prevailing criteria and lenses through which we have been invited to think about and judge the ECCC in Cambodia require scrutiny. They follow as epistemic lenses from the fields of transitional justice and human rights in ways that risk foreclosing other ways of appraising the court. Transitional justice has come to be dominated by two tendencies. Firstly, a form of *legalism* has been ascendant that is authorised through its normative denial and 'insulation' from 'politics'. Secondly, the institutional growth of transitional justice as field of *policy* has germinated approaches that seek 'best practice' – optimal solutions from a pre-existing armoury of approaches and techniques that are thought to offer redress for past violence. Such technocratic strategies can themselves be both deeply de-historicising and depoliticising of the contexts to which they are addressed. The ECCC has been widely denounced because it has been subjected to visible political interference from the Cambodian government, affronting the need for justice interventions to meet international standards of due process and independence. I agree that the ECCC is a deeply *political* institution and process. But this extends beyond the narrowly framed ledger of political interference by the Cambodian state. The ECCC is bound to and emerges from specific political histories and the political interests of various stakeholders – within and beyond Cambodia – that ensure that the justice it delivers is politically shaped. The ECCC acts on, calls upon, and purportedly renews memories in selective and politically contingent ways. This is, of course, a feature endemic to international criminal justice rather than specific to Cambodia. Yet, I argue, recognising this obliges us to rethink the wider language employed to justify and then evaluate how and why transitional justice mechanisms are or are not successful.

As important as the ECCC has been in working to authorise a specific and politically preferred reading of political violence in Cambodia, a second line of argument that I develop invites attention to the wider raft and assemblage of institutional groups and techniques that are deployed to act on memory. Transitional justice has tended to theorise 'cases' that are orientated around the role and efficacy of a central or centrepiece mechanism that has been deployed to renew a (principally national) social grouping. Here, through the lens of memory, I seek to analyse some of the wider projects, initiatives and techniques that are deployed in the name of ameliorating past violence. In these contexts, I argue, we begin to see a more complicated 'politics' of transitional justice, whereby techniques that are deployed to improve or remedy legacies of political violence are freighted with their own political consequences, foreclosing some ways of thinking about memories of atrocity just as others are enabled.

This book is fundamentally about the relationships that people are asked to establish with memories of political violence. The ECCC has been presented as an institutional mechanism that can enable a process of "moving forward through justice." This slogan implies a specific and progressive linear sequence from a state of disorder to a state of correction. Yet Cambodia does not have *one* relationship to its legacies of political violence. A prevailing language depicts Cambodia as a 'traumatised nation'[6] with a 'beleaguered' population,[7] but these are unhelpful representational tropes in this regard because they depict people as incapable of maintaining relationships with memories of atrocity, just as they are powerful frameworks for validating and obviating the *need* for transitional justice. Memories of Democratic Kampuchea, the various civil wars, foreign intervention and other experiences of suffering and violence are often interspersed, cued by differing political interests and obligations, as well as maintained through frameworks that are dislocated from the language of accountability and redress that is central to transitional justice. Cambodian communities have actively renegotiated relationships with memories of political violence in different ways and on different terms. Transitional justice – in Cambodia and beyond – would benefit from greater attention to and recognition of the terms on which such relationships are *actively* established and maintained, for good or bad.

Structure of the book

In the next chapter, I explore key literatures on memory and transitional justice to develop a picture of *how* memory works and the growth of memory as a field of ethical and political concern, before turning to examine and track changing approaches within transitional justice. I situate assumptions at work within transitional justice practice and scholarship in relief of memory studies, and I argue that we must appraise the nascent duty to remember – a claim that is foundational to the conceptual and normative 'grammar' of transitional justice – as a contingent feature of modern political life. In Chapter Three, 'Political violence in Cambodia', I turn to look at the history of atrocity, conflict and political order in closer detail. I develop a series of sketches of violence, atrocities and suffering during, before and after the years of Democratic Kampuchea. I then consider how these experiences fed into and made possible specific visions of justice and reconciliation that are at work at the ECCC today.

In Chapter Four, 'Moving forward through justice', I turn to ask some basic questions of the ECCC: What is the court? What is it doing? Why is it doing it? And who is it doing it for? I begin with a presentation of the ECCC's 'hybrid' structure and arguments for its establishment. I then review the ECCC caseload to date, while presenting some of the political implications of the sensitive prospective prosecutions in Cases 003 and 004. I then examine the ECCC jurisdiction in closer detail to highlight the selectivity and contingency of the appeals for justice that emanate from the court. In Chapter Five, 'Memory on trial', I look at forms of 'memory work' within the courtroom. I consider the lenses and registers through which memory is invoked, especially against criteria of reliability, accuracy and *truth*, as well as through the expressive power and spectacle of testimonial work. I then consider strategies employed by defence teams, specifically around 'denial' and 'rupture'. I argue that as the ECCC works to contain an account of past violence within its jurisdiction, defence teams are invited to appropriate and invoke Cambodia's experiences of political violence more broadly to contest the normative coherence and legitimacy of the court.

In Chapter Six, 'Complementary knowledge', I turn to examples of memory 'work', expertise and techniques operating outside of the ECCC. I show, through an examination of genocide education and trauma awareness–raising initiatives, how transitional justice interventions are constituted through specific assumptions and expertise that frame interventions seeking to redress experiences of atrocity as 'technical' exercises. In the cases at hand, I show how such interventions – where memory is invoked as an explicit object of transformation – carry important political consequences even as they seem to 'depoliticize' the past. Chapter Seven proceeds to analyse forms of memory work deployed in complement of the ECCC through public outreach and education events. I consider the resources that are put to work in licensing claims over memory – especially visits to memorial and museum sites – and the way these work to obviate both what must be 'known' and 'done' about the past. As I show through analysis of public forum transcripts, such exercises enjoy mixed results, often obliging ambivalent and resistant responses and claims over memory.

The penultimate chapter, 'Beyond the tribunal', explores Cambodian accounts of a genocide memorial at the Wat Thmey temple in Siem Reap. I consider the different frameworks that lay claim over genocide memory in Cambodia, working to pull memory in different, often seemingly conflicting directions. Yet the meanings of the memorial for the people I spoke to at and around the site often showed ambivalent and pragmatic relationships to the memories of the Khmer Rouge that the site called attention to. While Cambodian audiences were wary of the overtly 'political' messaging at work at the site, many welcomed the functional role the memorial played as a source of revenue for the monastic and wider community.

The final chapter, 'Remembering the Khmer Rouge Tribunal', attempts to bring together these strands to reprise an analysis of the ECCC. I argue that while the ECCC is 'flawed' and 'politically influenced' – as its critics contend – we need to rethink the language and terms through which transitional justice mechanisms are justified, celebrated and condemned, because such dialogues are critical for both engaging and, indeed, disappointing their constituents. I argue that there are instructive lessons to be gleaned for the wider landscape of transitional justice and memory studies in terms of expectation management, the ability of communities to negotiate relationships to memories of atrocity and the politics of transitional justice itself.

Notes

1 Law on the Establishment of the Extraordinary Chambers, with inclusion of amendments as promulgated on 27 October 2004 (NS/RKM/1004/006). Available at https://www.eccc.gov.kh/sites/default/files/legal-documents/KR_Law_as_amended_27_Oct_2004_Eng.pdf. Last accessed 21 September 2016.
2 See the ECCC publicity poster campaigns, available at https://www.eccc.gov.kh/en/public-affair/publication/poster. Last accessed 23 September 2016.
3 See "Cambodia's Khmer Rouge trials are a shocking failure," available at http://time.com/6997/cambodias-khmer-rouge-trials-are-a-shocking-failure/. Last accessed 23 September 2016.
4 See, for example, "Youk Chhang: Picking up the pieces in Cambodia," 22 April 2010, *Stanford Business*. Available at https://www.gsb.stanford.edu/insights/youk-chhang-picking-pieces-cambodia. Last accessed 23 September 2016.
5 See, for example, "The Khmer Rouge Tribunal: Cambodia's healing process," *Time*, 30 November 2009. Available at http://content.time.com/time/world/article/0,8599,1943373,00.html. Last accessed 23 September 2016.
6 "Second trial may be too little too late for traumatised nation" *The Times*, September 21, 2010. Available at http://www.thetimes.co.uk/tto/news/world/agenda/article2734395.ece. Last accessed 23 September 2016.
7 Picken, M. "The beleaguered Cambodians," *New York Review of Books*, January 13, 2011. Available at http://www.nybooks.com/articles/2011/01/13/beleaguered-cambodians/. Last accessed 23 September 2016.

References

Ainley, K., 2013. Transitional justice in Cambodia: The coincidence of power and principle. In *Transitional Justice in the Asia-Pacific*. R. Jeffery (ed). Cambridge, UK: Cambridge University Press.

Bernath, J., 2016. 'Complex political victims' in the aftermath of mass atrocity: Reflections on the Khmer Rouge tribunal in Cambodia. *International Journal of Transitional Justice, 10* (1): 46–66.

Chandler, D. P., 1991. *The Tragedy of Cambodian History: Politics, War, and Revolution since 1945*. New Haven, CT: Yale University Press.

Chandler, D. P. 1999. *Voices from S-21: Terror and History in Pol Pot's Secret Prison*. Berkeley, CA: University of California Press.

Ciorciari, J. D. and Heindel, A., 2014. *Hybrid Justice: The Extraordinary Chambers in the Courts of Cambodia*. Ann Arbor, MI: University of Michigan Press.

Ciorciari, J. D. and Heindel, A., 2016. Victim testimony in international and hybrid criminal courts: Narrative opportunities, challenges, and fair trial demands. *Virginia Journal of International Law, 56* (2): 265–338.

Elander, M., 2013. The victim's address: Expressivism and the victim at the Extraordinary Chambers in the Courts of Cambodia. *International Journal of Transitional Justice, 7* (1): 95–115.

Foucault, M., 2002. *Archaeology of Knowledge*. London, New York: Routledge.
Hacking, I., 1995. *Rewriting the Soul: Multiple Personality and the Sciences of Memory*. Princeton, NJ: Princeton University Press.
Hamber, B. and Wilson, R. A., 2002. Symbolic closure through memory, reparation and revenge in post-conflict societies. *Journal of Human Rights*, *1* (1): 35–53.
Hughes, C., 2003. *The Political Economy of the Cambodian Transition*. London, New York: Routledge.
Hughes, C., 2009. *Dependent Communities: Aid and Politics in Cambodia and East Timor* (No. 48). Ithaca, NY: SEAP Publications.
Hughes, R., 2015. Ordinary theatre and extraordinary law at the Khmer Rouge Tribunal. *Environment and Planning D: Society and Space*, *33* (4): 714–731.
Huyssen, A., 1995. *Twilight Memories: Marking Time in a Culture of Amnesia*. New York: Routledge.
Kent, A., 2007. Purchasing power and pagodas: The Sīma monastic boundary and consumer politics in Cambodia. *Journal of Southeast Asian Studies*, *38* (2): 335–354.
Kiernan, B. 2001. *The Pol Pot Regime: Race, Power, and Genocide in Cambodia Under the Khmer Rouge, 1975–79*. New Haven, CT: Yale University Press.
Kiernan, B., 2004. *How Pol Pot Came to Power: Colonialism, Nationalism, and Communism in Cambodia, 1930–1975*. New Haven, CT: Yale University Press.
Kritz, N. J., 1996. Coming to terms with atrocities: A review of accountability mechanisms for mass violations of human rights. *Law and Contemporary Problems*, *59* (4): 127–152.
Moon, C., 2007. States of acknowledgement: The politics of memory, apology, and therapy. In *Crime, Social Control and Human Rights: From Moral Panics to States of Denial, Essays in Honour of Stanley Cohen*. Downes, P., Rock, C., Chinkin, C. and Gearty, C. (eds) Devon, UK: Willan Publishing.
Norén-Nilsson, A., 2011. Children of former Khmer Rouge cadres. *Peace Review*, *23* (4): 462–468.
Olick, J. K., Vinitzky-Seroussi, V. and Levy, D., 2011. *The Collective Memory Reader*. Oxford and New York: Oxford University Press.
Olick, J. K., 2007. *The Politics of Regret: On Collective Memory and Historical Responsibility*. New York, London: Routledge.
Orentlicher, D. F., 1991. Settling accounts: The duty to prosecute human rights violations of a prior regime. *Yale Law Journal*, 2537–2615.
Radstone, S. and Hodgkin, K., 2005. *Memory Cultures: Memory, Subjectivity, and Recognition*. New Brunswick, NJ: Transaction Publishers.
Springer, S., 2011. Articulated neoliberalism: The specificity of patronage, kleptocracy, and violence in Cambodia's neoliberalization. *Environment and Planning*, *43* (11): 2554–2570.
Teitel, R., 2015. *Globalizing Transitional Justice*. Oxford: Oxford University Press.
Temple, B. and Edwards, R., 2002. Interpreters/translators and cross-language research: Reflexivity and border crossings. *International Journal of Qualitative Methods*, *1* (2).
Vickery, M., 1984. *Cambodia, 1975–1982*. Boston, MA: South End Press.
Zucker, E. M., 2013. *Forest of Struggle: Moralities of Remembrance in Upland Cambodia*. Hawaii: University of Hawaii Press.

2 Transitional justice and memory

In this chapter, we step back from the Cambodian context to examine key currents and developments in memory studies and transitional justice. My aim here is to track patterns and assumptions in thinking within the two fields that have gone on to coalesce powerfully in the case at hand, mapping frameworks for how memories of violence can and should be known and acted upon. Social scientific research on memory has been principally preoccupied with two questions (Brown 2008): Firstly, how does memory work (a social 'mechanics' of memory)? Secondly, why has memory emerged as such an important issue for and within contemporary societies? These two questions are important because they speak directly to the issues of how the past shapes who we are and the moral burdens that are invoked on the past in the name of renewing the present. Core concepts and scaffolds within the field – such as 'collective' memory – have been scrutinised, applied, discarded and reconsidered in the proliferation of scholarship that has marked the emergence of memory studies as a sub-disciplinary field over the past 20 years (Kansteiner 2010), reflecting a quickly changing landscape. My intention here, firstly, is to follow Jeffery Olick's invitation to problematise key areas that have hampered the study of collective or social memory: its unity or singularity, its authenticity, its tangibility and its conceptual autonomy and divisibility relative to other categories of analysis (2007: 89). In doing so, I thumbnail the roles of performance, place, history and discourse within explanations of how social memory is formed and reproduced. Within this account, I offer a brief reading of strands of the work of Michel Foucault, staking out an approach to memory that sees memory as a discourse that produces *subjects* – who we are – as well as promising itself as an *object* of expertise and transformation in its own right. I then return to reconsider the nascent urgency surrounding discourses of memory and the ethical imperative to remember.

The second half of this chapter thumbnails key debates within transitional justice, a field of scholarship and practice that is predicated on an interwoven set of normative, technical and ideological claims over what memory is and what must be done with it in the wake of atrocities and suffering. Transitional justice has grown rapidly over recent decades and it now represents a powerful field of advocacy, scholarship and practice that seeks to correct, redress and remedy social order in post-conflict settings. But transitional justice itself is also a contingent feature of international political order. Its central aims and techniques – which are not self-evidently coherent – reflect specific sets of assumptions and hopes for the forms of society that they seek to inaugurate, which are themselves politically freighted. Moreover, any case or 'episode' of transitional justice emerges and is framed subject to forces that shape and condition what redress, justice or restoration *can* look like in any given context.

A social mechanics of memory

A review of work on a social 'mechanics' of memory is obliged to start with Maurice Halbwachs' seminal work on the 'collective memory' (1992). Halbwachs' formative years were spent in France in the early decades of the twentieth century, and currents within French sociology and philosophy strongly shaped his writing. Halbwachs' central argument was that, while memory might appear to be the property of the individual psyche, it is our membership within social groups that arranges and orders the images of the past that are remembered and maintained, therefore contextualising and accomplishing individual memories as meaningful. Halbwachs suggests that memories are constitutive of group identities, furnishing the stories and narratives through which a sense of self and belonging are possible. Halbwachs was specifically writing against prevailing currents in psychology at the time that posited memory as a purely individual phenomenon. In this sense, the birth of the 'collective memory' as a social phenomenon emerged in relief of accounts that privileged the individual as the repository of memory, although one unifying convergence here was the premise that what we remember and forget constitutes who we are. While we should be wary of the tendency to canonise Halbwachs' work as *the* antecedent to memory studies – an *arts* of memory was longstanding prior to Halbwachs' writing, and his work emerged in relief of developments in the natural sciences, psychology and philosophy that took memory as their principal object of study (Olick *et al.* 2011: 5–9) – Halbwachs' thinking cues important and productive questions for our purposes here.

In several respects, Halbwachs' work mirrors wider currents that were emerging in social theory and thinking at that time. Halbwachs drew from the work of Durkheim, for example, in theorising the way the ritual affirmation of the past could constitute the social bonds of the present (2001). Indeed, Halbwachs has been subjected to many parallel critiques in this regard. Like Durkheim, Halbwachs' approach has been criticised for reifying a totalised understanding of the 'social' – that is, 'collective' – memory as an entity that exists in and of itself and in accordance to its own logic and that therefore risks an overdetermination of the individual and individual memory. Moreover, whilst Halbwachs suggested that there were as many collective memories as there were social groups, like Durkheim, he appears to present an account of the social world that quickly becomes coterminous with national collectivities or methodological nationalism (see Beck 2007 for a closer discussion of methodological nationalism). Despite these cautionary reflections, Halbwachs remains an important embarkation point because his work sensitises us to the way social groups can be constituted in the present through the maintenance of the past.

The relationship between memory and identity has been central to debates on social and collective memory. These debates have been characterised by a series of thorny oppositions concerning the way memories are constituted and how they are reproduced. Halbwachs' work can be read to assume the existence of a collective memory that might exist coercively beyond the individual, along the lines of Durkheim's famous *conscience collective* (1984). Against this, Olick has contrasted the development of 'collected' memory approaches, accounts of shared memories that might exist as the aggregated accretions of individual memory (2007: 23–27). In this tradition, for example, Schuman and Scott locate collected memories in the shared, aggregated experiences of generations (1989). The opposition between collective and collected memory invites us to choose between a framework that risks a cumbersome and totalising concept of collective memory, one that is implied to have an existence beyond individual psyches, and approaches to shared collected memories that might neglect the contingent and socially embedded forces at work in the maintenance of memories and therefore risk 'depoliticising' the past.

A second opposition prefigured within Halbwachs' writing is present here. Key approaches to social and collective memory have been keen to accommodate the role of memory in the realisation of cultural identity and the interface of 'vernacular', 'official' and 'public memory' (Bodnar 1993), situating the 'vernacular' as rooted within more authentic reflections of identity and experience. Theorists of nationalism might here point out that arguments that the past residually and authentically persists as 'traces' that constitute group identities are central to ethno-symbolist accounts of nations (see, e.g. Smith 1998). Against these are more critical accounts of memory that emphasise the constructed production and manipulation of social memory and history. Perhaps foremost in this line of thinking is Hobsbawm and Ranger's collection *The Invention of Tradition* (1983). For Hobsbawm and Ranger, the past can be a vehicle for the legitimation of elite and state power, particularly in the service of nationalistic beliefs, through commemorative activity. The opposition presented here is between, on the one hand, approaches that lean towards understanding collective memory as an authentic reflection of the past, versus, on the other, memory as synthetic, 'top-down' forms of mystification that conceal the 'real' past.

More recent scholarship in memory studies has sought to navigate these oppositions with further nuance. Wertsch (2002) and Olick (2007) have rejected the dichotomy between 'fictional' and 'authentic' and 'collective' versus 'collected' memories, instead emphasising that all acts of memory are active, practical, unfinished and socially mediated. Such arguments are indicative of a widespread reappraisal of the previous frameworks discussed. Olick points out, pragmatically, that approaches to memory from disciplines that are traditionally 'individualist' and 'physiologically' focused, such as neurobiology or psychology, are now keen to press that memory is cue dependent and networked and will often foreground social contexts rather than individual experience when individuals remember (2007: 26–27). Singer and Conway have argued, further, that even highly personalised traumatic memories are socially negotiated and contested, which enables and conditions processes of erasure and remembering (2014). Indeed, experimental and discursive strands of psychology increasingly foreground the role of interaction, culture and context in enabling memory (Brown and Reavey 2015). Conversely, from a sociological perspective, greater caution might be needed in locating exactly where the social conditioning of memory occurs. For example, as Gavriely-Nuri suggests (2014), we might reread Halbwachs' conception of collective memory as metaphorical rather than substantive category, pointing to the way that collective memory frameworks are invoked for and therefore constituted within political enunciations. In other words, as unsatisfactory a concept as a 'collective' memory might be as a substantive analytic category in its own right, collective memories – principally national ones – are frequently invoked as objects of intervention, transformation and discipline, affecting both what and how people remember.

Memories exist and are reproduced, then, neither as 'collective' nor 'collected' but as socially accomplished (Olick 2007: 26). On this basis, memory is seen as ongoing process of realisation between individuals, groups and social texts, representations and spaces (and accounts of memory here permit its realisation through relationships to material artefacts, places and technologies). These approaches to memory that seek to accommodate a 'dynamics' of remembering between agents, memory 'tools' and social contexts are fruitful because they do not recapitulate to naturalised conceptions of memory as purely archival, objectively locatable from a repository extraction, or prematurely dismiss the formative role that experience and agency may play in making memories persistent.

Crucibles and sites of memory

The reproduction of memory, according to 'dynamic' accounts, is therefore a practical process. On this basis, the active, 'performative' and spatial dimensions of memory are critical. Memory is topographically reproduced in its artefacts, institutions, agents and representations. It is maintained within 'everyday' landscapes (Tolia-Kelly 2004), as well as appearing rooted and embodied at sites implicated in specific histories including markers of memory, such as sites of atrocity (Koonz 1994). Memory is further invoked and affirmed at 'spectacular' forums, perhaps most visible in the seemingly unending proliferation of commemorative and memorial practices we see today (Frost and Laing 2013), especially in the service of the histories of nation states. Connerton suggests – drawing a connection between the body, bodily habits and performativity – that commemorations are pivotal in delineating pasts from presents, sedimenting 'bodily' memory and laying the contours within which social memory is possible (1989). The juncture of collective or shared social memories and individual minds therefore requires a bridging entity, which implies the constitutive role of embodiment, the body and performance (Narvaez 2006). As Winter notes, all acts of memory are more than just recollections, because in each performative, embodied iteration, memories are affected and affirmed rather than simply restated or 'verified' (2010: 11–12).

Memory performances, then, occur within specific social contexts and locations. The role of memorials and museums as markers of memory, in this regard, is rarely innocent because they always imply particular interests, preferred histories and wider patterns of inequality. In the minutiae, visual representations and displays at work in memorials and museums are thought to offer 'clusters' of meanings that communicate narratives about the past (Williams 2007), whereby memorials can act as 'texts' that can be read to condition and cue memory for visitors (Young 1993). The 'birth' of the museum as a nineteenth-century institution of historical documentation, taxonomy and display is deeply intertwined with a civilising mission, both 'inwardly' to discipline and animate social groups *as* cultural entities and 'outwardly' in the way it affirmed Western–European conceptions of (self-affirming) linear progress (Bennet 1995). Moreover, twentieth-century memorial and museum sites have long been implicated in the representation and reproduction of the preferred histories of states and state elites, even as they instigate discord over whom and what is depicted therein (see e.g. White 1997).

More recently, the proliferation of memorial sites and spaces that has marked the 'memory boom' over recent decades has been characterised by a more diverse range of memorial practices, identifying critically self-reflexive 'counter'-memorials (Young 1993: 45), and even calls for forgetting, or 'anti'-memorials (Ware 2008). Memory studies has increasingly analysed the relationships between material and technological objects and human consciousness as co-productive of memory (Schlunke 2013). The role of digital technology and networks is important to note here as it enables increasingly entropic and unpredictable archives that are constitutive of *more* memory (Hoskins 2013). Moreover, new forms of interaction are emergent through spaces and platforms that are constituted through archival memory repositories of photographs and personal experiences, such as Facebook (Schwarz 2014). In this sense, we see the emergence of new platforms and crucibles for social memory and memorialisation that are dislocated from key arbiters of memory such as the state, for example, visible in online YouTube memorials to fallen soldiers that entail more proximate and democratic contestations of memories (Knudsen and Stage 2013).

Specific spaces or sites of memory tend be bound to and licensed by wider systems of social and political regulation. The relationship between law and memory is an important case in this respect. Law provides a framework for coding, thinking about and acting on memory, and courtrooms are key socio-political site to these ends. Courtrooms and the criminal trials that they anchor are sites that operate for the adjudication of competing memories and public histories. Legal interventions that deliberate over past suffering, in this sense, converge with and constitute political techniques of memory. The relationship between trials and collective memory has been theorised as mutually constitutive: law provides a framework and coding for the reconstruction of memory, whilst memories shape and furnish the content and authority of law (Savelsberg and King 2007). Levy and Sznaider, for example, specifically point to the 'institutional' memory of the Nuremberg trials as a reference point for all subsequent tribunals (2010).

The use of trials and punishment as both a political technique for the construction of history and a means of rectifying violent pasts has been theorised in a number of ways. Within classical sociology, Durkheim suggested that the role of the trial is a ritual performance that affirms the norms and values of given collectivities (1984). In a similar vein, Osiel has pointed to the potential for trials to enable 'discursive solidarity' in the way trials act as a crucible for the resolution or accommodation of conflicting stories about the past (1997: 51). Misztal has further evaluated the varying contributions that ritual interventions on the past may yield for the promotion of democratic values (2005). Indeed, from Nuremberg to the more recent Milosevic trials, prosecutions for past injustices are now understood as much through their didactic function as history-writing exercises as through their discharging of *lex talionis* (Koskenniemi 2002).

The objects and subjects of memory

If, at this point, we recognise that all memory is social, unfinished and unstable; mediated and performed; materially and spatially situated; and therefore inescapably *political*, we are promised an avenue to critically reflect on a different yet crucial set of questions. Through what lenses and on what terms are memories animated? Who is permitted to act on or rally memory and where? To whom are such acts addressed and on what terms are they resisted? Here we can mine an important line of thinking that attends to such questions through the concept of discourse. To sensitise us to my intentions here, Antze and Lambek (1996) and Radstone and Hodgkin (2005) have called for an appreciation of the 'uses' of memory. Both sets of authors ground potential analysis of the way memory is situated as a field of knowledge to be 'known' and acted upon, as well as how memory 'itself' – the 'contents' of memory, its ontology – are a product of discourse. Two inter-related avenues for my argument are pertinent at this point. Firstly, that memory is constituted through discourse – talk, text and representation – and secondly, that memory can be the object and target of discourse through techniques that promise and target memory as a site of intervention. This is significant because it opens a space for the analysis of how collective memories are situated as objects of practice – within transitional justice contexts in particular – and intervened upon subject to fields of disciplinary knowledge and differing forms of practical expertise.

The value of the concept of discourse is indebted to the work of Michel Foucault, whose thinking informs much of the analysis presented in this book. According to Foucault (2002), a discourse is a body of knowledge and statements that shape the way we think about the world. They never do so absent of power. For Foucault, discourses obey specific 'regularities' that make potentially dispersed groups of statements intelligible and unified through 'rules' or 'formations' (2002: 32–42). In other words, discourse operates as a specific – but contingent – form of common underpinning knowledge of the world and its past; we might observe, in the case at hand, how discourses of 'nation', 'justice' or 'healing' make it possible – or even oblige us – to *think* about memory in specific ways. Two crucial issues follow from this. In *Politics and the Study of Discourse* (1991), Foucault examines the ways in which discourse defines the parameters of what is 'sayable', 'what it is possible to speak of' and 'those utterances that are destined to disappear without a trace'. He explicitly refers to 'the limits and forms of memory as it appears in different discursive formations', encouraging the recognition of those 'utterances' that have been marginalised or excluded as 'unmemorable' (1991: 59–61). In other words, if we treat memory as a form of knowledge of the past, Foucault draws our attention to how the 'contents' of memories – the detail of their stories, narratives and recollections – are discursively shaped. Foucault's corpus, directed to various other contexts, is broadly oriented to showing how discourse *produces* subjects, making us who we are. Here, in treating memory as a discursive product, we are further sensitised to how integral memory is to furnishing a sense of self, allowing us to tell stories of ourselves as individuals and social entities.

A second key thread at work within Foucault's corpus is crucial here. Memory itself is subjected to intervention through specific fields of expert knowledge – especially through the 'psy-sciences' – as an object of knowledge and transformation. Here we see *techniques* of memory deployed in the name of correcting, healing or managing memory. For Foucault, such operations and techniques are not straightforward exercises in 'domination'. At the level of the population, Foucault sees power at work in attempts to manage and maximise the very 'life', 'vitality' and health of the people (however *the people* are defined) (1998: 139). At the level of the body, the individual psyche, they constitute 'self-subjectivising' practices that allow individuals, by their own means, to effect power upon themselves, acting to correct 'abnormal', 'irregular' or 'deficient' social orders (and memories). For example, in Chapter 6, we examine techniques of memory deployed within Cambodia to enable individuals to self-diagnose trauma and post-traumatic stress disorder (PTSD). Such techniques of memory are inseparable from their wider institutional contexts and configurations. Foucault's concept of 'strategies' is particularly useful in this regard when linking memory and transitional justice. For Foucault, 'strategies' flow from particular 'discursive formations' (i.e. bodies of knowledge, sets of relational statements), that shape the way our choices are oriented to particular ends or outcomes (2002: 76–78). For example, as Moon has argued (drawing on Foucault) in relation to South Africa's Truth and Reconciliation Commission, a specific discursive strategy of 'reconciliation' emerged to act as a 'template-script' of what reconciliation should entail, animating the protagonists therein, and prescribing the techniques – such as testimonials and apologies – that would permit the realisation of such ends (2008: 54–55). We might anticipate how different discourses of 'justice', 'reconciliation', 'truth' or 'healing' might operate with similar regularities in Cambodia today.

Foucault suggests that strategies are deeply embedded within systems and networks of power but eschews the notion that strategies flow cleanly from a neat opposition of 'dominator' to 'dominated'. Rather, for Foucault, strategies and power should be understood as operating on potentially diverse, multiple platforms and layers, while retaining a 'more or less unitary strategic form' (1980: 142). Crucially, Foucault notes that 'there are no relations of power without resistances' and that these resistances are manifest at the point of the exercise of power (1980: 142). This is an important issue for an appreciation of an account of memory that recognises competing relationships laying claim over the past that are not omnipotent, determinant and totalising. Moreover, any failure of a particular 'strategy' – an attempt to bring about particular effects among the social body – can provide fertile terrain for analysis. As Gordon suggests, the imperfections in the correspondence of 'strategies', techniques and the effects they are enacted to bring about remains an area that is significant for the investigation of the 'real but unprogrammed effects' of strategies and technologies (1980: 247–248). In other words, when we see 'memory work' happening – within transitional justice and beyond – it rarely fulfils its aims or intended outcomes neatly or cleanly.

Memory and history

In marking an analytical distinction between what memory 'is' and how it is 'known', we can productively revisit another key and seemingly intractable opposition that has haunted scholarship in both memory studies and history. As Misztal points out, there is a purported conflict between the subjective and mythologizing qualities of memory, which necessarily subordinate clean distinctions between past and present; and the distanced, objective lens of history as a form of documentation and recording (2003: 99–100). This opposition is fundamentally bound to the specific histories of different disciplinary fields that were competing over 'the past', that is, memory and history, as objects of knowledge and enquiry. Historians working in the nineteenth century rallied to the prevailing positivisms of the time, which promised scientific truth, staking out the past as a field of excavation to be objectively disinterred and verified and positing individual memory as a questionable and unreliable repository of 'facts' (Klein 2000: 130). Indeed, the emergence of history as a science notably coincides and intersects with currents shaping the legal and penal system of the nineteenth century, which were predicated on assumptions of scientific *truth* – laying claim over memories specifically against registers of verification – that persist and organise exchanges in the courtroom today.

Yet memory obliges its own parallel history here rooted in the birth of the 'psy-sciences', which is also deeply connected to questions of truth, veracity and disclosure and is preoccupied by its imperfections therein. Hacking explains that the idea of memory was radically transformed in the late nineteenth century as it was brought into the sphere of medical knowledge, or 'medicalised'. Hacking here shows us how the 'grammar' of contemporary memory studies and 'memoro-politics' is constituted (1995: Chapter 15). In the work of Pierre Janet and Sigmund Freud, at the moment that the notion of trauma was translated from a category of purely bodily affliction to a psychic one, predicated on the possibility of suffering psychic wounds to the mind, a specific connection between self and memory was constituted in a constant and irreversible relationship: that what we remember and forget 'aetiologically' causes and constitutes both our character and our vitality. The assumption that, firstly, (faulty) memories can be objectively located and known; and secondly, that the disclosure and confrontation of memories of terrible experiences is the pathway to remedy present 'neuroses' was entrenched at this foundational moment. This is a premise that haunts memory studies and characterises scholarship and practice in transitional justice today.

If we return to the nearer present, the history of memory studies, as well as the cultural turn within history, should seem more familiar. In general, both the cultural turn and the birth of memory studies are emblematic of disciplinary labours that sought to destabilise and unmask authoritative historical narratives. This imperative itself draws on the assumption that marginalised and subaltern pasts must be uncovered. In this sense, one important way of approaching the distinction between history and memory is based on the assumption that they are themselves different epistemological lenses and registers that lay claim over the objective, genuine, sensory past, but just on different terms. They are not separable but neither are they interchangeable; history and memory *do* and are made to *do* different things.

The memory boom

A core set of questions that are central to (and in many ways constituted) memory studies are pertinent at this point: how and why has memory – and in particular, experiences of political violence – come to be such a vexed and urgent object of social and political practice today? The 1990s saw debates coalesce around a 'crisis' of memory. Terdiman argues that modernity centres memory in social life because the experience of modern world is predicated on forms of linear temporality, implying that there is no necessary connection between past and present (1993). Nora, similarly, diagnoses the rise of memory as a modern preoccupation (1989), famously claiming that the proliferation of 'memory', fixed in sites and objects or '*lieux de memoire*', emerges specifically from the absence of organic forms of community remembering that have been undermined by the conditions of late modernity. By this account, the decline of tradition inspires both the contemporary cultural and scholarly fascination with memory. Huyssen has argued that we have witnessed the 'twilight' of memory: as late modernity accelerates our experience of the world, the dislocation with a sense of past necessitates a reliance on memory as an anchoring social reference point (1995), key features of which are the growth in heritage and conservation industries and the proliferation of museum and memorial sites. These accounts have pointed to a broad cultural memory 'boom', limning the contingent currency of memory in modern life.

A defining aspect of the recent interest in memory is a focus on histories of suffering, conflict and atrocity. Glorified accounts of war, sacrifice and valour have been (and remain) central to national narratives (Hobsbawm and Ranger 1983; Renan 1990 [1882]; Gillis 1994; Anderson 2006). But as Olick has highlighted, the twentieth century witnessed a willingness of states and elites to acknowledge and disclose histories of political violence (2007: 165). Olick has described the entrenchment of an imperative to self-disclose, disinter, prosecute and apologise for histories of atrocity and suffering as bound to a nascent 'politics of regret', marking 'regret' as a new principle of political legitimacy (2007: 22). For Olick, an 'ethic' of regret is an emergent condition of modernity. Olick draws on both Weber and Nietzsche to mine the Enlightenment decline of religion, theodicy and the attendant demystification of public life as processes that worked to centre 'secular man' in time. Secular humanitarianism replaced theological calls for redemption as forms of '*ressentiment*' (a politics of protecting the vulnerable), and rational humanist 'progress' subsumed a Christian teleology as the prevailing moral narrative for the world view of (Western) man. For Olick, rational modernity and technological development produces and then obviates the arbitrary nature of human suffering resulting from conflict, as seen in the most dramatic form with 'total warfare' during World War II (WWII) and the experience of the Holocaust (2007: 172). Olick's account seeks to conceptually and empirically map how the thinking and experience of modernity germinates 'regret' as a moral and political imperative, obliging a 'duty' to remember.

Theories of the duty to remember tend to start with the experience of the Holocaust and WWII as reference points, underlining the significance of these events for the formation of an *ethic* of remembrance, signalled in the growth of post-war human-rights instruments, provisions and principles. We will turn to these shortly. The burdens and duties of memory, as framed emerging from these contexts, tend to be treated as self-evidently valuable. In particular, to remember suffering is necessary to counter forgetting, locating forgetting as a recapitulation to violence or a secondary injury. For example, from very different orientations in social theory, Adorno suggests that "(t)he abundance of real suffering tolerates no forgetting" (Adorno 1974: 84), while Baudrillard has written that "forgetting extermination is part of extermination, because it is also the extermination of memory, of history, of the social..." (1994: 49). Baudrillard is at the same time anxious to diagnose the way that the 'artificial' mass simulation of memory through cultural channels such as film and television debases and surrenders itself to the 'violence' of forgetting. The assumption that the past promises lessons for the present is the centrepiece of many such debates. Bauman's seminal *Modernity and the Holocaust* (2000), for example, diagnoses the Holocaust as the apotheosis of modernity – the accomplishments of rationalisation, efficiency and bureaucracy – revealing the immanent potential towards violence within modern social life that must be combated by a duty of memory.

The potential for memory work to yield ameliorative, educational or deterrent and socio-political outcomes in the present has become an axiom of modern human rights, even when the emergence of an ethic of memory is acknowledged to be historically contingent and conditioned; for example, accounts of the relationship of remembering to democratisation, trust, forgiveness and dignification (Misztal 2005, 2010, 2013) and the stabilisation of the modern human-rights project more broadly (Levy and Sznaider 2010). Levy and Sznaider have argued, along similar lines to Olick, that memories of the experiences of suffering during WWII and the Holocaust have engendered a 'cosmopolitanistion' of state sovereignty – the orientation of states' rational interests around human-rights principles of regret – premised on a willingness to remember and prevent the recurrence of such events

(Levy and Sznaider 2002, 2004, 2006, 2010). For Levy and Sznaider, the emergence of an ethic of regret is visible in the political–judicial responses to the Holocaust and WWII: the formalisation of the modern human-rights regime – specifically privileging the dignity of the individual victim – with the Universal Declaration of Human Rights, the United Nations Genocide Convention, the Geneva Conventions and the Nuremberg prosecutions for Nazi war crimes. The structure of these claims is significant because they imply a linear relationship between practices of memory furnishing social and political outcomes in the present, such as deterrence or democratisation. Moreover, through the 'sacralisation' of memory, these accounts imply and obviate that there are 'incorrect' practices of memory that are antithetical to specific and privileged constructions of dignity. Memory here begets remembering through a reading of cosmopolitanism that is arguably overly sanguine. As important as the Holocaust and WWII are as referents for an ethic(s) of memory, they conversely implicate questions over why a politics of regret, our account of it and, indeed, the modern human-rights project, did 'start' here, given the weight of experiences of slavery and colonial injustice before the wars. As Haraway notes (1992), the figuration of the "human" that emerged in the post-war period was a contingent, flattened category that could exclude and elide experiences of marginality and difference as much as redeem them.

It is notable that accounts connecting the formative experiences of the Holocaust, questions of memory and the modern human-rights regime are principally focused on the emergence of juridical instruments. This reading of the relationship between modern human rights and memory produces a fundamentally liberal, legalist and Western vision of human rights in character and tone. It privileges the individual as the key rights bearer, it is predicated on the purported deterrent potential of law and it is blind to hierarchies and politics that obviate some populations as entitled to human rights but not others. In this vein, Tony Evans has suggested that the colonization of human rights discourses and practices as a field of law (and lens of memory) requires a denial of its own political constitution, while foregrounding an inherently political and 'market'-driven vision of international social order (2005). While the premise of the modern human-rights project was based on the subordination of state sovereignty and the inauguration of forums for 'post-national' governance, the inconsistent and fragmented insertion of 'de-territorialized' techniques for the management of populations – transitional justice a key field therein – implies the very absence of universal 'rules' and accountability that were promised by the human-rights project (Chandler 2009). Indeed, as we will see, the state, sovereignty and national populations are clearly still fertile animating concepts for political life, if not the seemingly *a priori* and transcendent organising principles of political order, as early normative liberal and realist political theories imply. As human rights have now been used to justify military interventions and legitimate imperial ambitions across the globe, critical scholars have argued for the need to reclaim the cosmopolitan project on more genuinely utopian and emancipatory terms (Douzinas 2007).

At this juncture, where we have seen that memory promises to furnish human rights, offering truth, justice and redemption; and that human rights are thought to constitute international political order, we can turn to the historical changes and contingencies that have enabled the entrenchment of regret as a norm that informs the governance and management of post-conflict contexts. These events are central to the stories of both transitional justice and human rights. Whilst the Nuremberg prosecutions represent one of the first formal attempts to legally respond to atrocity – though equally embedding regimes of impunity for powerful international actors – the cementing of global norms and mechanisms that reckon with legacies of past political violence was impaired by the intractable bi-polar politics of the Cold War (Teitel 2003, 2005). The wider realisation of a 'politics of regret' was therefore only made possible by the fracturing of the international Cold War political landscape. The growth of specifically international non-governmental organisations (NGOs) institutionally embedded the human-rights project as a field of 'apolitical' advocacy (Moyn 2010), and the transitions to democracy across Latin America during the 1980s and in Eastern Europe from 1989 onwards have played a crucial role in shaping and cementing the current transitional justice regime in its often highly conflicted approaches and aims (Cohen 1995). I now turn to the relationship between memory and transitional justice-specific mechanisms in closer detail.

Transitional justice

Transitional justice is now a burgeoning field of scholarship and practice. It has grown alongside a proliferation of institutions and initiatives that seek to remedy and reckon with experiences of violence and suffering. The history of cases and mechanisms within transitional justice is itself vast and growing (see Hayner's account of truth commissions, 2002; Teitel 2003, 2015). Instead of reappraising cases and examples within transitional justice, I seek here to historicize and sketch some of the key assumptions at play in prevailing transitional justice scholarship and practice, examining tensions over what transitional justice has done and is *meant* to do. My aim, here, is to illustrate and present the contingency of its changing central assumptions. I then turn to reconnect and put into dialogue these approaches to the previous section on the mechanics and ethics of memory.

The term *transitional justice* came into use following the shifts away from authoritarian rule in Latin America and Eastern Europe in the 1980s and 1990s (Kritz 1996) and, constitutively, in the transition from apartheid in South Africa. Transitional justice has been broadly defined as a set of tools and strategies 'associated with periods of political change' (Teitel 2005: 837) that respond to the question of 'how to reckon with massive crimes and abuses' (Hayner 2002: 11). Transitional justice derives its normative authority from the field of human rights and a wider corpus of international criminal and humanitarian law, though it also reflects and nourishes specific (Western) taken-for-granted tropes about redress and justice that *must be done* in the wake of massive violence (Buckley-Zistel *et al.* 2014: 1). The scope of the field continues to be debated (Roht-Arriaza and Mariezcurrena 2006; Bell 2009), and despite attempts to develop 'models' of transition (see e.g. Winter 2013), scholarship has not yielded a 'general' theory of transitional justice or techniques for confronting past political violence (Arthur 2009); as Clark and Palmer question, transitional justice can be read to have authored itself 'too quickly', when its coherence remains inchoate (2012: 1). Transitional justice then – as a field of knowledge and practice – remains conflicted, contested and in flux.

Trevino-Rangel has identified three tendencies or 'clusters' within transitional scholarship that (loosely) map its conceptual and historical emergence (2012: Chapter 2; see also Teitel 2015). The first cluster was defined by the dilemmas and political trade-offs thought to characterise the first Latin American and Eastern European transitions. Transitional justice, first as a field practice, was initially preoccupied by two purportedly conflicting imperatives: the retribution and punishment of those that violate human rights, on the one hand; and the restoration and reconciliation of societies, on the other. Retribution follows from a legalist imperative to punish those that perpetrate violations of human rights. This retributive legalism was visible as it materialised at war crimes trials and tribunals (beginning at Nuremberg, more recently visible at the *ad hoc* prosecutions for crimes perpetrated in the former Yugoslavia and Rwanda, at the permanent International Criminal Court and present within Cambodia at the Extraordinary Chambers in the Courts of Cambodia [ECCC]). These approaches framed punishment through the lens of human rights (Kritz 1996; Mallinder 2007). Yet more broadly, the need to punish tends to be situated with greater complexity than a 'just deserts', located between and conjoining 'intrinsic' and 'consequential' human rights justifications for interventions. Intrinsic claims for justice assumed, simply, that injustice necessitated justice, thereby embodying a universal and absolutist retributivism that animates a clear and finite moral economy between crime and accountability. Consequentialist justifications, on the other hand, led advocates to add a raft of further outcomes of punishments as purported benefits: delineating individual and collective guilt for mass crimes (Méndez 1997), helping to establish the rule of law and foster democratic institutions (Borneman 1997), promoting memory and deterring the future perpetration of atrocity (Zalaquett 1990), enhancing social solidarity (Osiel 1997) and purportedly de-politicizing the treatment of perpetrators in the wake of political violence (Orentlicher 1991). These consequential justifications – increasingly framed as policy outcomes – prefigure the presence of a bureaucratic and institutionalised raft of bodies that act on and within transitional justice cases through the lens of 'best practice' today (Teitel 2015).

As an alternative approach to human-rights violations, restorative justice situated 'victims' as the site of civic renewal. These strategies emphasise approaches such as apology, reparation, and in particular, the recovery of 'truth' (through various techniques, i.e. public testimony at commissions, the disclosure of records from previous authorities and the production of reports). Restorative strategies were thought to better accommodate victims' needs (Hayner 2002), offer victims dignity (Minow and Rosenblum 2002), prevent further atrocity by virtue of truth (Rotberg and Thompson 2000), reform offenders (Braithwaite 1999) and reconcile and restore relationships between conflicted parties (Johnstone 2002). In doing so, they tend to animate and rely on clear aetiologies between past suffering and present 'disorder'. Restorative justice techniques – characterised by forms of disclosure manifest primarily at the site of truth commissions – have historically enmeshed discourses of reconciliation and the employment of amnesty agreements, visible (in early instances) in the institutional demands for 'truth' across the Latin American transitions and, most famously, at the South African Truth and Reconciliation Commission. In South Africa, amnesty was granted to perpetrators of crimes committed during South Africa's conflict in the name of 'truth', 'healing' and 'national reconciliation' (see Moon 2006, 2008). Reconciliation and restoration were thought to stand in conflict with retribution because they have tended to eschew punishment in the name of peace building.

The past two decades have seen a shift in research and practice within transitional justice that began to depart from early approaches in important ways. This shift especially coincides, on the one hand, with the configuration of a *continuous* and permanent site of international regulation at the International Criminal Court (ICC) with, on the other, the institutional embedding of (highly mobile) transnational institutions and bodies able to seek out, diagnose and *instruct* transitional justice as a de-territorialized field of knowledge and practice. Moreover, this shift has also coincided with contributions within research that tend to be more self-critical of the realisation of the goals of transitional justice whilst broadly still subscribing to the belief that interventions following political violence are imperative. They reformulate the debates about transitional justice through registers of the efficacy and outcomes yielded by the various approaches, rather than through a necessary trade-off between the imperatives to punishment, on the one hand, and restoration and reconciliation, on the other. Lastly, they shift the scope of debates in transitional justice to encompass a generalised and routine set of strategies for confronting political violence; they consider a broader range of techniques within the remit of the field; and they have focused on a wider range of problems (for example, incorporating the concept of 'historical injustice'). In this sense, a second 'cluster' of research within transitional justice reflects and embodies the proliferation of globally mobile leaders, ideas and institutions that reflect the way transitional justice has been presented as a continuous and transferable field of expertise (Trevino-Rangel 2012: 90–99).

The second cluster of research has critically departed from the concepts and dilemmas examined by the first in other important ways. While debates over peace versus justice persist – especially in the context of the ICC (Kersten 2016) – and, indeed, are appropriated for political gain by some stakeholders in transitional justice contexts, Vinjamuri notes that there has been a marked shift away from rationales for intervention based on the intrinsic value of justice towards more instrumental and outcomes framed validations (2010). The field, in some respects, obliged itself to undergo its own moral inventory. Core concepts such as reconciliation have been questioned and interrogated for their ambiguity (Pankhurst 1999; Clark 2010). And, as Weinstein stated in a recent special issue of the *International Journal of Transitional Justice*, no transitional justice initiative had discernibly achieved its goals:

> [W]e have focused entirely too much on the notions of closure and reconciliation. Member States of the UN and European Union have expended

> considerable amounts of money and human resources on chasing a will-o'-the wisp, adopting buzzwords that have no consistent definition or conceptual clarity and promoting mechanisms to achieve these obscure outcomes with little evidence that they will make a difference.
>
> (Weinstein 2011: 3)

At the same time, despite a more cautious and critical consensus emerging within transitional justice, the majority of work within the field over the past two decades largely remains haunted by the assumption that to do 'nothing' in the wake of political violence is no option, leaving societies that have experienced massive violence unable to 'develop' or 'move on' (Arenhövel 2008; Roehrig 2009). The inevitable failure of transitional justice interventions to deliver on their loftier headline ambitions has obliged scholars within the field to reframe research as a question of 'best practice' (demonstrating again the way that transitional justice has emerged as field that mutually implicates knowledge and practice). For example, in the South African context, Gibson sought to quantify and test the causal relationship between 'truth' (as a technique) and 'reconciliation' as an observable and measurable output (2004). Based on a large scale study of 854 cases held in 161 countries, Olsen *et al.* have claimed that, weighing positives and negatives, transitional justice has had a positive impact on human rights and democracy (2010). Leaving aside the validity of these claims, they are illuminating of the trend towards policy efficacy that has characterised scholarship in the field.

The preoccupation with maximising the beneficial social and political impacts of transitional justice interventions has emerged alongside and intertwined with other developments and forks in our story of the field (of which there might be many other variants). The field has proliferated over the last two decades 'vertically' along scales – from 'supra' or 'trans'-national groups, states, and non-governmental organisations (NGOs) to more proximate agents – as well as 'horizontally' attending to new legal and political contexts and concerns (Hansen 2014). On the one hand, in the shadow of the ICC and galvanised by the International Criminal Tribunal for the former Yugoslavia (ICTY) and International Criminal Tribunal for Rwanda (ICTR) precedents, *legalism* has taken on a renewed ascendancy in the field, seductive because it purports to offer an 'apolitical' and 'common sense' set of responses to violence (McEvoy 2007; Teitel 2015). On the other hand, nourished by the institutional growth of the field and fuelled by critiques of the ICTY and ICTR as 'remote' from the populations that it sought to address, an increasing interest in 'localising' justice initiatives emerged. This trend seeks to accommodate 'holistic' approaches and legal pluralism. Calls for 'grassroots' justice initiatives suggest that transitional justice mechanisms are most meaningful when they are sensitive to the variety and richness of the experiences they are intended to redress and embedded within the communities that they are intended to renew (Arriaza and Roht-Arriaza 2008; Shaw *et al.* 2010). As is visible with the Cambodian case, hybrid institutions were rationalised on the basis of their ability to provide 'international' standards of justice whilst rendering resonant, meaningful verdicts for the local population and enhancing local judicial capacity (Urs 2007; Gellman 2008; Stensrud 2009). Moreover, one further development is marked here as research on transitional justice began to expand its scope in two additional senses. Firstly, the targets of transitional justice strategies were broadened to include the wider category of 'historical injustice' (Torpey 2007). This extends the scope of the field to include questions of redress for crimes many years previous, in post-colonial contexts such as slavery (Posner and Vermeule 2003), or the treatment of aboriginal communities (Short 2007), principally through mechanisms of apology or compensation. Secondly, as indicated by the aforementioned interest in the use of apology and compensation, research into the techniques of the field expanded to specifically include, for example, memorialisation (Jelin 2007; Barsalou and Baxter 2007), or the public education system and school curricula (Cole 2007). The widening of the field points to the normalisation of a generalised, continuous set of claims for the governance of societies that have suffered political violence.

A third and more recent tendency within transitional justice research is characterised by a more critical approach to the assumptions, concepts and frameworks underpinning transitional justice as a field of knowledge and practice. In many respects, this reflects a maturing of the field too long dominated by *practice* (Clark *et al.* 2012: 2), affording a necessary and productive disaggregation between analysis and advocacy that is too often confused. Bell, for example, disputes that transitional justice has a self-evident coherence, suggesting that its various normative, legal and political frictions and contradictions are concealed by its purported inter-disciplinarity (2009). Such a line of enquiry helps us move beyond the important question of whether transitional justice mechanisms do – or even are able to do – what they claim to do (Mendeloff 2004), gesturing to the recognition that denouncing and reframing the past cannot prevent unconnected forms of violence in the present. Rather, at the heart of recent, more critical scholarship is an interest in power. Instead of offering an institutional 'de-politicization' of confronting past political violence (see Orentlicher 1991), transitional justice interventions emerge and work subject to and conditioned by hierarchies of power (Short 2007; Moon 2008; Nagy 2008; Ainley 2011). Recognising the way power both shapes and *constitutes* transitions and interventions is important because it gestures to the way that practitioners and scholars treat the vocabulary and concepts of transitional as neutral, stable and apolitical. Indeed, Wilson's work on reconciliation in South Africa specifically showed that the language of human rights had the effect of concealing a (pragmatic) politics of nation building, which was at points in conflict with locally embedded imperatives for retributive justice (2001). More recently, Loyle and Davenport have pointed out that it is entirely possible for states to utilise the mechanisms of transitional justice with no interest in enacting the beneficial outcomes that are thought bound to them (e.g. truth, healing or democracy), coining the term transitional 'injustice' (2016). Furthermore, the recognition that transitional justice can be 'iatrogenic', representing a cure that does more harm than good, has been shown to be common across and not incidental within the field (Trevino-Rangel 2012; Millar 2015).

In appreciating the role of power and hierarchy in shaping specific interventions, we are historically better sensitised to the specific interests and actions that shape each case. Subotić has argued that the "norm" of doing justice was initially driven by cases with strong local appetites for intervention, which in turn came to entrench wider assumptions and expectations *of* post-conflict or transitional contexts. Now, Subotić points out, transitional justice mechanisms are often not straightforwardly implemented for the reasons that they are said or meant to be, and often on terms contrary to their public presentation (2014, 2009). Indeed, as Short argues, claims advanced within transitional justice must be understood as mediated by political interests and not necessarily benevolent (2007).

Such critiques have consequences for how we approach the concepts at play in researching transitional justice. Comparative analysis of transitional justice mechanisms across cases, for example, can be valuable if clear, empirical variables are easily pinpointed. But given that such variables are often both assumed and remain conceptually and politically contingent (i.e. the make-up of a given mechanism and its relation to, say, rates of human-rights violation or measures of 'democratisation'), we have reason to remain cautious. It might be premature to dismiss the value of deeper case based analysis, which can still be instructive of the wider field. Moon, for example, examines discourses of reconciliation in South Africa to show that it is more fruitful analytically to interrogate the specific architecture of reconciliatory claims as they are propagated on a case-by-case basis rather than presuming a universal end or process that can be observed and judged, as if reconciled states can be observed (or not) across contexts (2008). Indeed, Tony Evans has shown how the language of human rights is discursively contested and appropriated, buttressing relationships of domination and resistance (Evans 2005), while Franzki and Olarte point out that the social orders transitional justice seeks to inaugurate are specifically 'neoliberal' and market friendly (2014); transitional justice is equally complicit therein, and we should be wary of whether the headline 'deliverables' of transitional justice are either observable or even valuable in each particular context.

A second crucial issue concerns the representation of transitional justice contexts, bearing in mind Foucault's claim that how we come to *know* problems tends to shape and obviate the tools and strategies for its resolution. Transitional justice tends to conceptualise (national) societies as singular objects. A question of memory arises on this basis, because 'individual' qualities about the psyche are ascribed onto and read from collective groupings when arguments for the need to intervene are advanced (Moon 2007). As Hamber and Wilson note, this is problematic because it positions memory as a 'static and collective *object*' (2002: 36). The first issue here is that interventions are justified in ways that treat their objects as homogenous, singular, passive entities, particularly in the way that they tend to be bound to political nation-building projects (Wilson 2001). As a field of practice, then, transitional justice coincides with assumptions about memory that treat past violence as aetiologically generative of potential socio-political dysfunction in the present. Transitional justice presents its techniques and interventions as necessary and inevitable, and in the absence of which societies are unable to properly engage experiences of suffering (Trevino-Rangel 2012: 102). In other words, the absence of transitional justice is seen as evidence of the need for transitional justice. This premise is fraught because it establishes and relies on teleological schemas that objectify states of suffering or 'progression' on a linear registers. Societies, conceptualised as objects to intervene on, are not 'corrected' until transitional justice is *done*, but only through the mechanisms and lenses of transitional justice. It is on this basis that societies that have experienced political violence are framed and represented through the language of transitional justice in dichotomous functional/dysfunctional terms, as 'traumatised', 'broken', 'fragmented', implicating the need for or purported success of particular techniques of intervention and often animating supervisory relationships of the international over the domestic (see Hughes and Pupavac 2005, specifically on Cambodia).

Conclusion

We might here briefly revisit the way that the core approaches and frameworks of transitional justice relate to, invoke and imply memory. The vocabularies of transitional justice treat memory in different ways, but they are unified in the way they situate the past as a site that can renew, resolve and ameliorate the social and political conditions of the present. This is a significant overlap with the prevailing currents within memory studies that locate an ethics of memory. Punishment and the spectacle of the war-crimes trial looks to the past to furnish its narrative content through the way it reckons with past conflict. It bids to produce an account of past crimes through the techniques and interplays of evidence, interpretation, performance and contextual political interests. Retribution simultaneously has one eye on the future, in the way it asks trials to act as both didactic agents (e.g. enhancing the rule of law or deterring future crimes) and bodies that can affirm social solidarity (Osiel 1997: 18). The prevailing vocabulary of healing and renewal more explicitly invokes memory as an object that must be ameliorated; as Moon (2009) notes, adopting a more critical lens, the South African Truth and Reconciliation commission specifically drew its authority from a medicalised and therapeutic language of (memory) repression, denial, trauma and catharsis in the way it represented the national body politic (and its collective memory). Crucially, in the way they make demands of, act upon and (re)produce memory, both retributive and restorative vocabularies and frameworks presume to act on objectively locatable 'collective memory', especially as they invoke, animate and address national psyches. Moreover, as each initiative seeks to 'reckon with' and 'settle' the past, its resonance tends to presuppose the broad acceptance of its particular version of events, in either the provision of a sense of justice or the realisation of bids to reconciliation around social rupture.

There are two key common problems arising within the literatures on memory studies and transitional justice that premise my approach here. Firstly, prevailing assumptions within transitional justice and memory studies assume the need to confront, disinter and intervene in memories of political violence as a means of social progression, primarily through the formal processes and mechanisms of transitional justice (broadly defined). This obliges lenses for 'seeing' the absence or deficiencies of transitional justice as obviating the need for more or 'better' transitional justice, obliging further regimes of supervision and management. My intention in this book is to query the sequence and the singularity of relationships between memories of past violence and techniques of remedy in the present that they presuppose. Secondly, in the wake of atrocity, the need for a formal mechanism that inaugurates a society's ability to 'move on' – and those benefits it purports to yield – has been naturalised as a self-evident, de-contextualised imperative for the governance of post-atrocity societies. But social orders in the present are not singularly determined by any one episode of past violence, and the assumption that particular transitional justice mechanisms can and will redress them through a clear relation of present to past is problematic; social orders are actively maintained to conceal or preserve experiences of violence or the inequalities that generate them. Moreover, transitional justice interventions do not occur in a vacuum. They emerge from and are shaped by specific relationships and hierarchies of power at play. They do not operate neutrally or void questions of power. Transitional justice can conceal as much as it discloses. And it can also do harm as well as much-needed good.

References

Adorno, T. 1974. Commitment. *New Left Review*, 87–88.

Ainley, K. 2011. Excesses of responsibility: The limits of law and the possibilities of politics. *Ethics & International Affairs*, *25* (4): 407–431.

Anderson, B. R. O. G. 2006. *Imagined Communities: Reflections on the Origin and Spread of Nationalism*. London, New York: Verso.

Antze, P. and Lambek, M. 1996. *Tense Past: Cultural Essays in Trauma And Memory*. New York, London: Routledge.

Arenhövel, M. 2008. Democratization and transitional justice. *Democratisation*, *15* (3): 570–587.

Arriaza, L. and Roht-Arriaza, N. 2008. Social reconstruction as a local process. *International Journal of Transitional Justice*, *2* (2): 152–172.

Arthur, P. 2009. How 'transitions' reshaped human rights: A conceptual history of transitional justice. *Human Rights Quarterly*, *31* (2): 321–367.

Barsalou, J. and Baxter, V. 2007. The urge to remember: The role of memorials in social reconstruction and transitional justice. *Stabilisation and Reconstruction Series* (5). United States Institute for Peace.

Baudrillard, J. 1994. *Simulacra and Simulation*. Ann Arbor: University of Michigan Press.

Bauman, Z. 2000. *Modernity and the Holocaust*. Ithaca, NY: Cornell University Press.

Beck, U. 2007. The cosmopolitan condition: Why methodological nationalism fails. *Theory, Culture & Society*, *24* (7–8): 286–290.

Bell, C. 2009. Transitional justice, interdisciplinarity and the state of the 'field'or 'non-field'. *International Journal of Transitional Justice*, *3* (1): 5–27.

Bennett, T. 1995. *The Birth of the Museum: History, Theory, Politics*. London, Routledge.

Bodnar, J. 1993. *Remaking America: Public Memory, Commemoration, and Patriotism in the Twentieth Century*. Princeton, NJ: Princeton University Press.

Borneman, J. 1997. *Settling Accounts: Violence, Justice, and Accountability in Postsocialist Europe*. Princeton, NJ: Princeton University Press.

Buckley-Zistel, S., Beck, T. K., Braun, C. and Mieth, F. (eds) 2013. *Transitional Justice Theories*. New York, Routledge.

Braithwaite, J. 1999. Restorative justice: Assessing optimistic and pessimistic accounts. *Crime and Justice*: 1–127.

Brown, S. D. 2008. The quotation marks have a certain importance: Prospects for a 'memory studies'. *Memory Studies*, *1* (3): 261–71.
Brown, S. D. and Reavey, P., 2015. Turning around on experience: The 'expanded view' of memory within psychology. *Memory Studies*, *8* (2): 131–150.
Chandler, D. 2009. Critiquing liberal cosmopolitanism? The limits of the biopolitical approach. *International Political Sociology*, *3* (1): 53–70.
Clark, P. 2010. *The Gacaca Courts, Post-Genocide Justice and Reconciliation in Rwanda: Justice without Lawyers*. Cambridge, UK: Cambridge University Press.
Clark, P., Palmer, N. and Granville, D. 2012. *Critical Perspectives in Transitional Justice*. Antwerpen: Intersentia.
Cohen, S. 1995. State crimes of previous regimes: Knowledge, accountability, and the policing of the past. *Law & Social Inquiry*, *20* (1): 7–50.
Cole, E. A. 2007. Transitional justice and the reform of history education. *International Journal of Transitional Justice*, *1* (1): 115–137.
Connerton, P. 1989. *How Societies Remember*. Cambridge, UK: Cambridge University Press.
Douzinas, C. 2007. *Human Rights and Empire: The Political Philosophy of Cosmopolitanism*. New York: Routledge.
Durkheim, É. 1984. *The Division of Labour in Society*. Basingstoke: Macmillan.
Durkheim, É. 2001. *The Elementary Forms of the Religious life*. Oxford: Oxford University Press.
Evans, T. 2005. International human rights law as power/knowledge. *Human Rights Quarterly*, *27* (3): 1046–1068.
Foucault, M. 1980. Power and strategies. In *Power-Knowledge: Selected Interviews and Other Writings, 1972–1977*. C. Gordon (ed). Brighton, Harvester Press.
Foucault, M. 1991. Politics and the study of discourse. In *The Foucault effect: Studies in Governmentality; With Two Lectures by and an Interview with Michel Foucault*. G. Burchell, C. Gordon, P. Miller and M. Foucault (eds). London, Chicago: University of Chicago Press.
Foucault, M. 1998. *The History of Sexuality, Vol. 1: The will to knowledge*. London: Penguin.
Foucault, M. 2002. *Archaeology of Knowledge*. London, New York: Routledge.
Foucault, M. and Gordon, C. 1980. *Power-Knowledge: Selected Interviews and Other Writings, 1972–1977*. Brighton: Harvester Press.
Franzki, H. and Olarte, M. C. 2014. Understanding the political economy of transitional justice. In *Transitional justice theories*. Buckley-Zistel, S., Beck, T. K., Braun, C. and Mieth, F. (eds), 2014. New York: Routledge. 201–221.
Frost, W. and Laing, J. 2013. *Commemorative Events: Memory, Identities, Conflict*. New York: Routledge.
Gavriely-Nuri, D. 2014. Collective memory as a metaphor: The case of speeches by Israeli prime ministers 2001–2009. *Memory Studies*, *7* (1): 46–60.
Gellman, M. 2008. No justice, no peace? National reconciliation and conflict resolution in Cambodia. *Asian Perspective*, *32* (2): 37–57.
Gibson, J. L. 2004. Does truth lead to reconciliation? Testing the causal assumptions of the South African truth and reconciliation process. *American Journal of Political Science*, *48* (2): 201–217.
Gillis, J. R. 1994. *Commemorations: The Politics of National Identity*. Princeton, NJ: Princeton University Press.

Gordon, C. 1980. Afterword. *Power-Knowledge: Selected Interviews and Other Writings, 1972–1977*. C. Gordon (ed). Brighton: Harvester.

Hacking, I. 1995. *Rewriting the Soul: Multiple Personality and the Sciences of Memory*. Princeton, NJ: Princeton University Press.

Halbwachs, M. 1992. *On Collective Memory*, edited and translated by Lewis Coser. Chicago: University of Chicago Press.

Hamber, B. and Wilson, R. A. 2002. Symbolic closure through memory, reparation and revenge in post-conflict societies. *Journal of Human Rights*, *1* (1): 35–53.

Hansen, T. O. 2014. The vertical and horizontal expansion of transitional justice. In *Transitional justice theories*. Buckley-Zistel, S., Beck, T. K., Braun, C. and Mieth, F. (eds). New York, Routledge. 105–124.

Haraway, D. 1992. Ecce homo, ain't (ar'n't) I a woman, and inappropriate/d others: The human in a post-humanist landscape. In *Feminists Theorize the Political*. Butler, J. and Scott, J. (eds). New York: Routledge. 86–100.

Hayner, P. 2002. *Unspeakable Truths: Facing the Challenge of Truth Commissions*. New York: Routledge.

Hobsbawm, E. J. and Ranger, T. O. 1983. *The Invention of Tradition*. Cambridge: Cambridge University Press.

Hoskins, A. 2013. The end of decay time. *Memory Studies*, *6* (4): 387–389.

Hughes, C. and Pupavac, V. 2005. Framing post-conflict societies: International pathologisation of Cambodia and the post-Yugoslav states. *Third World Quarterly*, *26* (6): 873–889.

Huyssen, A. 1995. *Twilight Memories: Marking Time in a Culture of Amnesia*. New York: Routledge.

Jelin, E. 2007. Public memorialization in perspective: Truth, justice and memory of past repression in the southern cone of South America. *International Journal of Transitional Justice*, *1* (1): 138–156.

Johnstone, G. 2002. *Restorative Justice: Ideas, Values, Debates*. Cullompton: Willan.

Kansteiner, W. 2010. Memory, media and Menschen: Where is the individual in collective memory studies? *Memory Studies*, *3* (1): 3–4.

Kersten, M. 2016. *Justice in Conflict: The Effects of the International Criminal Court's Interventions on Ending Wars And Building Peace*. Oxford: Oxford University Press.

Klein, K. L. 2000. On the emergence of memory in historical discourse. *Representations*, *69*: 127–150.

Knudsen, B. T. and Stage, C. 2013. Online war memorials: YouTube as a democratic space of commemoration exemplified through video tributes to fallen Danish soldiers. *Memory Studies*, *6* (4): 418–436.

Koonz, C. 1994. Between memory and oblivion: concentration camps in German memory'. In *Commemorations: The Politics of National Identity*. Gillis, J. (ed). Princeton, NJ: Princeton University Press. 93–107

Koskenniemi, M. 2002. Between impunity and show trials. *Max Planck Yearbook of United Nations Law*, *6* (1): 1–32.

Kritz, N. J. 1996. Coming to terms with atrocities: A review of accountability mechanisms for mass violations of human rights. *Law and Contemporary Problems*, *59* (4): 127–152.

Levy, D. and Sznaider, N. 2002. Memory unbound: The Holocaust and the formation of cosmopolitan memory. *European Journal of Social Theory*, *5* (1): 87–106.

Levy, D. and Sznaider, N. 2004. The institutionalization of cosmopolitan morality: The Holocaust and human rights. *Journal of Human Rights*, *3* (2): 143–157.

Levy, D. and Sznaider, N. 2006. Sovereignty transformed: A sociology of human rights. *The British Journal of Sociology, 57* (4): 657–676.
Levy, D. and Sznaider, N. 2010. *Human Rights and Memory*. University Park: Pennsylvania State University Press.
Loyle, C. E. and Davenport, C., 2016. Transitional injustice: Subverting justice in transition and postconflict societies. *Journal of Human Rights, 15* (1): 126–149.
Mallinder, L. 2007. Can amnesties and international justice be reconciled? *International Journal of Transitional Justice, 1* (2): 208–230.
Méndez, J. E. 1997. Accountability for past abuses. *Human Rights Quarterly, 19* (2): 255–282.
Mendeloff, D. 2004. Truth-seeking, truth-telling, and postconflict peacebuilding: Curb the enthusiasm? *International Studies Review, 6* (3): 355–380.
Millar, G. 2015. Performative memory and re-victimization: Truth-telling and provocation in Sierra Leone. *Memory Studies, 8* (2): 242–254.
Minow, M. and Rosenblum, N. L. 2002. *Breaking the Cycles of Hatred: Memory, Law, And Repair*. Princeton, NJ: Princeton University Press.
Misztal, B. 2003. *Theories of Social Remembering*. Maidenhead: McGraw-Hill Education/Open University Press.
Misztal, B. A. 2005. Memory and democracy. *American Behavioral Scientist, 48* (10): 1320–1338.
Misztal, B. A. 2010. Collective memory in a global age: Learning how and what to remember. *Current Sociology, 58* (1): 24–44.
Misztal, B. A. 2013. The idea of dignity: Its modern significance. *European Journal of Social Theory, 16* (1): 101–121.
McEvoy, K. 2007. Beyond legalism: Towards a thicker understanding of transitional justice. *Journal of Law and Society, 34* (4): 411–440.
Moon, C. 2006. Narrating political reconciliation: Truth and reconciliation in South Africa. *Social & Legal Studies, 15* (2): 257–275.
Moon, C. 2007. States of acknowledgement: The politics of memory, apology, and therapy. In *Crime, Social Control and Human Rights: From Moral Panics to States of Denial, Essays in Honour of Stanley Cohen*. Downes, P., Rock, C., Chinkin, C. and Gearty, C. (eds). Devon, UK: Willan Publishing.
Moon, C. 2008. *Narrating Political Reconciliation: South Africa's Truth and Reconciliation Commission*. Lanham: Lexington Books.
Moon, C. 2009. Healing past violence: Traumatic assumptions and therapeutic interventions in war and reconciliation. *Journal of Human Rights, 8* (1): 71–91.
Moyn, S. 2010. *The Last Utopia*. Cambridge: Harvard University Press.
Nagy, R. 2008. Transitional justice as global project: Critical reflections. *Third World Quarterly, 29* (2): 275–289.
Narvaez, R. F. 2006. Embodiment, collective memory and time. *Body & Society, 12* (3): 51–73.
Nora, P. 1989. Between memory and history: Les lieux de mémoire. *Representations, 26*: 7–24.
Olick, J. K. 2007. *The Politics of Regret: On Collective Memory and Historical Responsibility*. New York, London: Routledge.
Olick, J. K., Vinitzky-Seroussi, V. and Levy, D. 2011. *The Collective Memory Reader*. Oxford and New York: Oxford University Press
Olsen, T., Payne, L. and Reiter, A. 2010. Transitional justice in balance. *Comparing Processes, Weighing Efficacy*. Washington, DC: United States Institute of Peace.

Orentlicher, D. F. 1991. Settling accounts: The duty to prosecute human rights violations of a prior regime. *Yale Law Journal*, 2537–2615.

Osiel, M. 1997. *Mass Atrocity, Collective Memory, and the Law*. New Brunswick, NJ: Transaction Publishers.

Pankhurst, D. 1999. Issues of justice and reconciliation in complex political emergencies: Conceptualising reconciliation, justice and peace. *Third World Quarterly*, *20* (1): 239–255.

Posner, E. A. and Vermeule, A. 2003. Reparations for slavery and other historical injustices. *Columbia Law Review*, 689–748.

Radstone, S. and Hodgkin, K. 2005. *Memory Cultures: Memory, Subjectivity, and Recognition*. New Brunswick, NJ: Transaction Publishers.

Renan, E. 1990. What is a nation? In *Nation and Narration*. H. K. Bhabha (ed). London: Routledge.

Roehrig, T. 2009. Executive leadership and the continuing quest for justice in Argentina. *Human Rights Quarterly*, *31* (3): 721–747.

Roht-Arriaza, N. and Mariezcurrena, J. 2006. *Transitional Justice in the Twenty-First Century: Beyond Truth Versus Justice*. Cambridge, UK; New York: Cambridge University Press.

Rotberg, R. I. and Thompson, D. 2000. *Truth v. Justice: The Morality of Truth Commissions*. Princeton, NJ: Princeton University Press.

Savelsberg, J. J. and King, R. D. 2007. Law and collective memory. *Annu. Rev. Law Soc. Sci.*, *3*: 189–211.

Schlunke, K. 2013. Memory and materiality. *Memory Studies*, *6* (3): 253–261.

Schuman, H. and Scott, J. 1989. Generations and collective memories. *American Sociological Review*, *54* (3): 359–381.

Schwarz, O. 2014. The past next door: Neighbourly relations with digital memory-artefacts. *Memory Studies*, *7* (1): 7–21.

Shaw, R., Waldorf, L. and Hazan, P. 2010. *Localizing Transitional Justice: Interventions and Priorities after Mass Violence*. Stanford: Stanford University Press.

Short, D. 2007. The social construction of indigenous native title land rights in Australia. *Current Sociology*, *55* (6): 857–876.

Singer, J. A. and Conway, M. A. 2014. The varieties of remembered experience: Moving memory beyond the bounded self. *Memory Studies*, *7* (3): 385–392.

Smith, A. D. 1998. *Nationalism and Modernism: A Critical Survey of Recent Theories of Nations and Nationalism*. New York: Routledge.

Stensrud, E. E. 2009. New dilemmas in transitional justice: Lessons from the mixed courts in Sierra Leone and Cambodia. *Journal of Peace Research*, *46* (1): 5.

Subotić, J. 2014. Bargaining justice: A theory of transitional justice compliance. In *Transitional Justice Theories*. Buckley-Zistel, S., Beck, T. K., Braun, C. and Mieth, F. (eds), 2014. New York: Routledge. 125–143.

Subotić, J. 2009. The paradox of international justice compliance. *International Journal of Transitional Justice*, *3* (3): 362–383.

Teitel, R. 2003. Transitional justice genealogy. *Harv. Hum. Rts. J.*, *16*: 69.

Teitel, R. 2005. The law and politics of contemporary transitional justice. *Cornell International Law Journal*, *38*.

Teitel, R. 2015. *Globalizing Transitional Justice*. Oxford and New York: Oxford University Press.

Terdiman, R. 1993. *Present Past: Modernity and the Memory Crisis*. Ithaca, NY: Cornell University Press.

Tolia-Kelly, D. 2004. Locating processes of identification: Studying the precipitates of re-memory through artefacts in the British Asian home. *Transactions of the Institute of British Geographers*, *29* (3): 314–329.

Torpey, J. 2003. *Politics and the Past: On Repairing Historical Injustices*. Lanham, MD: Rowman & Littlefield.

Trevino-Rangel, J. 2012. *Policing the Past: Transitional Justice and the Special Prosecutor's Office in Mexico, 2000–2006*. PhD thesis. The London School of Economics and Political Science (LSE).

Urs, T. 2007. Imagining locally-motivated accountability for mass atrocities: Voices from Cambodia. Sur. *Revista Internacional de Direitos Humanos*, *4*: 58–99.

Vinjamuri, L. 2010. Deterrence, democracy, and the pursuit of international justice. *Ethics & International Affairs*, *24* (2): 191–211.

Ware, S. 2008. Anti-memorials and the art of forgetting: Critical reflections on a memorial design practice. *Public History Review*, *15*.

Weinstein, H. M. 2011. The myth of closure, the illusion of reconciliation: Final thoughts on five years as co-editor-in-chief. *The International Journal of Transitional Justice*, *5* (1): 1–10.

Wertsch, J. V. 2002. *Voices of Collective Remembering*. Cambridge: Cambridge University Press.

White, G. 1997. Museum/memorial/shrine: National narrative in national spaces. *Museum Anthropology*, *21* (1): 8–26.

Williams, P. H. 2007. *Memorial Museums: The Global Rush to Commemorate Atrocities*. Oxford, New York: Berg

Wilson, R. 2001. *The Politics of Truth and Reconciliation In South Africa: Legitimizing the Post-Apartheid State*. Cambridge, New York: Cambridge University Press.

Winter, J. 2010. The performance of the past: Memory, history, identity. In *Performing the Past: Memory, History, and Identity in Modern Europe*. Tilmans, K., van Vree, F. and Winter, J. M. (eds). Amsterdam: Amsterdam University Press. 1–11.

Winter, S. 2013. Towards a unified theory of transitional justice. *International Journal of Transitional Justice*, *7* (2): 224–244.

Young, J. E. 1993. *The Texture of Memory: Holocaust Memorials and Meaning in Europe, Israel, and America*. New Haven, CT: Yale University Press.

Zalaquett, J. 1990. Confronting human rights violations committed by former governments: Applicable principles and political constraints. *Hamline L. Rev.*, *13*: 623.

3 Political violence in Cambodia

Where should we begin to tell the story of political violence in Cambodia? The horrors of the Democratic Kampuchea regime might be neatly bracketed from 1975 to 1979, but they were prefigured by years of serious and sustained political violence, and the decades after the Khmer Rouge regime were marked by persistent conflict, violence and atrocities. Analytically, the question of how to *write* a history of violence in Cambodia is challenging because complex episodes of violence resist neat periodisation. Moreover, this is an especially troubling task given that my intention in this book is, in part, to scrutinize the terms on which different accounts of the past become authoritative, notwithstanding the very present, routine and urgent questions of political violence in Cambodia today. Providing a foundational, comprehensive or definitive record of violence in Cambodia is beyond the aims or scope of my work here, and such analyses have been accomplished by more qualified historians in thorough and extensive accounts (Chandler 1991, 1999; Kiernan 2001, 2002, 2004; Vickery 1984). My intention here is to present an analytical exercise, through a series of historical outlines, to illustrate the contingency, narrowness and selectivity of the prevailing claims of justice and reconciliation that are embodied and mobilised around the Extraordinary Chambers in the Courts of Cambodia (ECCC) today, as well as to empirically map the key points of 'rupture' and continuity across successive regimes in Cambodia (Thion 1986; Cunha *et al.* 2015). This chapter proceeds through sketches of the nearly 50 years of war, conflict, atrocity and genocide that Cambodia has experienced, though I have deliberately eschewed the chronological ordering of these episodes in deference to the need to devote specific attention to political violence and flux prior to 1975 and the politics of genocide recognition after 1979 as substantive concerns in their own rights. I hope to offer both a background of events in Cambodia for unfamiliar readers, while preparing the ground for a wider analysis that reads appeals for justice, truth and reconciliation as politically contingent claims for memory. On this basis, the chapter then directly pivots to try to connect these experiences to the negotiations over the establishment of the ECCC.

Democratic Kampuchea

On April 17th 1975, Khmer Rouge forces captured Phnom Penh. Over the following 3 years, 8 months and 20 days, an estimated 1.6 million Cambodians died of starvation or disease or were executed (Kiernan 2001: 459). A preliminary sketch of this period might focus on the ideological aims of the Khmer Rouge 'Communist Party of Kampuchea' (CPK) leadership. These were, during their ascent to power and early years in rule, communist in tone and overtly oriented toward the establishment of a self-sufficient, agrarian economy. Upon seizing power, the Khmer Rouge evacuated city centres and transferred the urban population to the countryside by force, proclaiming the newly founded 'Democratic Kampuchea' state. The evacuation of Phnom Penh in April 1975, under the pretext of the safety and wellbeing of the population, cost the lives of an estimated 10,600 people alone (Kiernan 2001: 48). The Khmer Rouge hailed the establishment of Democratic Kampuchea as marking 'year zero', and the first weeks of Khmer Rouge rule were characterised by attempts to dismantle and destroy the institutions and remnants of the former 'bourgeois' republican regime and its associated imperial sponsors, the United States (US). Money and markets were abolished, organised religion prohibited and books burned. The Khmer Rouge demanded absolute loyalty and obedience to the *Angkar* or 'organisation'. During the evacuations of Phnom Penh and other cities, former members of the republican establishment, army and civil service were sieved from the population and executed in order to 'cleanse' the population.

Members of the urban population forced to the countryside were termed 'new' people or 'depositees'. Those liberated before April 1975 in areas outside the capital were known as 'base' or 'old' people (Kiernan 2001: 164). This division enacted a basic set of differentiated entitlements and privileges, though both Kiernan (2001) and Vickery (1984) have suggested that the experience of the regime varied across regions. Broadly, 'base' people, who the Khmer Rouge thought embodied a more authentic image of true and 'untainted' Khmer identity, received more favourable treatment. 'New' groups were sent to less well-resourced areas, were subject to greater surveillance and were more likely to be detained and executed in one of the Khmer Rouge network of security centres. For Vickery, the opposition between peasants and urban elites – which pre-existed the Khmer Rouge rise to power – was the central cleavage generative of violence under Democratic Kampuchea rather than the product of a premeditated set of policies (1984). Life in the cooperatives was punishing, organised around forced heavy labour and rice production, with food and basic medicine in short supply. Infant mortality rocketed. By 1977, centrally imposed quotas for rice production and export – requiring an average national output double the levels of even the most productive regions – drove large parts of the country from hunger into famine, in turn exacerbating problems of disease (Chandler 1991: 1). Indeed, Tyner and Rice point out that rationing food supplies under Democratic Kampuchea was a technique that maintained political control by effecting vulnerability, contradictorily imposing death while maintaining life (2016).

An alternative sketch of Khmer Rouge rule might emphasise the racialised and xenophobic language and practices of the CPK leadership, particularly in the latter stages of the regime. Through this reading of Democratic Kampuchea, we see violence perpetrated in the name of racialised nationalism as much as communism

(Frieson 1988; Kiernan 2001). (Here we can further see the central planks of the prosecutions for the crime of genocide that are proceeding at the ECCC today). On taking power in 1975, the Khmer Rouge set about purifying the Cambodian polity of racial 'contaminant' groups, targeting the Cham Muslim minority, ethnic Thai and Chinese communities and particularly the ethnic Vietnamese, who were murdered in their entirety. Cambodia's relationship with neighbouring Vietnam would become increasingly vexed as the regime aged. From 1977 onward, the CPK leadership were increasingly animated by the threat they perceived to be posed by their former ally, Vietnam. Khmer Rouge troops began to launch border raids into Vietnamese territory from 1977, skirmishing with Vietnamese troops and massacring civilians in border villages. These provocations would eventually be the downfall of the regime. Vietnamese and rebel Cambodian forces invaded from the Eastern border on Christmas Day 1978.

From 1977, *Angkar* began a series of internal purges in the Cambodian interior against anyone suspected of collaboration with the Vietnamese, labelling suspects "Khmer bodies with Vietnamese minds" (Kiernan 2001: 4). The eastern zones of Cambodia that bordered Vietnam were hardest hit. Pol Pot had long been suspicious of the leadership in the eastern zones, some of whom maintained ties to Vietnamese communists and had until then provided relatively favourable conditions under the regime. The purges began with the installation of new organisational structures across the region, with troops from the central, south west and north zones sent in to suppress dissent. Some members of the Eastern zone authorities anticipated what was to follow and fled across the border with their troops. Among these were Hun Sen, Chea Sim and Heng Samrin, figures who would soon dominate – and today still loom over – Cambodian politics. Pol Pot considered the dissent in the east a vindication of his suspicions and intensified the purges of the hierarchy through 1978. The *Santebal* security apparatus tortured suspected "enemies" in a network of prisons, including at the infamous S-21 site in Phnom Penh, extracting an ever proliferating chain of 'confessions' that implicated a fictitious Vietnamese (or CIA) conspiracy. Many of these victims were themselves Khmer Rouge cadre; many were also women and children.

One aspect of the violence suffered under Democratic Kampuchea that has only recently garnered full attention was its gendered distribution, dynamics and implications. Henri Locard has noted that while the number of killings was greater among men than women, the burden of household responsibility during the difficult period of recovery after Democratic Kampuchea disproportionately fell on the shoulders of women (2005). Gender-based violence was also routine under the Khmer Rouge. Opportunistic sexual violence against women was widespread, including rape, sexual assault and sexual slavery. In particular, though, enforced marriage was practiced systematically throughout Democratic Kampuchea, denying basic rights of sexual choice to victims and precipitating marital rape (De Langis 2014). Forced marriage was deployed particularly as a means of disciplining ethnic and religious minority groups (Braaf *et al.* 2014). Such techniques – deployed to regulate the most private and individual bodily conduct – are reflective of a wider vision that laid claim over the life and vitality of the population.

We might here scrutinise Cambodia's perpetrators in more detail. Who were the Khmer Rouge? And how do historical accounts implicate specific readings of their guilt? While levels of violence varied between 1975 and 1979 and across different regions in Cambodia, Kiernan's work makes clear that the Khmer Rouge leadership developed centrally directed eliminatory policies (2001). Today, establishing a record of high-level, intentional and directed policy has been the central focus of the prosecutors at the ECCC. The role of lower-level perpetrators remains cloudier. Hinton, for example, seeks to develop an explanation of perpetrator actions beyond arguments of obedience to authority, which perpetrators of atrocities often invoke retrospectively because it implies that the violence they might have perpetrated occurred under duress. Hinton claims that Khmer Rouge brutality was conditioned through culturally framed moral economies of revenge that were fed by longstanding resentment of urban elites and their perceived corruption and collusion with the US-backed predecessor regime among the rural poor (1998). A closer examination still might invite us to trouble the perpetrator category further. Ea and Sim (2001), for example, have highlighted how making a clear distinction between victims and perpetrators under the Khmer Rouge is difficult. Firstly, the levels of self-directed purges by the Khmer Rouge meant that perpetrators often became victims. And secondly, because perpetrators were often themselves either children or adolescent, undergoing indoctrination and bearing witness to violence and suffering, space must also be afforded to recognise their victimhood.

In developing these sketches of life and death under Democratic Kampuchea, we have foregrounded different sets of victims as they were targeted on the basis of their class, 'race' and gender. This is important because it illuminates the importance of the lenses and rationalities through which perpetrators see their victims and violence as much as the legal categories that actions might retrospectively be coded within. Moreover, while developing a broader picture of the experience of Democratic Kampuchea, we can see a specific biopolitical vision for the management of life (and death) in Cambodia, animated by the image of the chaste and self-sufficient integrity of the (racialised) rural poor. In other words, the Khmer Rouge years were not simply a peasant revolution motivated singularly by spite, revenge or ignorance. The Khmer Rouge perpetrated violence as part of a wider and systematic vision prescribing social, economic and moral order that obviated criteria for those entitled to live and die.

Before Democratic Kampuchea

Confining our sketches of historical political violence in Cambodia to the experience of Democratic Kampuchea, as the ECCC principally does, poses a number of problems. Firstly, periodising Cambodian history in this way, while privileging and highlighting the severity of Khmer Rouge rule, also tends to obfuscate serious episodes of human-rights abuse that were perpetrated before and after Democratic Kampuchea. As I show in Chapter 4, 'Moving forward through justice', this raises serious questions about the selectivity and politics of international and transitional justice interventions. Moreover, as we reflect on a near-continuous experience of conflict and violence in Cambodia from the 1960s through to the turn of the millennium, we should reflect on the pertinent question about when (and if) exactly Cambodia experienced any *transition(s)* and what any transition represented. As Caroline Hughes has pointed out, while Cambodia has undergone transitions to democratic rule, from war to peace and from a command to a market economy, none of these shifts have been coherent, uniform, continuous or settled (C. Hughes 2003). Secondly, a series of contextual issues arise here. Focusing only on the 3 years, 8 months and 20 days of Democratic Kampuchea elides important questions concerning how the Khmer Rouge came to power, why they have not until now been held accountable for the crimes perpetrated 1975–1979 and the attendant questions of responsibility arising from these failures.

The Cambodian communist movement was born in the struggle for independence from French colonial rule after WWII. In 1945, nationalist resistance groups in Cambodia and Vietnam – Issarak (Independent Khmer) and the Viet Minh respectively – were galvanised following the Japanese surrender and the restoration of French protectorate rule, sparking the first Indochina war (1946–1954). Khmer Issarak groups, who were comprised of both communist and non-communist factions, launched low-level, primarily rural campaigns against French oversight throughout the late 1940s. Sections of the non-communist Khmer Issarak factions also burnished their nationalist credentials during this period, promising to protect Cambodia from Vietnamese influence and massacring Vietnamese civilians on occasion (Kiernan 2004: 74). From 1950, Vietnamese communists gained more influence within the Khmer Issarak movement, utilising Cambodian territory in their own war against French rule. The Vietnamese communists played a key role in founding their sister Khmer People's Revolutionary Party in 1951.

Meanwhile in Phnom Penh, the Cambodian monarchy was engaged in a delicate political balancing act. Norodom Sihanouk had inherited the throne in 1941 while Cambodia was under Japanese occupation. After the war, Sihanouk bargained concessions from the French, ensuring a degree of autonomy within the French Union, a written constitution that allowed for a democratically elected assembly in 1947 and, later, powers to set Cambodia's foreign policy in 1949. Sihanouk, in turn, sought to marginalise the democratic domestic opposition, and dissolved the national assembly in 1953 under the pretext of a national emergency (Chandler 1991: 65). From this point, enjoying *de facto* self-government, Sihanouk turned his attention more directly to the campaign against French oversight, declaring full independence in November 1953, appropriating 'indigenised' Buddhist tropes to project himself as restoring former glories (Keyes 1994). After proclaiming independence, the bulk of the non-communist Khmer Issarak groups had disbanded (Kiernan 2004: 131). In 1954, following defeat at Dien Bien Phu at the hands of the Viet Minh and peace negotiations in Geneva, France withdrew from Indochina entirely. Sihanouk exploited this political capital in 1955, cementing a popular mandate through a referendum, before offering a surprise abdication from the throne in order to contest the 1955 National Assembly elections as head of a newly formed party, Sangkum. As prime minister, Sihanouk established Cambodia as a constitutional monarchy, though this did not prevent him resuming the throne in 1960.

Sihanouk was committed to maintaining a neutral foreign policy. This ambition was bound to be disappointed as Indochina became a key arena of Cold War proxy politics. Sihanouk firstly faced domestic pressure to manage a growing communist movement. The Geneva peace negotiations in 1954 forced Vietnamese communists out of Cambodian territory, drawing with them Khmer factions with closer ties to Hanoi. This enabled the colonisation of the Khmer People's Revolutionary Party by more radical members such as Pol Pot and other leaders of Democratic Kampuchea such as Son Sen, Nuon Chea, Khieu Samphan and Ieng Sary, who had all returned from university in Paris where they had been exposed to more radical strands of leftist thinking, orienting their beliefs around idealised plans for self-sufficiency, with nationalist and racist inflections (Kiernan 2004: 176). In 1962, having seized the leadership of the Khmer People's Revolutionary Party, Pol Pot fled Phnom Penh and started an underground resistance from the rural East. Sihanouk, in turn, cracked down on more mainstream leftist dissent, further generating new supporters for the cause of the communists. In 1967, localised protests broke out in rural Samlot in western Cambodia against government-backed rice purchasing schemes, fed by longstanding resentment of government clientelism, corruption and inequality. Villagers seized arms, destroyed government property and killed several government officials, sparking unrest in other provinces among the disaffected rural poor. Sihanouk ordered a fierce clampdown on the rebellion, killing dozens, while coining the term *Khmer Rouge* for the insurgents (Chandler 1991: 164–166). For many among the rural poor, the connection between localised experiences of state and elite repression and the attraction of a growing communist insurgency, who had called for a nationwide uprising earlier that year, was sealed at this juncture.

Meanwhile, Cambodia's proximity to the intensifying Vietnam conflict meant that Sihanouk faced international pressure to take sides within the wider landscape of Cold War politics. The US had escalated the Vietnam War in 1965, destabilising Cambodia's eastern border and inadvertently inviting Vietnamese communists to use Cambodian territory as a safe haven as the conflict developed. US and South Vietnamese troops began to engage communist forces within Cambodian territory, and in 1969, President Nixon escalated large-scale bombing raids on Cambodian territory. Sihanouk had long been suspicious of US intentions regarding Cambodia – having stifled several attempts to depose him by right-leaning political groups that enjoyed US backing – and edged towards a more welcoming stance to the North Vietnamese, allowing communist troops sanctuary in the east. Facing economic paralysis and mounting domestic discontent, Sihanouk could not maintain his conflicted positioning for long. In 1970, while Sihanouk was touring Europe, republican forces in Phnom Penh under the orders of General Lon Nol staged a military coup, founding the Khmer Republic. Sihanouk fled to Beijing and quickly threw his endorsement to the Cambodian communist rebels, galvanising their support further in the countryside.

The years between 1970 and 1975 in Cambodia were remarkably bloody. Lon Nol's forces, backed by US air power, fought a brutal campaign against the Khmer Rouge and North Vietnamese forces in the interior. Lon Nol's own brand of racist nationalism led to pogroms against Vietnamese civilians living in Cambodia, massacring hundreds and forcing a further 300,000 to flee to Vietnam (Kiernan 2002: 485). Worse was faced at the hands of the US bombing campaigns. Between 1965 and 1973, the US dropped 2.75 million tons of munitions on Cambodian territory, often without discriminating targets (Kiernan and Owen 2006). From February 1973, Nixon secretly resumed and escalated carpet bombing in Cambodia, bidding to halt the Khmer Rouge march on Phnom Penh; this was despite the January 1973 Paris Peace Accords, which had mandated the withdrawal of Vietnamese troops from Cambodia, marking the end of cooperation between the Khmer Rouge and Vietnamese communists and an end to hostilities. Kiernan and Owen offer an estimate of 150,000 killed in the US bombing (2006), though an earlier Finnish enquiry placed this figure higher, claiming that as many as 600,000 Cambodians were killed in the US raids, with nearly 2 million displaced (Kiljunen 1984). Nicole Barrett has suggested that the carpet bombings present a *prima facie* case of war crimes in their own right (2000). The bombing would also have profound consequences for the trajectory of the war, as the US attacks generated further popular support for the Khmer Rouge. The death toll and abundant suffering fuelled resentment and a desire for revenge among recruits. Moreover, the bombing served to harden, radicalise and legitimise the extreme policy ambitions in the minds of the Khmer Rouge leadership (Kiernan 2004: 390).

If we recognise, here, that there are outstanding questions of accountability for human-rights violations perpetrated before Democratic Kampuchea, as well as questions around responsibility for the rise of the Khmer Rouge, we might also reflect on the continuing patterns of human-rights violations after the Vietnamese intervention. These occurred within both domestic and international contexts that precluded accountability for the Khmer Rouge leadership. It is worth reminding ourselves that the demise of the regime was largely self-inflicted. The Khmer Rouge had escalated attacks on Vietnamese villages and troops along the eastern border from 1977, gambling that their allegiance with China would guarantee their security (China did indeed go on to launch a brief invasion of Vietnam in early 1979 that was beaten back). By 1978, Vietnam had had enough. On Christmas day, 150,000 Vietnamese troops and Cambodian rebels, operating under name the United Front for the National Salvation of Kampuchea, invaded from the east, driving the Khmer Rouge west to the forests and mountains along the Thai border. Phnom Penh was captured on 7th January 1979, marking the founding of the People's Republic of Kampuchea. Heng Samrin, Chea Sim and the current prime minister, Hun Sen, who had defected from the Khmer Rouge eastern zones in 1977, would occupy leading positions in the new government. The Third Indochina war would last another ten years, and conflict within Cambodia would persist until 1998.

After Democratic Kampuchea

Upon taking power in 1979, the government of the newly founded People's Republic of Kampuchea confronted an extraordinary challenge in the scale and scope of social reconstruction. The Khmer Rouge had systematically destroyed a functioning state apparatus, and the new government confronted the need for near-total institutional reconstruction as well as widespread food shortages. International isolation within the bifurcated Cold War political landscape and the prospect of further civil war with a coalition of Khmer Rouge and other anti-Vietnamese Cambodian factions exacerbated these challenges. Domestically, the population was torn between relief at the demise of the Khmer Rouge, a desire to search for family and survivors, suspicion of the occupying Vietnamese forces and the fear of impending famine. Moreover, in maintaining a commitment to state socialism, the basic rights to free speech, assembly, religious practice and private commerce were, in the early years of the People's Republic of Kampuchea, heavily restricted, undermining the popularity of the regime. Thousands fled across Khmer Rouge lines on the Thai border, following the thousands the Khmer Rouge had marched at gunpoint during their retreat and swelling the numbers in refugee camps to 300,000 in late 1979 (Gottesman 2003: 42). Many of the refugees would not return from Thailand until the mid-1990s.

The new government was eager to establish its legitimacy for both international and domestic audiences. In doing so, the state of the People's Republic of Kampuchea sought recourse to some of the core techniques in transitional justice and memory management that are so familiar to us today. After capturing Phnom Penh, Vietnamese troops quickly found the S-21 prison centre, based in a former high school in the south of the capital. S-21 was one of a network of prisons used by the *Santebal* security apparatus where 'enemies' of the regime were tortured and executed. At S-21, some 14,000 had been interred and subsequently killed, many of whom were Khmer Rouge cadre who became victims of internal purges (Chandler 1999: 36). The new government invited foreign journalists and delegations to tour the site and witness the *proof* of the genocidal character of the Khmer Rouge leadership, while promoting the corollary legitimacy of the Vietnamese intervention as an act of humanitarianism. The site was formally curated as a museum a year later, displaying chemically treated human remains and the 'primary' artefacts of Khmer Rouge violence as evidence, such as shackles, cages and torture instruments (R. Hughes 2003; Ledgerwood 1997).

A second key government initiative connecting the proof of the atrocities suffered under the regime specifically to the responsibility of the Khmer Rouge leadership and their international patrons was held later in 1979. Gottesman explains that in 1979, the newly founded People's Republic of Kampuchea had an interest in offering public redress for the atrocities perpetrated under Democratic Kampuchea as a means of cleanly demarcating a new era of government and symbolically discharging the popular anger against the Khmer Rouge regime (2003: Chapter 3). In August, a trial of the 'Pol Pot and Ieng Sary clique' *in absentia* was convened, hearing testimony from survivors, convicting the Khmer Rouge leaders of genocide and implicating China in their support and patronage of Democratic Kampuchea. While Western governments denounced the People's Revolutionary Tribunal as a political show trial that failed to meet basic legal standards, Fawthrop and Jarvis point out that the tribunal offered the first genuine opportunity for survivors to express and affirm their experiences of Democratic Kampuchea (2004: 49). The prevailing state narrative of the experience of the Khmer Rouge crystallised at exactly this point: a handful of genocidal leaders could be blamed for hijacking an otherwise benign revolution, and lower-level members of the Khmer Rouge should expect reintegration and exculpation (Gottesman 2003). The guilt of the Pol Pot–Ieng Sary clique would be the focus of further memorial initiatives across Cambodia through the 1980s, deployed with one eye on maintaining popular support in the face of the Khmer Rouge insurgency. Hundreds of mass grave sites were disinterred across the country, with human remains chemically treated and displayed as proof of the genocide (R. Hughes 2005). Provincial grave sites would become the focus of an annual 'Day of Hate' commemoration held every May 20th, during which victim representatives would denounce the Khmer Rouge leadership (R. Hughes 2000). This reading of responsibility for the crimes of Democratic Kampuchea would play an important role in the state-led reconciliatory initiatives that ended the war and, as I show, would be powerfully reanimated in the work of the ECCC today.

The People's Republic of Kampuchea relied on Vietnamese military support throughout the 1980s. The presence of Vietnamese troops and civil officials was a contributing factor behind the uneven public support the new government enjoyed and, despite the overwhelming evidence of their atrocities, it was a key rallying appeal for the Khmer Rouge to recruit more and more new members to wage the insurgency. The regrouping and resurgence of the Khmer Rouge along the Thai border placed the People's Republic of Kampuchea in a challenging situation. The new government was worried about Khmer Rouge infiltration, and many former Khmer Rouge members were imprisoned without trial in the early 1980s and often tortured on the pretext of security grounds. Despite internal conflicts about the prospect of integrating former Khmer Rouge members but lacking both civilian and military authority in the provinces, the newly established administration was forced to make compromises. Lower-level Khmer Rouge cadre and fighters deemed not to hold 'blood debts' were enticed to defect to the government side (Gottesman 2003: Chapter 3), laying a template for informal and formal amnesty programs deployed later in the 1980s and 1990s.

The wider civilian population was not exempt from the needs of the new state either. The urgent need for troops also meant that large numbers of adult men were conscripted into militia initially, then into the new Kampuchean People's Revolutionary Armed Forces. In 1984, the People's Republic of Kampuchea launched a strategy to 'seal' the Thai border from the insurgents, known as the K5 project. The K5 project required the mass mobilisation of civilian labour between 1985 and 1989, calling up both men and women, with recruits set digging trenches, building fortifications, deforesting and laying minefields. By 1985, some 400,000 mines had been planted (Slocomb 2001: 198). Conditions working on K5 were abject, and the plan became deeply unpopular. The border areas were highly malarial, food was in short supply and the authorities failed to provide basic medicine, with as many as 50,000 conscripts succumbing to illness (Luciolli, quoted in Slocomb 2001: 202). Thousands also died laying and inadvertently triggering mines and traps along the border, and many more lost limbs. The border regions of Cambodia remain contaminated by unexploded mines, claiming victims to this day despite two decades of demining efforts.

International isolation

From its establishment in 1979, the international political landscape weighed heavily against the People's Republic of Kampuchea. Despite overwhelming evidence of the atrocities perpetrated under Democratic Kampuchea, Western governments widely condemned the Vietnamese intervention, and the regrouped Khmer Rouge continued to enjoy regional support and patronage from China and members of the Association of South East Asian Nations (ASEAN). China continued to supply arms and military equipment to the Khmer Rouge via Thailand throughout the 1980s, estimated to be worth $100 million a year (Kiernan 2002: 488). Western humanitarian aid and support earmarked for Cambodia was directed through Khmer Rouge and rebel-controlled border camps rather than Phnom Penh, further fuelling the insurgency. From 1979 until 1982, the Khmer Rouge maintained the Cambodian seat at the United Nations (UN), before formally forming the 'Coalition Government of Democratic Kampuchea' against the People's Republic of Kampuchea with other resistance factions including anti-communist forces and royalists led by Sihanouk. No Western government would vote against the Khmer Rouge representation on Cambodia's seat at the UN until 1988. Conspicuously absent throughout this period were international appeals or initiatives for accountability for the atrocities perpetrated by the Khmer Rouge. Genocide justice was not, at this point, a legal problem. The one notable exception to this embargo were efforts by the Australian Foreign Minister, Bill Hayden, who in 1986 pushed for a mechanism to try the Khmer Rouge leadership at the UN but was thwarted by pressure from the US (Fawthrop and Jarvis 2004: 78–79). The international political climate Cambodia faced in the 1980s was not simply disinterested in the violence perpetrated by the Khmer Rouge. Powerful international states and groupings like China, the US and ASEAN actively muted efforts to redress it, while contributing to the civil war that would preclude initiatives for accountability for a further two decades (Jones 2007). The Khmer Rouge were only sustained as military force through international support and patronage, ensuring that any substantive accountability process remained impossible.

The late 1980s saw several political developments that were precipitant to an eventual peace process. From 1979 to 1984, Heng Samrin had led Cambodia's reconstruction. However, in 1985, power shifted within domestic politics. Hun Sen was promoted from foreign minister to prime minister, exploiting his ability to manage both domestic patronage networks and ties with the Vietnamese. Hun Sen's ascent inaugurated a move away from the ideological rigidity of Heng Samrin's socialism, allowing and embedding basic forms of market enterprise, for example, where it suited productive and influential patronage networks (see Gottesman 2003: Chapter 9). Hun Sen also embarked on more direct moves to initiate peace, recognising that the Vietnamese military presence in Cambodia was not indefinite, and that a political settlement would likely be the only feasible way of ending the war. Domestically, the government redoubled efforts to entice defections from the Khmer Rouge under the aegis of national reconciliation, promising integration and forgiveness for lower-level cadres willing to change sides. Then in 1987, Hun Sen reached out to Sihanouk and the anti-communist groups to initiate peace talks but not to the Khmer Rouge, seeking to drive a wedge between the rebel factions. In December 1987, Hun Sen and Siahnouk met for the first time, and a peace process finally started.

Peace processes

Hun Sen was determined that any peace settlement should not include the Khmer Rouge, but the international mood was conflicted and often hostile to his position. By 1988, the US was beginning to soften regarding the Khmer Rouge, recognising – at least – that they should be prevented from returning to power. China, however, remained insistent that any negotiated political settlement should include the Party of Democratic Kampuchea. A 1989 Paris Peace Conference brought the conflicted groups together but floundered on the issue of genocide recognition for the crimes perpetrated under Democratic Kampuchea and broke down without progress (Um 1990). Several developments triggered an end to the impasse, accelerating the peace process. Vietnam had long been eager to extricate itself from the Cambodian conflict, and it finally honoured commitments to fully withdraw troops from Cambodian territory in September 1989. The Union of Soviet Socialist Republics (USSR) and Vietnam were increasingly inclined to encourage a political settlement with Phnom Penh, which had initiated its own transition from state socialism by this point, renaming the country the 'State of Cambodia' and signalling its own measures to liberalise the economy and acquiesce to the discipline of market order. Meanwhile, the Khmer Rouge continued to perpetrate violence, launching raids on several passenger trains in Cambodia in July 1990, massacring over 100 civilians (Fawthrop and Jarvis 2004: 92). The attacks served to harden attitudes against the Khmer Rouge in Western capitals, before the UN General Assembly finally rescinded their occupation of the Cambodian seat at the UN, leaving it temporarily vacant.

Finally, Hun Sen inched towards conceding ground regarding the question of genocide recognition, softening towards the loose prescription of the need to avoid the "policies and practices of the past" preferred by the UN. At a meeting of the parties in Jakarta in September 1990, a new 'Supreme National Council' was formed, comprised of representatives from the State of Cambodia and the opposition factions and tasked with hammering out the details of an internationally sponsored framework to implement a transition to elections under the supervision of a UN authority. The final Paris Peace Accords, co-chaired by Indonesia and France, were signed by 19 governments and all parties to the Cambodian conflict in October 1991, promising a comprehensive end to the Cambodian conflict and urging the need for national reconciliation. The agreements mandated a ceasefire, the withdrawal and non-interference of foreign actors, a new constitution embodying principles of human rights and a United Nations Transitional Authority (UNTAC) and peacekeeping force to oversee democratic elections. UNTAC began work in Phnom Penh in February 1992.

Did the UNTAC period mark a *transition* for Cambodia? UNTAC was widely hailed as a peacekeeping success story, having overseen the first democratic elections in 1993, enabling the repatriation of refugees from the border camps and enshrining certain human-rights principles in the constitution. UNTAC also powerfully inserted Cambodia into the international aid economy, for better and worse, while carving out a continuing political space for a raft of non-governmental organisations (NGOs) (C. Hughes 1996: 86; see C. Hughes 2003 for a thorough account of political economy through the 1990s in Cambodia). UNTAC's prescription of market discipline was invariably ripe for appropriation by local elites, affecting the continuing coproduction of market order and political power that characterises Cambodia today (Springer 2011). Moreover, UNTAC was in itself expensive: in 2 years of operations alone, UNTAC cost over $3 billion (Fawthrop and Jarvis 2004: 107). UNTAC also starkly failed to deliver the peace that it promised. The Khmer Rouge – increasingly self-reliant on the black-market trade on the Thai border rather than on Chinese patronage – refused to adhere to the Paris agreements (Fawthrop and Jarvis 2004: 103–107). UN peacekeepers were refused entry to Khmer Rouge zones and increasingly came under attack in the run up to the vote, which the Khmer Rouge had boycotted and tried to prevent. The UNTAC mission ended in September 1993 with the civil war unresolved.

The 1993 elections produced a coalition of Hun Sen's rebranded Cambodian People's Party (CPP) and royalists of the Front uni national pour un Cambodge indépendant, neutre, pacifique et coopératif (FUNCINPEC) under Siahnouk's son, Prince Norodom Ranaridh, forming the first 'Royal Government of Cambodia' (RGC). Sihanouk was crowned king once more, in a largely ceremonial role, and Cambodia enjoyed the peculiar situation of having two prime ministers. While royalist and the remaining anti-Vietnamese troops were now within the government fold, the Khmer Rouge had continued attacking civilians during the UNTAC years, particularly Vietnamese communities, and retained significant stretches of territory along the Western border. In 1994, the National Assembly passed legislation 'Outlawing of the Democratic Kampuchea Group'.[1] The new law reanimated and formalised the principles of previous amnesty programs used under the People's Republic of Kampuchea, bidding to reintegrate and reconcile lower-level Khmer Rouge while excluding their leaders. The law granted an amnesty period of 6 months from July 1994, though informally this was extended to defectors throughout the mid 1990s. Amnesty was specified for "crimes they have committed," loosely formulated, perhaps, to encompass crimes perpetrated in the Democratic Kampuchea period, as well as the newly criminalised membership of the Khmer Rouge organisation (perhaps understandably, given that, by 1994, much of the Khmer Rouge fighting force were born during and after Democratic Kampuchea).

The Khmer Rouge continued their guerrilla campaign in spite of the new law, laying mines, killing civilians, attacking government and agricultural infrastructure and kidnapping for ransom. However, serious fault lines and tensions within the movement began to emerge. A major breakthrough came in 1996, when Ieng Sary, the former foreign minister of Democratic Kampuchea, defected to the government along with his substantial forces based in Pailin and Malai in Cambodia's west (Kiernan 2002: 491). In return for his surrender, Ieng Sary was offered a royal pardon for his conviction for genocide at the 1979 People's Revolutionary Tribunal. The Khmer Rouge were now split, having lost the strategic footholds and the black-market trade provided by the western border, leaving their remaining forces under Ta Mok and Pol Pot isolated in the north around the town of Anlong Veng.

In 1997, Phnom Penh faced another bout of political turbulence. The 1998 elections were on the horizon, and both Hun Sen and Ranaridh had discretely worked to secure defections from the remaining Khmer Rouge faction. Tensions were high between the coalition parties, and in July, fighting broke out on the streets of Phnom Penh. Hun Sen then removed his coalition partners by force under the pretext of their collaboration with the Khmer Rouge (Peou 1998); he would subsequently reconvene a coalition with Ranaridh after the 1998 elections gave the CPP the largest number of seats in the National Assembly. Meanwhile, the last of the Khmer Rouge were thrown into a final set of convulsions in 1997. Having ordered the execution of another remaining leader, Son Sen, and his entire family on the suspicion that they too would defect, Pol Pot was deposed by Ta Mok, a leading military figure within the Khmer Rouge (and responsible for some of the worst atrocities of the Democratic Kampuchea period). Pol Pot was placed under house arrest by the Khmer Rouge, where he is thought to have committed suicide in April 1998. Ke Pauk, another leading figure under Democratic Kampuchea, defied Mok and defected in March 1998. Then in December, Khieu Samphan and Nuon Chea, the most senior surviving leaders of Democratic Kampuchea, surrendered to the government, leaving only Ta Mok and a small rump of loyal Khmer Rouge troops at large. The Royal Cambodian Armed Forces captured Ta Mok in January 1999. After over 40 years of near-continuous war, violence and upheaval, Cambodia was at peace.

Negotiating the ECCC

Advocacy and scholarship in human rights tends to present the normative injunction to 'do justice' after atrocity and conflict as a universal, apolitical and ahistorical imperative. Yet the Extraordinary Chambers in the Courts of Cambodia (ECCC) and its emergence cannot be understood outside of the pervasive conflicts and violence, shifting international and regional alliances, domestic factionalisms, political compromises and social upheavals that have shaped Cambodia over the last 60 years, as well as the growth and entrenchment of a field of thought and practice that is premised on its expertise in remedying post-conflict societies, as discussed in the last chapter. This history profoundly shaped the negotiations over the establishment of the ECCC and, consequently, the contours of what prevailing – yet contingent – accounts of justice and reconciliation look like in Cambodia today, as well as some of the conflicts and frictions that have troubled the work of the court.

1994 was an important year for the future shape of the ECCC. It was the beginning of a translation of the legacy of Democratic Kampuchea – in the minds of key international stakeholders – from a principally *political* issue into a potentially *legal* problem. Throughout the 1980s, the US government had faced domestic pressure from NGOs, Cambodian and US activists and leading scholars regarding its support for the Coalition Government of Democratic Kampuchea and the issue of accountability for Khmer Rouge crimes. However, US Cold War strategy had dictated that the Khmer Rouge could be accommodated and tolerated because they were hostile to Vietnam, and they served to check their purported expansionism. The end of the Cold War inaugurated a new international environment that promised the resolution of previous proxy conflicts, as well as precipitating more proactive approaches in international liberal interventionism. Within this new milieu, the US Congress was more receptive to the campaign for Khmer Rouge accountability and reconfiguring policy toward Cambodia. After pressure from campaigners, the Cambodian Genocide Justice Act was initiated in 1991 and formally passed in the Senate and signed into law by Bill Clinton in 1994. The new law mandated the investigation and documentation of the crimes perpetrated under Democratic Kampuchea and signalled that efforts to bring Khmer Rouge leaders to justice were now US foreign policy. The Cambodian Genocide Justice Act further generated a raft of institutional and discursive initiatives that would set the tone and shape later dialogue on the establishment of the ECCC. Alongside the Cambodian Genocide Program, hosted at Yale University, the Cambodian Genocide Justice Act also provided funding for the establishment of a research and documentation centre in Phnom Penh, first as a field office, then as an independent research and advocacy group in and of its own right. The Documentation Centre of Cambodia led a series of projects, including mass-grave mapping, archival preservation and oral history work, oriented to an eventual legal reckoning with Khmer Rouge violence.

The 1994 Cambodian Genocide Justice Act was not, however, innocent. The mandate for research and investigation into the events of April 17th 1975 to January 7th 1979 neatly circumscribes the years of Democratic Kampuchea, precluding scrutiny of the periods of more direct US involvement in the Cambodian conflicts. It is important to bear in mind that such a periodisation of Cambodian history is reflected in the work of the ECCC today. Moreover, the about turn in US policy stands in relief of the fact that the Cambodian government had been promoting Khmer Rouge accountability throughout the 1980s, notwithstanding the initiation of the1979 People's Revolutionary Tribunal and its formal procedural flaws. The newly found interest in Khmer Rouge accountability represented an implicit view that Cambodia must have justice 'done' to and for it rather than leading it, mirroring the massive expansion of aid and development projects that bloomed in Cambodia in the late 1990s to rehabilitate social order, which were supervised, guided and managed within networks of international expertise. Animating images of Cambodia as a dysfunctional political space that must be supervised and managed through aid and developmental supervision – visible first in validations for the UNTAC intervention (Hughes and Pupavac 2005) – had and still has important consequences. Firstly, it nourished diagnostic tropes of 'amnesia' and 'denial' that posit Cambodia as politically incapable and therefore pathologically forgetful. Secondly, it animated and reflects an Orientalist logic, visible still in the prevailing critiques of the ECCC today, that affirms the procedural hygiene of international justice in relief of the failings and corruption of Cambodian counterparts.

In June 1996, Thomas Hammarberg was appointed special representative of the secretary general for human rights in Cambodia. The early 1990s had seen the establishment of UN-backed *ad hoc* tribunals to prosecute atrocities perpetrated in the former Yugolsalvia and Rwanda under international law, and Hammarberg immediately sought to initiate discussion around a similar mechanism intended to deal with outstanding Khmer Rouge crimes. In 1997, Hammarberg persuaded (then) co-prime ministers Hun Sen and Ranaridh to formally request assistance from the UN, noting the efforts in the former Yugoslavia and Rwanda. The secretary general responded by appointing a Group of Experts, who would conduct preliminary investigations around the scale of evidence of crimes committed under Democratic Kampuchea, assess the feasibility of prosecutions and evaluate the different options for the composition and location of a tribunal. The Group of Experts reported back in 1999, recommending the formation of an *ad hoc* tribunal resembling that implemented for the former Yugoslavia. The Group of Experts suggested that any tribunal should be wholly international in composition, thereby 'insulated' from Cambodian politics; that it should be located outside Cambodia; and, while suggesting that prosecutions should keep one eye on stability and 'national reconciliation', that between 20 and 30 suspects should be tried. The report proposed a jurisdiction of April 17th 1975 to January 7th 1979 on the basis that an expanded time frame could include actions that would distract from the 'unique' and 'extraordinary' violence suffered under Democratic Kampuchea.[2]

The proposals of the Group of Experts were met with hostility by the RGC. The Cambodian side objected to the plans on several grounds, including the ex-situ location and full international control of the planned court. More significantly, the government fiercely opposed the proposed scope of prosecutions to include 20–30 former Khmer Rouge as a threat to peace, citing the need for 'national reconciliation'. Notably, the defections of Nuon Chea and Khieu Samphan in December 1998 under informal assurances against prosecution were secured while the Group of Experts investigation was ongoing. Hun Sen had welcomed the two Khmer Rouge leaders under the need for peace and 'national reconciliation', providing the fuel for the accusation that he was disingenuous in his moves to create a process of accountability in the first place. Whether the Cambodian government's insistence on narrower prosecutions was based on worries and anxieties over reconciliation and stability in good faith – and we should note that unease over the peace process was represented in the Group of Experts report too – is now moot. Hun Sen happily recycles far-fetched concerns over peace and stability in objections to ECCC prosecutions he does not agree with to this day, despite the unlikely resumption of war. And yet, conversely, our understanding of the formation of the ECCC is hindered by a tendency to read the Cambodian approach to the negotiations as conspiratorially predetermined against the formation of the tribunal, rather than accommodating the possibility that the RGC might have had conflicted and changing perspectives after decades of war.

It is telling that in anticipating the negotiations over the establishment of the ECCC, Cambodian and international stakeholders were reproducing and bargaining over positions within prevailing debates over purportedly necessary and inevitable trade-offs between peace and prosecutions. These trade-offs were characteristic of thinking in transitional justice in the mid to late 1990s, conceptually implying that justice and peace were finite and exclusive registers that could be balanced in the number of prosecutions delivered, rather than politically contingent claims for social ordering *in all enunciations*. In turn, the negotiations over the ECCC would themselves begin to influence and configure debates in transitional justice around the 'localisation' of mechanisms. The report of the Group of Experts had led to an impasse, and in 1999, and following the arrest of Ta Mok, a leading Khmer Rouge figure, Hun Sen openly began suggesting holding purely domestic trials for Khmer Rouge leaders (Scheffer 2008). One of the key objections from the Cambodian side was towards full international control of the ECCC, as well as the location of any tribunal outside Cambodia. Perceived limitations of the tribunals established for Rwanda and Yugoslavia were important reference points here. The tribunals for the former Yugoslavia and Rwanda were situated away from victim constituencies and were thought to remote and dislocated in the benefits they might yield. A repeated criticism contends that such complaints purely reflected the Cambodian government's determination to retain political control and oversight of any Cambodian mechanism.

The Cambodian side was also under pressure from international donors, NGOs and the domestic opposition to engage with the UN. Negotiations continued to stall until US-sponsored plans based on a "mixed" formula were tabled in late 1999, providing for an 'Extraordinary Chamber' within Cambodia's court system, international and Cambodian co-staffing across the tribunal organs and a 'supermajority' decision-making formula to balance the majority of Cambodian judges in trial chambers. For the Cambodian side, the mixed model protected their sovereignty. For the UN, the mixed model could be justified as an exercise in capacity building, transferring legal skills and experience to the local judiciary and providing a less expensive but more resonant and visible process than those for Rwanda and Yugoslavia (Ciorciari and Heindel 2014: 27).

The UN retained serious reservations about the mixed-model proposal and the implications of ceding control to the Cambodian government, and it had sought assurances from the Cambodian side that 'international standards' of justice would be maintained. Meanwhile, the Cambodian government had proceeded to formalise and legislate for the prospective tribunal, passing the Law on the Establishment of the Extraordinary Chambers in 2001, despite unresolved disagreements with the UN over how many former Khmer Rouge figures to prosecute. The ongoing conflicts visible today over prospective prosecutions in Cases 003 and 004 were prefigured at exactly this point. In 2002, the United Nations abruptly walked away from the process, citing concerns over the prospective impartiality and independence of the court. The UN move was applauded by leading human-rights organisations and the opposition Sam Rainsy Party, and the Cambodian government again suggested proceeding with purely domestic prosecutions. The UN withdrawal, however, raised eyebrows among several interested governments, including Japan, the US, Australia and France, who were all keen to see trials take place (Ciorciari and Heindel 2014: 33). After the Cambodian side signalled willingness to amend the 2001 Law on the Establishment of the ECCC, international pressure mounted and eventually forced the UN back to the negotiating table in 2003. A revised Law on the Establishment of the EC was passed in October 2004.

Conclusion

The ECCC cannot be appraised outside of the histories presented here because they have deeply shaped the scope, focus and very possibility of its prosecutions. Tracking this story is important for several reasons. In the first instance, these are histories that reveal ruptures as well as strong continuities within Cambodian political orders. Conflict, violence and suffering has characterised the latter half of the twentieth century in Cambodia, notwithstanding the exceptionally grave crimes of the Democratic Kampuchea, and while there are clear 'breaks' across regimes, the instrumental use of violence, the concentration of power in the hands of a narrow factional leadership and an 'extractive' relationship of leaders to the social order seems continuous across regimes (Cunha *et al.* 2015; Thion 1986). Secondly, within these histories, the ECCC attends to the past selectively, prosecuting some (but not all) perpetrators of political violence, as well as examining some (but not all) episodes of atrocity that *could* be scrutinised as criminal. Appeals for justice, truth and reconciliation, then, must be approached as politically contingent claims for memory. The terms on which the ECCC attends to these histories – and the subjects of memory animated thereupon – are the focus of the next two chapters. The fact that Cambodian communities have established and are invited into a variety of social and political relationships to these histories is the focus of the latter half of the book.

Notes

1 "Law on the Outlawing of the 'Democratic Kampuchea Group'" (1994). Available at https://www.eccc.gov.kh/sites/default/files/legal-documents/Law_to_Outlaw_DK_Group_1994.pdf. Last accessed September 23rd 2016.
2 Report of the Group of Experts for Cambodia established pursuant to General Assembly resolution 52/135. Available at http://hrlibrary.umn.edu/cambodia-1999.html. Last accessed 23 September 2016.

References

Barrett, N. 2000. Holding individual leaders responsible for violations of customary international law: The US bombardment of Cambodia and Laos. *Colum. Hum. Rts. L. Rev.*, *32*: 429.

Braaf, R., Kim, T., de Langis, T., Strasser, J. and Taing, S. 2014. *Like Ghost Changes Body: A Study on the Impact of Forced Marriage under the Khmer Rouge Regime*. Phnom Penh: Transcultural Psychosocial Organisation.

Chandler, D. P. 1991. *The Tragedy of Cambodian History: Politics, War, and Revolution Since 1945*. Yale University Press.

Chandler, D. P. 1999. *Voices from S-21: Terror and History in Pol Pot's Secret Prison*. Berkeley, CA: University of California Press.

Ciorciari, J. D. and Heindel, A. 2014. *Hybrid Justice: The Extraordinary Chambers in the Courts of Cambodia*. Ann Arbor, MI: University of Michigan Press.

Cunha, M. P. E., Rego, A., Silva, Á. F. D. and Clegg, S. 2015. An institutional palimpsest? The case of Cambodia's political order, 1970 and beyond. *Journal of Political Power*, *8* (3): 431–455.

De Langis, T. 2014. A missed opportunity, a last hope? Prosecuting sexual crimes under the Khmer Rouge Regime. *Cambodia Law and Policy Journal*, *2*: 61–78.

Ea, M. T. and Sim, S. 2001. *Victims and Perpetrators? Testimony of Young Khmer Rouge Comrades*. Phnom Penh, Cambodia: Documentation Center of Cambodia.

Fawthrop, T. and Jarvis, H. 2004. *Getting Away with Genocide? Elusive Justice and the Khmer Rouge Tribunal*. London; Ann Arbor, MI: Pluto Press.

Frieson, K. 1988. The political nature of Democratic Kampuchea. *Pacific Affairs*, 405–427.

Gottesman, E. R. 2003. *Cambodia after the Khmer Rouge: Inside The Politics Of Nation Building*. New Haven: Yale University Press.

Hinton, A. 1998. A head for an eye: Revenge in the Cambodian Genocide. *American Ethnologist*, *25* (3): 352–377.

Hughes, C. 1996. *UNTAC in Cambodia: The Impact on Human Rights*. Singapore: Institute of Southeast Asian Studies, No. 92.

Hughes, C. 2003. *The Political of the Cambodian Transition*. London, New York: Routledge.

Hughes, C. and Pupavac, V. 2005. Framing post-conflict societies: International pathologisation of Cambodia and the post-Yugoslav states. *Third World Quarterly*, *26* (6): 873–889.

Hughes, R. 2000. "Remembering May 20 Day of Anger". *Searching for the Truth*. *12*: 39–42.

Hughes, R. 2003. Nationalism and memory at the Tuol Sleng Museum of Genocide Crimes, Phnom Penh, Cambodia. In *Contested Pasts: The Politics of Memory*. K. Hodgkin and S. Radstone (eds). New York, London: Routledge. 175–192.

Hughes, R. 2005. Memory and sovereignty in post-1979 Cambodia: Choeung Ek and local genocide memorials. In *Genocide in Cambodia and Rwanda: New Perspectives*. S. Cook (ed). New Haven, CT: Yale University Center for International and Area Studies.

Jones, L. 2007. ASEAN intervention in Cambodia: From Cold War to conditionality. *The Pacific Review*, *20* (4): 523–550.

Keyes, C. F. 1994. Communist revolution and the Buddhist past in Cambodia. In *Asian Visions of Authority: Religion and the Modern States of East and Southeast Asia*. Honolulu, HI: University of Hawai'i Press, pp. 43–73.

Kiernan, B. and Owen, T. 2006. Bombs over Cambodia: New information reveals that Cambodia was bombed far more heavily than previously believed. *The Walrus*, October.

Kiernan, B. 2001. *The Pol Pot regime: Race, power, and genocide in Cambodia under the Khmer Rouge, 1975–79*. New Haven, CT: Yale University Press.

Kiernan, B. 2002. Introduction: Conflict in Cambodia, 1945–2002. *Critical Asian Studies*, *34* (4): 483–495.

Kiernan, B. 2004. *How Pol Pot Came to Power: Colonialism, Nationalism, and Communism in Cambodia, 1930–1975*. New Haven, CT: Yale University Press.
Kiljunen, K. and Kampuchea Inquiry Commission. 1984. *Kampuchea: Decade Of The Genocide: Report of a Finnish Inquiry Commission*. London: Zed.
Ledgerwood, J. 1997. The Cambodian Tuol Sleng Museum of Genocidal Crimes: National Narrative. *Museum Anthropology*, *21* (1): 82–98.
Locard, H. 2005. State violence in Democratic Kampuchea (1975–1979) and retribution (1979–2004). *European Review of History—Revue européenne d'Histoire*, *12* (1): 121–143.
Peou, S. 1998. Cambodia in 1997: Back to square one? *Asian Survey*, 69–74.
Scheffer, D. 2008. The Extraordinary Chambers in the Courts of Cambodia. *International Criminal Law*, *3*: 219–255.
Slocomb, M. 2001. The K5 gamble: National defence and nation building under the People's Republic of Kampuchea. *Journal of Southeast Asian Studies*, *32* (02): 195–210.
Springer, S. 2011. Articulated neoliberalism: the specificity of patronage, kleptocracy, and violence in Cambodia's neoliberalization. *Environment and Planning*, *43* (11): 2554.
Thion, S. 1986. The pattern of Cambodian politics. *International Journal of Politics*, *16* (3), 110–130.
Tyner, J. A. and Rice, S. 2016. To live and let die: Food, famine, and administrative violence in Democratic Kampuchea, 1975–1979. *Political Geography*, *52*: 47–56.
Um, K. 1990. Cambodia in 1989: Still talking but no settlement. *Asian Survey*, 96–104.
Vickery, M. 1984. *Cambodia, 1975–1982*. Boston, MA: South End Press.

4 Moving forward through justice

The Extraordinary Chambers in the Courts of Cambodia (ECCC) opened its doors to start the process of investigating and prosecuting the "senior leaders" and "most responsible persons" of the Democratic Kampuchea regime in 2006. To date, after 10 years, the ECCC has delivered verdicts against three former Khmer Rouge figures, and there is a sense emanating from the court that those three defendants will be its last. The court has attracted a range of fierce criticism, facing accusations from commentators of procedural failings, technical flaws and, especially, political interference from the Cambodian government. As I argued in the previous chapter, the ECCC *is* a distinctively political institution and a product of a specific political history. Negotiations over the establishment of the ECCC reflected competing interests, none of which were wholly innocent. The ECCC attends to just one period of violence, ignoring the perpetration and commission of violence by external actors before and after the Khmer Rouge regime, and it represents a marker of institutional continuity for a longstanding legitimating trope preferred by the Cambodian government, offering both a domestic reminder of the role of the ruling Cambodian People's Party (CPP) within Cambodia's darkest period of history and international legitimacy according to human-rights standards. Yet the ECCC is also a product of transnational ideas and assumptions about justice, redress and renewal, as well as active diplomacy and lobbying from both state and non-governmental bodies. This assemblage is freighted with a raft of expectations around the benefits of promoting the prosecution of crimes against humanity, effecting a 'disciplining' of societies into states of order.

The ECCC, then, does have *a* politics, but that politics seem more expansive than objections to political interference account for or accommodate. In this chapter, I aim to ask some basic, foundational questions about the ECCC. Precisely what is the ECCC? What is the ECCC doing? Why is it doing it? And who, exactly, is it doing it for? In each of these questions, I argue, we see that memory is implicated in varied ways that are instructive of the wider *politics* of transitional justice and memory in Cambodia.

Stewarding memory

The ECCC is a complex set of organs that, it should be noted, do not pull in one direction with great harmony. As an exercise in international justice, the ECCC is one example of the movement toward 'hybrid' or 'mixed' courts that gained traction in the early 2000s, visible also, for example, at the Special Court for Sierra Leone, the Lebanon Tribunal or the Special Panels for Serious Crimes in East Timor. Hybrid bodies, in varying formulations, mix international and domestic legal systems, procedures and judicial and administrative appointments. Hybrid approaches became popular in transitional justice thinking – and international criminal justice – because they were thought to remedy problems arising at the 1990s ad hoc international courts for Yugoslavia and Rwanda concerning the accessibility and resonance of proceedings for domestic constituencies. In particular, reflective of the advent of 'best practice' and outcomes-driven approaches in transitional justice, proponents of hybridity promised that mixed mechanisms could deliver specific socio-political benefits: localising 'ownership', enhancing the rule of law and local judicial capacity building, for example. These outcomes-driven justifications were pivotal in presenting and justifying the ECCC, and I will return to reappraise them in the latter sections of the chapter.

While the ECCC is a hybrid institution, it has a stronger domestic weighting and character than other mixed mechanisms. As Ciorciari and Heindel point out, the ECCC remains a United Nations (UN)-backed body but its establishment was specifically instigated and formalised in domestic Cambodian legislation (2014a: 371).[1] The ECCC draws principally from a French civil law heritage, meaning, in the simplest terms, that procedures move from a prosecutorial submission, through an investigative phase to trial and then to subsequent appeals, though the civil tradition also prefigures a novel ECCC victim participation mechanism, whereby formally recognised victims become 'Civil Parties' within cases. The ECCC was designed to balance, where possible, international and domestic staff within its organs. While the ECCC enjoys parallel international and national personnel in key investigative and prosecutorial bodies, weighting is balanced toward the Cambodian side within adjudicative organs under a 'super majority' decision-making mechanism. Cambodian judges – appointed by the Cambodian Supreme Council of Magistracy – outnumber their international counterparts – nominated by the UN Secretary General and approved by the Cambodian Supreme Council of Magistracy – in the Pre-Trial, Trial, and Supreme Court Chambers, though any final judgement must include at least one international member. Robert Petit, the first international co-prosecutor working at the ECCC, points out that, in its whole, the ECCC is principally a national court with international support and parts (2010: 195).

Commentators have repeatedly highlighted the hybrid structure of the court as a key fault line and pitfall for the efficacy and workings of the court. Ciorciari and Heindel (2014b), for example, point to the practical and technical difficulties confronting the integration of differing legal procedures, driven often by the varying personalities of frequently changing judicial staff, while highlighting the vulnerability of the national side of the court to domestic political interference. Indeed, the international and domestic bifurcation of organs and personnel at the court has, in many senses, been made to stand as *the* key site of 'politics' at the court. Indeed, much commentary on the court has posited the ECCC's exposure to the 'weak' Cambodian judiciary as, generously, a brake on the judicial process and, more often, an impediment to its fulfilment, accusing the ECCC of being subject to outright political determination by the Cambodian government and claiming that the court is a 'show trial' (see, e.g. Bowman 2006; Morris 2010; c.f. Hughes 2015, for a critical appraisal of the 'show trial' attribution to the ECCC).

Cases to date

The first ECCC trial was Case 001 against Kaing Guek Eav, also known by the alias Duch. Duch faced charges of crimes against humanity and grave breaches of the Geneva Conventions arising from his role overseeing the S-21 prison centre in Phnom Penh. After the fall of the Democratic Kampuchea regime, Duch lived in the camps along the Thai border before returning to settle in western Cambodia, where he converted to Christianity in the mid-1990s and began working as a teacher. In 1999, Duch was identified for his role at S-21 and was arrested by Cambodian authorities. He would be held without trial until his indictment at the ECCC. At S-21 an estimated 12,000 – many of whom were Khmer Rouge personnel – were tortured and then executed between 1976 and 1979, marking Duch under the "most responsible persons" framing of the ECCC jurisdiction. Sixty-four Civil Parties were initially admitted to the case. Initial hearings were held in 2008 and substantive hearings in 2009, before guilty verdicts were delivered in 2010. Duch was found to have overseen interrogations of prisoners, directed torture and sanctioned executions.

Ciorciari and Heidel suggest that the Duch trial was the 'easiest' the ECCC would oversee: the S-21 site provided substantial and detailed evidence of Duch's station, key witnesses were forthcoming, Duch himself had offered several statements of admission and the proceedings were the least politically delicate the ECCC would broach (2014b: 104–106). The Duch verdict was heralded as a landmark success for the ECCC. Ledgerwood and Un have weighed the value of proceedings positively against the wider challenges of transforming Cambodia's judicial system, suggesting that the case catalysed public outreach and engagement work; that the case attracted broad domestic media coverage of proceedings; that Duch's contrition and remorse during proceedings were symbolically significant; and that S-21 could stand, emblematically, for broader experiences of suffering, therefore encouraging wider conversations about the period (2010: 4–5). Others have erred towards more critical positions. Mohan suggests, for example, that Duch's basic pre-trial rights were broadly subordinated under the weight of retributive expectations surrounding the court (2009: 18–19). Moreover, as I have argued elsewhere, the claim that S-21 can be representative of Cambodia's wider experiences of the Khmer Rouge – a claim that was mobilised throughout the 1980s by the People's Republic of Kampuchea government and is also pronounced today at the ECCC – does not resonate among all constituents (Manning 2012).

While Duch's defense had previously been oriented to cooperation with the court, during closing arguments Duch's national defense counsel abruptly pivoted from statements of admission to deny ECCC jurisdiction over his client, requesting a not guilty verdict. Moreover, Duch's initial sentence of 35 years – calculated thereupon to include a 5-year reduction to compensate for his illegal detention from 1999 and factoring in time served – angered some victim groups. The initial sentence was subsequently quashed after an appeal from the co-prosecutors and, given the gravity of the crimes at hand, Duch would be sentenced to a life term. Reparations were ordered to include the compilation of Duch's statements of apology, as well as the inclusion of the names of Civil Parties in the verdict, which disappointed Civil Parties, who had sought more extensive memorial and commemorative reparations, and troubled the accessibility of reparations for wider victims groups who were not party to the case (Ciorciari and Heindel 2014b: 131).

The 'headline' ECCC prosecutions against "senior leaders" charged in Case 002 have faced more significant challenges. ECCC co-investigating judges issued a closing order in September 2010 indicting four defendants who had occupied leadership positions in the Democratic Kampuchea hierarchy. These included Nuon Chea, former deputy secretary of the Communist Party of Kampuchea Standing Committee, thought to be second in command to Pol Pot; Khieu Samphan, once head of state of Democratic Kampuchea; Ieng Sary, the former minister of foreign affairs; and Ieng Thirith, the minister of social affairs. Each of these senior leaders had surrendered or defected to the government side from the mid-1990s. The indictments specified charges of crimes against humanity, genocide and grave breaches of the 1949 Geneva Conventions, examining allegations of population transfer, targeting of minority communities and members of the former regime, internal purges and overseeing gender-based violence. Given that the scope of Case 002 was set to examine a broader universe of events and locations than Case 001, co-prosecutors sought to try the four defendants together to expedite proceedings (Ciorciari and Heindel 2014b: 135–136).

One early litmus test for the purported independence of the ECCC arose from the applicability of a Royal Pardon granted when Ieng Sary defected to the government in 1996. Human-rights groups had worried that the pardon and amnesty would become too politically sensitive for the court. Ieng Sary had been found guilty of genocide *in absentia* at the 1979 People's Revolutionary Tribunal. Moreover, defecting in the context of a 1994 amnesty law that provided vague exemptions for Khmer Rouge and the 'crimes which they have committed' – but specifically not to *senior* leaders – led to thorny legal questions.[2] Ieng Sary's defense team argued along several fronts that the pardon and amnesty provided a general exemption to prosecutions, and that the pardon provided evidence of 'double jeopardy', that is, that he could not face the same charges again (Ciorciari and Heindel 2014b: 138). The ECCC Trial Chamber ruled that the amnesty and pardon should be set aside before – following a defense appeal – the Supreme Court kicked the issue into the long grass, deciding that the matter was beyond the remit of its oversight capacity. Ieng Sary died in March 2013, ensuring that a definitive resolution of the arguments over his pardon and amnesty would not be achieved. The timing of Ieng Sary's death followed, just 6 months earlier, the discharge of his spouse and co-defendant from proceedings, Ieng Thirith, who had been found unfit to stand trial. Suffering from dementia, Ieng Thirith was released from provisional detention under judicial supervision in September 2012. She would die aged 83 in western Cambodia in August 2015.

The ailing health of the defendants – notwithstanding the long list of former Khmer Rouge leaders who had prematurely evaded scrutiny for their roles in Democratic Kampuchea by virtue of their mortality – alongside the burgeoning potential scope of Case 002 had already led the ECCC Trial Chamber to take unprecedented steps to expedite proceedings in order to maximise the chance of verdicts in their headline case, even before the demise of Ieng Thirith and Ieng Sary. In 2011, Case 002 was 'severed' into segments that focused on a particular period, locale and group implicated in the initial closing order. Williams points out that although the severance was ordered to expedite proceedings, it instigated several rounds of lengthy appeals, complicating the trial process further (2015). The first segment, Case 002/01, would principally examine events surrounding the evacuation of Phnom Penh in 1975, the forced transfer of populations up to 1977 and the question of crimes against humanity arising therein.[3] A total of 3869 Civil Parties were admitted to the case. Co-prosecutor and defense opening statements were heard in late 2011, followed by nearly 2 years of evidential and testimonial hearings, before closing arguments were proffered in October 2013. For Ciorciari and Heindel, the sheer scope and scale of Case 002/01 itself brought the limitations of the ECCC hybrid structure into sharper relief: co-investigating judges suffered problems of capacity management, having developed a weighty corpus of evidence in the investigative phase that balanced inculpatory and exculpatory items poorly, while national judicial staff stonewalled defense requests to summon politically sensitive witnesses, leading to question marks over fair-trial rights for the accused and renewed accusations of government interference (2014b: 144–146).

In August 2014, Nuon Chea and Khieu Samphan were found guilty of crimes against humanity and sentenced to life imprisonment for their role overseeing the 1975 evacuation of Phnom Penh and population transfer in the subsequent 2 years. Civil Party teams had laid the groundwork to show the financial feasibility of a raft of proposed reparations, allowing the Trial Chamber to endorse a range of initiatives and avoid some of the disappointments arising from reparations ordered in Case 001 (Williams and Palmer 2016: 322–323), though these were funded externally rather than by the accused:

> the institution of a National Remembrance Day project; the construction of a memorial in Phnom Penh to honour victims of forced evacuations; a testimonial therapy project; self-help groups; a permanent exhibition; a mobile exhibition and education project; the inclusion of a chapter on forced population movement and executions at Tuol Po Chrey within the Cambodian school curriculum; the construction of a peace learning centre; a booklet on adjudicated facts and Civil Party participation at the ECCC; two editions of the verdict in Case 002/01; and inclusion of Civil Party names on the ECCC website.[4]

The verdict against the remaining two "senior leaders" of Democratic Kampuchea was hailed as a landmark, though the ECCC, at such crunch moments, is visibly pulled in different directions. At a press conference after the verdict, David Scheffer, UN Special Expert for the ECCC, proclaimed that the moment had seen "the winds of international justice swept through the fields, forests, and towns of Cambodia where millions perished."[5] Yet concerns were voiced regarding the standards of the legal process in particular, as well as the scope of the verdict. Cohen and Hyde, for example, objected to the severance of Case 002 as a prioritisation of an "expeditious trial" over "fair trial rights," labelling the judgement a "poorly organized, ill-documented, and meandering narrative in lieu of clearly structured legal writing" (2015: vi–viii). Perhaps more importantly, while the focus of the Case 002/01 verdict was narrowly framed for the sake of expediency, the story of evacuation and population transfer examined in the first segment seemed dislocated from the proclamations of a comprehensive justice that followed from the verdict. As with Case 001, a wider universe of experiences was, at best, partially reflected.

One consequence of these limitations is that there is a burden on the second part of Case 002 to deliver both a more comprehensive and resonant verdict. Case 002/02 began in October 2014 and is currently examining – alongside further evidence of crimes against humanity – the politically significant charges of genocide. The charges remain sensitive because the international community failed to recognise genocide in Cambodia throughout the 1980s and the UNTAC period, while the Cambodian government has reaped continuous political currency from usage of the term since 1979. But genocide recognition in Cambodia remains politically fraught beyond this divergence. The fulcrum of genocide prosecutions under Case 002/02 are allegations of violence directed at Cham Muslims and ethnic Vietnamese communities *on the basis of their membership within religious and ethnic groups as such*, a requirement under the notoriously narrow provisions of the UN Genocide Convention. As Giry has observed (2015), the charges do not refer to or encompass the wider experience of the majority of Cambodian survivors, who went on to witness the 1979 tribunal that prosecuted *genocide*, and who have since described the years of Democratic Kampuchea as an episode of genocide. The ECCC, Giry suggests, is set to disappoint one way or the other: either Case 002/02 does not recognise that genocide happened in Cambodia, disappointing all constituents; or it recognises the genocide of minorities under the Khmer Rouge but, necessarily, not the wider experience of other survivors on those terms. Such a finding would risk stoking tensions between minority and majority communities. The politics of genocide recognition are vexed.

Despite its critics, the ECCC has remained an open door for stakeholders to actively shape and author the scope and content of its work. While the recognition of minority experiences carries political baggage, Nguyen and Sperfeldt point to how ethnic Vietnamese Civil Parties to Case 002/02 are appealing for reparations to alleviate entrenched socio-political problems of the present, specifically appealing for the tribunal to order the encoding of new citizenship rights (2014). Moreover, while the scope and verdict of Case 002/01 disappointed many in the way it flattened experiences of violence and harm that may have specifically gendered dimensions (Sankey 2016; Studzinsky 2013), criticism from advocacy groups and stakeholders has pressed the Trial Chamber to examine cases of forced marriage and rape under the Khmer Rouge on a specifically nationwide basis within Case 002/02 (De Langis 2014: 43). Co-prosecutors seem alive to the need to better address the specifically gendered dimensions of Khmer Rouge violence and have filed submissions to consider sexual violence within and beyond forced marriage under prospective Cases 003 and 004 (Sankey 2016). The future of both of these cases is, however, far from certain.

Cases 003 and 004 have become a key fault line in the work of the ECCC. In November 2008, Robert Petit, the then international co-prosecutor, submitted a request for judicial investigations into five suspects beyond those indicted under Cases 001 and 002 without the agreement of the national co-prosecutor, Chea Leang. The disagreement between co-prosecutors was passed to the ECCC Pre-Trial Chamber for resolution. After deliberation, in August 2009 the Pre-Trial Chamber split along national and international lines without a conclusive decision. As a result, specifically in the absence of a 'super-majority' that transcended domestic and international members, the Pre-Trial Chamber was obliged to sanction further investigations by default. In September 2009, the introductory submissions to Cases 003 and 004 were forwarded to co-investigating judges. The handling of the investigatory phases of Cases 003 and 004 has attracted great criticism, which I will discuss after briefly outlining the scope of each case.

Case 003 was initially set to examine the role of two suspects for their alleged involvement in genocide and crimes against humanity perpetrated between 1975 and 1979, namely Sou Met, former commander of the air force under Democratic Kampuchea; and Meas Muth, former commander of the navy. Meas Muth was charged *in absentia* in March 2015 but appeared before the ECCC later that year. Sou Met died in 2013 without facing charges. Case 004 would examine the role of three suspects for a range of allegations: Im Chaem, a district secretary in the North West Zone under Democratic Kampuchea, was charged with crimes against humanity in absentia in March 2015; Ao An, alias Ta An, a deputy secretary of the Central Zone, was charged with crimes against humanity in March 2015, though a charge of genocide against the Cham Muslim minority was subsequently added in March 2016; and Yim Tith, alias Ta Tith, was charged with crimes against humanity and genocide against the Khmer Krom minority in December 2015. While investigations into Ao An and Ta Tith continue, co-investigating judges concluded investigations into Im Chaem in December 2015. Accordingly, in February 2016, proceedings against Im Chaem were severed into a new file, Case 004/01, to oblige the defendant's rights to a swift resolution of charges. At the time of writing, closing orders that would send Cases 003, Case 004/01 or 004 to trial had not been issued.

The Office for Co-Investigating Judges has been the site of greatest friction between the international and domestic sides of the ECCC, especially so in investigative work on Cases 003 and 004. From 2009, after initiating investigations into the additional suspects, Marcel Lemonde, the then international co-investigating judge, voiced concerns over reluctance from his Cambodian counterpart, You Bunleng, to proceed with work on Cases 003 and 004. Lemonde resigned in late 2010. His successor, Siegfried Blunk, adopted a very different tack with regard to Cases 003 and 004. In February 2011, the co-investigating judges publicly qualified that investigations into Cases 003 and 004 were ongoing but based on documents included in Cases 001 and 002 only, rather than through field investigations or further witness interviews. Outside the court, the belief that the investigative work was at best superficial and perfunctory grew when the co-investigating judges promptly closed Cased 003 in April 2011, attracting widespread criticism from court monitoring and advocacy groups, as well as court staff, including the newly appointed international co-prosecutor, Andrew Cayley (Ciorciari and Heindel 2014b: 179–180). Blunk resigned later that year. The Cambodian authorities – and national members of the Office for Co-Investigating Judges – pointedly refused to recognise the authority of Blunk's replacement, Laurent Kasper-Ansermet, who would resign in May 2012. In October 2012, Mark Harmon was sworn in as the fourth international co-investigating judge. Harmon would occupy the role until July 2015. While Harmon made headway with both Cases 003 and 004, reopening the former and continuing more expansive investigations into the latter – without the support of his national counterparts – he eventually resigned amid disputes over an arrest warrant he issued in June 2015 for Meas Muth, which national judicial police have so far refused to execute.

Cases 003 and 004 remain items within the latest ECCC Completion Plan.[6] Yet the prospect of either coming to trial appears unlikely. For the Cambodian government, Cases 003 and 004 are unwanted: they overstep the personal jurisdiction mandated to the court and represent a breach of the spirit of negotiations over the ECCC that had anticipated the prosecution of only a handful of former Khmer Rouge figures from the outset. Moreover, Hun Sen has publicly declared that Cases 003 and 004 cannot happen as they are a threat to peace, stability and reconciliation.[7] Human rights and advocacy groups see government reticence over Cases 003 and 004 as cover for an interest in protecting favoured officials and clients within domestic political networks from scrutiny for their roles under Democratic Kampuchea. For advocacy groups, the willingness to prosecute Cases 003 and 004 has become the key touchstone of judicial independence at the ECCC and a mark of its legacy as an effective judicial mechanism (Open Society Justice Initiative 2012).

How should we appraise these starkly opposed public positions? It is worth pointing out that both appear overstated. There is no realistic prospect of the ECCC instigating civil conflict on its own; in fact, lower-level Khmer Rouge – themselves ageing – who might still celebrate their former leaders are often supportive of the ECCC project (Manning 2015). Conversely, the idea that more prosecutions will offer more justice, more reconciliation or more judicial transformation seems wishful. As advocacy and human rights groups idealise 'apolitical' unfettered prosecutions, they reproduce a form of legalism that must deny it has *any* politics at all. Such a position seems peculiar, given that political pragmatism was an axiom that shaped the field of transitional justice from its birth. It is also fair to say, given the record of the UN and international community supporting the Khmer Rouge in the 1980s up to UNTAC, that the Cambodian government is entitled to ask whose place it is to define the scope of prosecutions. At its heart, what is unsaid in these debates is perhaps important: Cases 003 and 004 would represent the subordination of the position of the national, sovereign government yielding to the purported imperatives of human rights, yet such a public subordination of national prerogative would represent a serious instance of 'losing face' and is likely a not insignificant reason why these cases are now opposed.

It is likely that the ECCC will not attend to Cases 003 and 004 for other reasons too. The sense that Case 002/02 will be the last the ECCC prosecutes is now felt acutely among stakeholder groups. To date, the ECCC has spent nearly $300 million. Financial problems have plagued the ECCC, especially as the national sections of the court are donor funded, working according to the varying willingness of international patrons to maintain the exercise. In March 2013, for example, staff working as interpreters walked out after going unpaid for several months. Donor fatigue has become an issue for the court as well as for partnered non-governmental organisations (NGOs) supporting the work of the court (Sperfeldt 2012a). As one former ECCC outreach staff explained recently, "Lots of people have lost interest in the court now. It's not like it was a few years ago. There is less money for the public work now... If they aren't directly involved, people know little about the court."[8]

Troubling the jurisdiction

How should we evaluate the relationship between the ECCC and memory? Legal interventions to punish past crimes can converge with and constitute political techniques of memory. In the most obvious sense, they can do so through a straightforward rendering of a 'purely political' victor's justice that offers predetermined or fabricated historical accounts (Elster 2004: 84–85). Writing on the Eichman prosecution, Arendt remarks that a trial in such circumstances is more concerned with the production of public memory than with the deliberative interplays of law (Arendt 2006). Indeed, Wilson has recently argued that international criminal trials are today increasingly burdened with the expectation of history writing (2011). From Nuremberg to the more recent Milosevic trials, prosecutions for past atrocities are often now understood as much through their didactic and historical functions as through their basic discharging of *lex talionis* (Koskenniemi 2002).

Yet the relationship between law and memory tends to be more complicated than the imposition of one specific reading of the past. Memory shapes and furnishes the content and authority of law through the reproduction of precedent, practice and procedure that is further affirmed and authorised as legitimate through its performance. In turn, law provides a framework for the reconstruction of memory through registers of verification, of 'what happened', deliberating a record of events as *true* and authorising a wider account that frames socially embedded recollections more broadly. This is not to discount the role of power, politics and sovereignty in delimiting what can and cannot be remembered within the courtroom. The ECCC is 'contained' and shaped in the way it produces memory around certain political possibilities, the first of which being that, like all political trials, for it to *acquit* the accused, it would be deemed a failure

(Koskenniemi 2002). Yet it is open to contestation, has seen unanticipated outcomes and is 'redeemed' as a deliberative, adjudicative spectacle: as Christodoulidis argues, "What becomes possible… is not just the containment of the trial but also the redemption of that containment through democratic categories. Containment and justification stand and fall together" (2009: 132).

The ECCC is mandated to prosecute crimes under relevant Cambodian and international law, including the gravest international violations, namely, war crimes, crimes against humanity and genocide. The ECCC has a jurisdiction allowing the prosecution of "senior leaders" and "most responsible" persons for crimes perpetrated within Cambodia during the Democratic Regime between 1975 and 1979.[9] The jurisdiction and mandate of the ECCC are important starting points for reflecting on the relationship of prosecutions to memory because they anchor, rather than pre-determine, processes of *disclosure* and *concealment* of past violence, with memories coded within and against specific criminal categories. In other words, the application of such bodies of law consolidates a field of objects representing a field of memorable events that are potentially impressed within categories of human-rights violation. These categories are themselves normatively freighted with the memories of past global experiences and prosecutions of political violence (Levy and Sznaider 2010: 14).

In the first instance, we should bear in mind that the ECCC jurisdiction is itself a contingent and politically furnished product. We might reflect, for example, on the omission of events before and after the mandated temporal jurisdiction. One foundation for negotiations of the establishment of the ECCC was the 1997 UN Group of Expert Report, which specifically posited the 1975–1979 jurisdiction so as to not "detract from the unique and extraordinary nature of the crimes committed by the leaders of Democratic Kampuchea."[10] In other words, negotiations over the establishment of the ECCC began through precluding the scrutiny of potential international crimes before and after the Khmer Rouge held power. Acknowledging the extraordinary nature of Khmer Rouge violence does not necessarily attenuate the inconsistency posed here. Given that the ECCC is an institution that is normatively predicated on retributivist principles that oblige the prosecution of *all* perpetrators of human-rights violations, this is a political contingency that should not be dismissed. The ECCC, as a product of specific negotiations, was not feasible if it were to seriously scrutinise the United States (US) bombing campaigns through the early 1970s, Chinese patronage of the Democratic Kampuchea group during and after the regime or periods including Lon Nol's pogroms against ethnic Vietnamese or episodes of Vietnamese and People's Republic of Kampuchea violence perpetrated after the Khmer Rouge fell. As Bartholomew notes, the history of international law (and international tribunals in particular) is characterised by powerful states specifically suspending their own regulation *by law* (2006). In calling attention to some episodes of atrocity while neglecting others, the ECCC enacts an uneven politics of recognition and acknowledgement. In other words, the justice that the ECCC provides is of a very specific kind.

The ECCC personal jurisdiction encompassing "senior leaders" and "most responsible" persons also begs further scrutiny. Negotiations over the establishment of the ECCC were fraught partly because of disagreements over the number of figures to prosecute, and today, as discussed, the application of the current formulation of "most responsible persons" remains contentious. The initial Group of Experts Report had envisaged prosecutions of 20–30 Khmer Rouge figures, while the Cambodian government, invoking the imperatives of peace and reconciliation, sought a far narrower range of figures. On the one hand, critics of the Cambodian government have viewed such claims for national reconciliation as made in bad faith, working as a tool for the Cambodian People's Party to protect senior members from scrutiny of their own roles during the Khmer Rouge years. On the other hand, the Cambodian government today still maintains that a wide raft of prosecutions will undermine processes of reconciliation, and that its conditions for the establishment of the ECCC – that only a handful of figures would be indicted – were clear from the start.[11] These fault lines have been realised in debates over the uncertain future of prospective prosecutions in Cases 003 and 004.

As Hughes invites, it is worth pausing here to reflect on the continuities and parallels between the 1979 People's Revolutionary Tribunal and the current ECCC prosecutions (2015). In 1979, the People's Republic of Kampuchea initiated prosecutions of the 'Pol Pot–Ieng Sary clique', finding the two senior Khmer Rouge leaders guilty of genocide *in absentia*. The People's Revolutionary Tribunal crystallised the state sponsored narrative of the atrocities of Democratic Kampuchea, focusing on the guilt of the Khmer Rouge leadership only, and it still today mirrors Cambodian government representations of blame. One important consequence of this restriction was that the culpability of lower-level Khmer Rouge figures became, in the first instance and again today at the ECCC, obscured and exculpated in the name of national reconciliation. The restriction of both sets of prosecutions can be read to enact a *de facto* amnesty in this regard, a key technique of managing memory that was mobilised formally and informally through reconciliatory initiatives throughout the 1980s and 1990s to erode the capacity of the Khmer Rouge insurgency. In this sense, as the ECCC today targets "senior leaders" while assuring lower-level Khmer Rouge that they "have nothing to fear,"[12] the ECCC reproduces a longstanding politics of 'national' reconciliation and memory – just *one* discursive claim for reconciliation at work in Cambodia – that hinges upon a specific reading of guilt. Hughes goes on to point out that critiques levelled at the 1979 tribunal – specifically, that it was a politically determined 'show trial' – are further mirrored within critiques of the ECCC today that deem the Cambodian People's Party to have interfered with or directed the judicial process for political purposes (2015). Hughes queries objections to the ECCC as a form of 'theatre' that is distinct from the apparent purity of an idealised discourse of unhindered and objective law partly because they animate an image of Cambodia as dysfunctional space that is incapable of 'justice', while importantly noting that politically winnowed prosecutions are the norm rather than exception within international prosecutions. In other words, all tribunals of this kind intervene in political pasts at the service of highly political presents. For Hughes, the critiques of both the People's Revolutionary Tribunal and the ECCC serves as representational tropes through which "Cambodia is condemned to the recurrent trauma of international illegitimacy" (2015: 719).

The narrow remit for prosecutions at the ECCC also reflects a wider tendency to individualise proceedings at international tribunals. This reflects the way that law, as a discursive system, pivots on the premise of individual rational responsibility. As Koskenniemi suggests, the tendency to individualise prosecutions – because of expediency, logistics or politics – is not neutral in its effects (2002). In the broadest sense, because international law is predicated on a universalist imperative that *all* perpetrators of human-rights violations be punished, restricted prosecutions necessarily furnish symbolic rather than comprehensive ledgers of accountability. The underpinning legal lens that sees, first and foremost, individual agents as rational actors with particular intentions and 'free will' obfuscates wider contexts and meanings that might be fruitful for understanding the events at hand and therefore the reconstruction of any coherent public record (Koskenniemi 2002: 13–14). In this sense, one unintended consequence of the attempts to delimit what is and is not counted as 'memorable' is that legal defense teams in political trials reach to wider historical contexts in order to contest the legitimacy of trials as arbiters of memory and truth. I return to how this generates strategies of 'rupture' and 'denial' in the next chapter, though notable examples include the defense appealing to periods of political violence beyond the mandate of the ECCC such as the 1970s US bombing campaigns or the role of current leading political figures (who have refused calls to participate at the ECCC) during the Khmer Rouge years.

In sum, the ECCC jurisdiction, as with the jurisdiction of all tribunals, is an important technique of memory. We should note that its application and implementation are not entirely determinant or uncontested processes, within the courtroom and beyond. Yet the jurisdiction does *work* to contour and frame practices of memory because it furnishes and anchors an institutional landscape of formal (and informal) subjects that are constituted within its parameters, even as it provokes frictions and discord as both a judicial and political process. Within the remit of violence perpetrated between 1975 and 1979 and the classification of "senior leaders" and "most responsible persons," specific sets of perpetrators and victims become possible, if disputed and unfinished. Through the judicial process, as they participate, testify, confess or resist, they are realised as both agents and objects of memory. In the next chapter, I examine the minutiae of this process in greater detail. Here, though, alongside the narrow remit of potentially culpable suspects, I turn to examine one highly novel and celebrated feature of the ECCC that attends to the process of recognising and licensing specific kinds of victim.

Victims as Civil Parties

The emergence and composition of the ECCC is entangled with wider currents in international and transitional justice that promise to integrate a more substantial focus and role for victims within criminal proceedings (Sperfeldt 2012b). Establishing the ECCC within Cambodia was thought to present a prime opportunity for engagement with victim constituencies, and in 2007, specific rights for victim groups were written into the procedural 'Internal Rules' governing the work of the court. Not only would the ECCC mechanism allow for the formal recognition of victims as 'Civil Parties', providing 'unique' and 'unprecedented' roles for victim participation within trial proceedings (Bair 2008), victims were granted the possibilities of 'collective and moral reparation' arising from guilty verdicts.[13] The process of 'producing' and recognising victims groups has, however, been uneven. As McEvoy and McConnachie suggest (2013), attention must be paid to the way victims are formally recognised within transitional contexts as an active process because the consolidation of victim categories can elide and flatten experiences and agency. Indeed, our treatment of the category of victimhood itself can be fraught because it risks dichotomising blame, obviating perpetrator guilt in singularity, when victims and perpetrators may have more complex experiences (see Bernath 2016 on 'complex political victims' at the ECCC). I examine the way Cambodians navigate and negotiate their positioning within these brackets within the courtroom and at ECCC public forum events in closer detail in the next chapters. In the context of the ECCC Civil Party process, the animation, recognition and mobilisation of victim claims has been mediated within a changing institutional landscape with mixed consequences.

The ECCC allows scope for any person who experienced the Democratic Kampuchea regime to file complaints to the co-prosecutors, who may use the information detailed within their investigations. The ECCC Internal Rules, however, further enact and specify the category of 'Civil Party' through which victims may seek formal recognition by the ECCC, participate within court proceedings, and thereupon seek collective and moral reparations. As the ECCC Internal Rules state, "In order for Civil Party action to be admissible, the Civil Party applicant shall: be clearly identified; and b) demonstrate as a direct consequence of at least one of the crimes alleged against the Charged Person, that he or she has in fact suffered physical, material or psychological injury upon which a claim of collective and moral reparation might be based."[14] The "clearly identified" ability of victims to "demonstrate" their injury is assessed, in the first instance, by the co-investigating judges during the investigative stages of ECCC proceedings. Immediately prior to a case closing order, indicating the start of trial proceedings or the case dismissal, co-investigating judges rule on the final admissibility of Civil Party applications. Under initial formulations, the ECCC's internal rules prescribed Civil Parties with a range of participatory rights, broadly on a par with the defense and prosecution. These rights were conceived to include access to case files and investigative input, the right to address the pre-trial and trial chambers and, as an outcome of guilty verdicts, the right to collective and moral reparations. The distinction between complainants, who may have suffered violence, and formally recognised Civil Parties (as those who are entitled to reparation) represents a notable point of arbitration within the official category of victimhood because it enacts a hierarchy of entitlements based on the demonstration of suffering, which carries important consequences. On the one hand, as Bernath points out, the category of victim animated here is inclusively produced through the lens of collective suffering in relief of the way the ECCC frames guilt around the Khmer Rouge leadership; this obscures the fact that there may be formally recognised Civil Parties who themselves may also have victimised others (2016: 54). On the other hand, as Pham *et al.* show, while Civil Parties recognised at the ECCC broadly spoke positively about their experiences, those not recognised indicated feelings of shame, worthlessness and anger (2011). The inclusions and exclusions produced here are not neutral.

Civil Party applications accepted to a case (i.e. those able to prove injuries resulting from a link to the criminal proceedings) are amalgamated prior to trial proceedings commencing. The process of grouping and administering Civil Party applications is overseen by the ECCC 'Victims Support Section' (VSS, formerly the Victims Unit). The Civil Party process necessarily entails amalgamating individual complaints into collective stories, reframing memory and bridging of individual, collective and national stories. The specificities and detail of individual experiences of suffering are recast and defined by collective frameworks. The VSS further coordinates victim support, witness protection and access to Civil Party lawyers, though much of this work has occurred in conjunction with advocacy and civil society groups. The agents constructing the category of victim are, in this instance, actively furnishing and renegotiating memory within the frameworks afforded by the ECCC law, a process I examine in closer detail in the coming chapters.

The prominence of victims within the ECCC process has evolved over the life of the court. Elander outlines how a specified 'Victims Unit' at the ECCC, tasked with the collation and administration of Civil Party applications, was not institutionalised until 2008 and commenced work with limited resources (2013: 107). While the initial procedures for Civil Party participation licensed broad participatory rights, following delays and procedural teething problems during early hearings, these were increasingly curtailed and the internal rules subsequently reformulated to provide a narrower role (Werner and Rudy 2009). In particular, the rights of Civil Parties to address the court chambers were reduced, shifting from individual opportunities to speak to forms of address through collective representation (Elander 2013: 109), subordinating the participatory role of 'victims' within the legal process that had become a key selling point of the court. In this light, it is worth remaining attentive to the changing constraints and demands legal processes place on victims (Dembour and Haslam 2004). While Pham *et al.* (2011) found broadly favourable responses among Civil Party participants towards their experience of early proceedings, Mohan has drawn on interviews with Civil Parties to suggest that the mechanism for participants was as bounded as it was enabling, denying the victims the very forms of agency and empowerment that they were promised (2009).

The process of *recognising* formal victims has generated frictions. Khmer Krom and Vietnamese minority groups – communities targeted in violent purges during Democratic Kampuchea – sought recognition as Civil Parties in the headline ECCC Case 002 against "senior leaders" but were initially rejected by the co-investigating judges on the grounds that the incidents were beyond the scope of the charges. Writing in 2008, Mahdev Mohan, who worked as a Civil Party lawyer at the ECCC, noted that the marginalisation of the Khmer Krom within the legal process reflected a process of writing difference out of the tribunal narrative, eliding them within the Cambodian "social memory" (2008: 54). Concerted efforts by the NGO Civil Party lawyers acting on behalf of Khmer Krom and Vietnamese applicants led to a reconsideration of the admissibility of their status in 2011, and now Khmer Krom and Vietnamese experiences are central within the prosecution of genocide in the ongoing Case 002/02. Today, the ECCC genocide prosecutions offer a hugely symbolic charge that may not have been sustainable without attention to the experiences of Khmer Krom and Vietnamese communities and their corollary admission as Civil Parties. We must note, still, that victims' suffering is formally recognised through a contingent process that can itself have problematic consequences in the way it can deny the memories and experiences of some communities.

A more recent set of innovations at the ECCC has been seen with the introduction of 'Victim Impact Hearings' and the ability of Civil Parties to offer 'Statements of Suffering' to the court and accused. In some respects, these innovations can be read to show that judicial staff within the court are reflexively adjusting the work of the court in response to the critiques of victim participation levelled at earlier hearings. Ciorciari and Heindel note that these techniques were not provided for within the initial mandate or rules of the ECCC, having been improvised and introduced to proceedings in Case 002 from 2013, prior to which Civil Party testimony had been offered subject to specific time constraints (2016). How have such developments been rationalised? Writing for an ECCC blog, Civil Party lead co-lawyers Mr. Pich Ang and Ms. Elisabeth Simonneau sought to explain the purpose of the impact hearings and statements from the perspective of Civil Parties:

> This evidence will assist the Trial Chamber in assessing the gravity of the crimes, placing them in their proper context, and determining the appropriateness of the reparations claimed to remedy these harms. Accordingly, the Hearings on Impact are an essential mechanism for bringing the human toll of these crimes into the proceedings.
>
> Second, though not the raison d'être for these hearings, another undeniably important aspect of these hearings is the opportunity they provide for at least a limited number of Civil Parties to tell their stories in an official, judicial setting with the presence of (and sometimes exchange with) one or more of the Accused. Under the right circumstances, this can be a meaningful, empowering and healing experience for Civil Parties wherein the process itself provides a reparative benefit—in the broader meaning of the term.[15]

As uncontested, uninterrupted and highly personalised accounts of suffering harm, the opportunity to testify, disclose suffering and be *heard* is here freighted with a range of assumed emotional and psycho-therapeutic benefits, reflective of the increasing centrality of victims as a key site of purpose within (otherwise principally) retributive transitional justice interventions. These adaptations suggest that staff at the ECCC are eager to implement the kinds of truth-seeking techniques that stakeholders have hoped it will deliver. While Ciorciari and Heindel stress that Civil Parties offering 'Statements of Suffering' were appreciative of the opportunity afforded, they caveat that we should recognise the tensions between such mechanisms and the fair trial rights of the accused (2016). Moreover, we must remain cautious of the process of how and on what terms specific victims are chosen to speak within the courtroom, as well as being mindful of the weight of expectation that comes with such an experience.

Who for and why?

This last section gives pause for thought for some of the justifications that have been offered for the work of the ECCC. Different stakeholders have mobilised different arguments for the need for the ECCC, the benefits it will yield and the constituents it will help. These arguments have themselves changed over the life of the court. In the broadest terrain, as Rachel Hughes has shown, international media coverage of the ECCC has tended to animate images of Cambodia as a traumatised, singular and passive space, casting the court as a mechanism that intervenes in to rehabilitate (but is obstructed by) a dysfunctional body politic (2015: 723–724). Such a flattening of Cambodian subjectivity mirrors and reproduces longstanding discourses of international management and supervision that have circulated around Cambodia since the United Nations Transitional Authority (UNTAC) intervention in the 1990s (C. Hughes and Pupavac 2005). When David Scheffer, UN Special Expert for the Khmer Rouge Trials, proclaimed that the Case 002/01 verdict represented the moment the "winds of international justice swept through the fields, forests and towns of Cambodia," the sense that international justice was a force *done to* rather than *by* Cambodia was telling.

What is crucial here is that forms of justification for the ECCC based on rehabilitating the public sphere, especially around rule of law, 'democratisation' and judicial capacity – influential in transitional justice scholarship (see e.g. Olsen *et al.* 2010) – present instrumental benefits as neatly sequenced consequences of the ECCC prosecutions. These often include a combination of claims that the ECCC will deter the perpetration of future atrocities (establishing a relationship between the past, present action and the future, implicating assumptions about the progressive, linear sequence of memory work), enhancing the rule of law and challenging a 'culture' of impunity (offering an assumed pathology of 'uncorrected' post-conflict memory cultures). These also tend to be notable markers that would discipline a specific vision of liberal order. The United Nations Office for the High Commissioner for Human Rights suggested, for example, that the key legacy of the ECCC would be through its role as a 'model court' that could transfer skills and expertise to the local judiciary through a 'demonstration effect',[16] contributing to domestic judicial reform, transparency and independence. The classical 'civilising' mission law has played in developing contexts appears present again.

It is, of course, difficult to observe the traction of such arguments, but anecdotally, some Cambodian staff at the ECCC have suggested that they felt they have benefited from their time working at the court.[17] Notwithstanding such gains, it seems that instrumental arguments justifying the ECCC lost favour over time. Writing at the time of the Case 002/01 verdict in 2014, Ainley argues that the deteriorating human-rights situation in Cambodia made it harder to publicly proclaim the ECCC as an agent of judicial transformation and democratisation (2014), given that the past years had been marked by political turmoil afflicting both democratic processes and the judiciary. Instead, arguments about the intrinsic value of prosecutions furnishing justice and truth resurfaced in lieu of any discernible ECCC impact on the overall human-rights situation. As Ainley points out, these in turn attracted criticism precisely because the 'quantity' of justice has been narrow and apparently poorly dispensed; that is, Cases 003 and 004 have not progressed because of government opposition to wider prosecutions, marking a 'tarnished' judicial process.

It is important to disentangle justifications for the ECCC further because they invoke and naturalise multiple constituencies, helping us reflect on the question of who this process is for. These tend to be registered through the language of individual victims as a specific grouping, a nationally framed call to *Cambodian* victims or smothering appeal to all Cambodians as *victims*, or through a broader presentation of internationalised criminal categories and jurisprudence. These three constituencies are, of course, not mutually exclusive. Yet it is telling that they point to, crudely, both the national and cosmopolitan audiences and stakeholders that the work of the court animates and addresses. Indeed, as layers of memory claim – and claims made on behalf of constituencies of memory – we might note here that all transitional justice processes variously and unevenly call for individual, national and cosmopolitan subjects as the beneficiaries of justice projects. Within the ECCC, firstly, we have seen that a specific universe of formally recognised Civil Parties through individual and collective experiences is enacted as victims, licensed to speak and be heard within the courtroom. The ECCC Public Affairs Office invokes and reinforces a wider undifferentiated national audience as a constituency of memory through a language of national wounds, suffering and renewal. In this second reading, Cambodia becomes a collectivised psycho-social category that is permitted to "move forward through justice" within and by the ECCC. And cosmopolitan inflections are added in these justifications, with Cambodia and the ECCC foregrounded in the gaze of the international community, as the normative weight of the international human rights landscape is invoked through categories of international jurisprudence, and monitoring NGOs judge and appraise the work of the ECCC against the criteria of 'international standards'. The ECCC is thus inscribed as a further mechanism on the list of international(ised) criminal tribunals, bolstering the place of transitional justice as a continuous – rather than exceptional – set of practices and assumptions for post-conflict governance, constituting "international community" out of the "tragedies of others" (Koskenniemi 2002: 34).

Conclusion

I began this chapter by pointing to some of the (frequently damning) criticism that the ECCC attracts. Given that the edifice of the court is itself the contingent outcome of a distinctly international political history, it seems peculiar that the ECCC has been condemned so unconditionally on the basis of apparent political interference. Here I have tried to attend to its political architecture a little more carefully. As a technique of memory, the ECCC jurisdiction allows for and generates specific sets of victims and perpetrators, marking the terrain from which they can speak about the past. In doing so, it works to conceal the formal *possibility* of other victims and politically sensitive perpetrators. The ECCC is presented and demanded as an apolitical, deliberative and unresolved exercise at the same time as serious constraints act on its possible outcomes. It must be deliberative, because it is meant to enhance the rule of law and act as an agent of democratisation; it must be contained, because the political interests that sanctioned its existence dictate so; and yet it must also deliver justice *and* reconciliation as civic harmony, outcomes purported to follow from *both* deliberation and containment. Given that such a process is inextricably bound to processes of inclusion, exclusion and power – politics as such – it seems that the appraisals of ECCC on the basis of its insulation from politics seem to be read through a narrow set of optics. Such optics themselves have consequences because they are, as a reflection of legalism, both de-historicising and de-contextualising, preventing us from thinking about the ECCC against other criteria and registers of success or, indeed, failure.

Notes

1 Law on the Establishment of the Extraordinary Chambers, with inclusion of amendments as promulgated on 27 October 2004 (NS/RKM/1004/006). Available at https://www.eccc.gov.kh/sites/default/files/legal-documents/KR_Law_as_amended_27_Oct_2004_Eng.pdf. Last accessed 21 September 2016.
2 Article 6 of the "Law on the Outlawing of the 'Democratic Kampuchea Group'" suspends amnesty for leaders. Available at https://www.eccc.gov.kh/sites/default/files/legal-documents/Law_to_Outlaw_DK_Group_1994.pdf. Last accessed 23 September 2016.
3 The summary of the Case 001 judgement is available at https://www.eccc.gov.kh/sites/default/files/articles/20140807%20FINAL%20Summary%20of%20Judgement%20ENG.pdf. Last accessed 23 September 2016.
4 The summary of the judgement in Case 002/01, including reparation orders, is available at https://www.eccc.gov.kh/sites/default/files/articles/20140807%20FINAL%20Summary%20of%20Judgement%20ENG.pdf. Last accessed 23 September 2016.
5 "Press Conferences Detail Triumphs, Defeats, and Plans in the Aftermath of Case 002/01". Available at http://www.cambodiatribunal.org/2014/08/07/press-conferences-detail-triumphs-defeats-and-plans-in-the-aftermath-of-case-00201/. Last accessed 23 September 2016.
6 The July 2016 completion plan (Revision 9) is available at https://www.eccc.gov.kh/sites/default/files/Completion%20Plan-Final-Rev9%20.pdf. Last accessed 23 September 2016.
7 See 'Hun Sen Warns of Civil War', *Cambodia Daily*, February 27th 2015. Available at https://www.cambodiadaily.com/archives/hun-sen-warns-of-civil-war-if-eccc-goes-beyond-limit-78757/. Last accessed 23 September 2016.
8 Personal interview, Former ECCC Outreach Staff, Phnom Penh, March 2016.
9 Law on the Establishment of the Extraordinary Chambers in the Courts of Cambodia, with inclusion of amendments as promulgated on 27 October 2004 (NS/RKM/1004/006).

Available at https://www.eccc.gov.kh/sites/default/files/legal-documents/KR_Law_as_amended_27_Oct_2004_Eng.pdf. Last accessed 23 September 2016.

10 Report of the Group of Experts for Cambodia established pursuant to General Assembly resolution 52/135. Available at http://hrlibrary.umn.edu/cambodia-1999.html. Last accessed 23 September.

11 For example, at the 'Dealing with a Past Holocaust and National Reconciliation: Learning from Experiences' conference (2006), Sean Visoth (a government appointment ECCC administrator) specifically tempered appraisals of the need for the ECCC against imperatives of peace and reconciliation. Available at https://www.eccc.gov.kh/sites/default/files/media/Finding_the_Truth_and_Reconciliation.pdf. Last accessed 23 September.

12 See, for examples, the ECCC poster campaigns. Available at https://www.eccc.gov.kh/sites/default/files/publications/poster-senior-big%20EN.jpg Last accessed 23 September.

13 Internal Rules (Rev.8), 3 August 2011, Rule 23. 1 b) 'General Principles of Victims Participation as Civil Parties' Available at https://www.eccc.gov.kh/sites/default/files/legal-documents/ECCC%20Internal%20Rules%20(Rev.8)%20English.pdf. Last accessed 23 September 2016.

14 Internal Rules (Rev.8), 3 August 2011, Rule 23 bis. 1. 'Application and admission of Civil Parties'. Available at https://www.eccc.gov.kh/sites/default/files/legal-documents/ECCC%20Internal%20Rules%20(Rev.8)%20English.pdf. Last accessed 23 September 2016.

15 Available at https://www.eccc.gov.kh/en/blog/2013/06/07/purpose-hearing-victims-suffering. Last accessed 23 September 2016.

16 See United Nations Office for the High Commissioner for Human Rights, 'Supporting the Legacy of the Extraordinary Chambers in the Courts of Cambodia'. Available at http://cambodia.ohchr.org/en/rule-of-law/promotion-eccc-legacy. Last accessed 23 September 2016.

17 Personal interview, former ECCC staff, Phnom Penh, April 2016.

References

Ainley, K. 2014. Justifying justice: Verdicts at the ECCC. *Justice in Conflict*, (16 Sep 2014) Blog entry.

Arendt, H. 2006. *Eichmann in Jerusalem: A Report on the Banality of Evil*. New York: Penguin.

Bair, J. P. 2008. From the numbers who died to those who survived: Victim participation in the Extraordinary Chambers in the Courts of Cambodia. *U. Haw. L. Rev.*, *31*: 507.

Bartholomew, A. 2006. Empire's law and the contradictory politics of human rights. In *Empire's Law: The American Imperial Project and the War to Remake the World*. A. Bartholomew (ed). London: Pluto Press.

Bernath, J. 2016. 'Complex political victims' in the aftermath of mass atrocity: Reflections on the Khmer Rouge Tribunal in Cambodia. *International Journal of Transitional Justice*, *10* (1): 46–66.

Bowman, H. D. 2006. Not worth the wait: Hun Sen, the UN, and the Khmer Rouge Tribunal. *UCLA Pac. Basin LJ*, *24*: 51.

Christodoulidis, E. 2009. Strategies of rupture. *Law and Critique*, *20* (1): 3–26.

Ciorciari, J. D. and Heindel, A. 2014a. Experiments in international criminal justice: Lessons from the Khmer Rouge Tribunal. *Michigan Journal of International Law*, *35* (2).

Ciorciari, J. D. and Heindel, A. 2014b. *Hybrid Justice: The Extraordinary Chambers in the Courts of Cambodia*. University of Michigan Press.

Ciorciari, J. D. and Heindel, A. 2016. Victim testimony in international and hybrid criminal courts: Narrative opportunities, challenges, and fair trial demands. (Forthcoming) *Virginia Journal of International Law*, *56* (2).

Cohen, D. and Hyde, M. 2015. A well-reasoned opinion? Critical analysis of the first case against the alleged senior leaders of the Khmer Rouge (Case 002/01). East West Center. Available at http://www.eastwestcenter.org/publications/well-reasoned-opinion-critical-analysis-the-first-case-against-the-alleged-senior. Last accessed 23 September 2016.

De Langis, T. 2014. A missed opportunity, a last hope? Prosecuting sexual crimes under the Khmer Rouge Regime. *Cambodia Law and Policy Journal*, *2*: 61–78.

Dembour, M. B. and Haslam, E. 2004. Silencing hearings? Victim-witnesses at war crimes trials. *European Journal of International Law*, *15* (1): 151–177.

Elander, M. 2013. The victim's address: Expressivism and the victim at the Extraordinary Chambers in the Courts of Cambodia. *International Journal of Transitional Justice*, *7* (1): 95–115.

Elster, J. 2004. *Closing the Books: Transitional Justice in Historical Perspective*. Cambridge, UK: Cambridge University Press.

Giry, S. 2015. The genocide that wasn't. *The New York Review of Books*. Available at www.nybooks.com/blogs/nyrblog/2014/aug/25/khmer-rouge-genocide-wasnt. Last accessed 23 September 2016.

Hughes, C. and Pupavac, V. 2005. Framing post-conflict societies: International pathologisation of Cambodia and the post-Yugoslav states. *Third World Quarterly*, *26* (6): 873–889.

Hughes, R. 2015. Ordinary theatre and extraordinary law at the Khmer Rouge Tribunal. *Environment and Planning D: Society and Space*, *33* (4): 714–731.

Koskenniemi, M. 2002. Between impunity and show trials. *Max Planck Yearbook of United Nations Law*, *6* (1): 1–32.

Ledgerwood, J. and Un, K. 2010. Is the trial of 'Duch' a catalyst for change in Cambodia's court? *Asia Pacific Issues*, *95*. East-West Center.

Levy, D. and Sznaider, N. 2010. *Human Rights and Memory*. University Park: Pennsylvania State University Press.

Manning, P. 2012. Governing memory: Justice, reconciliation and outreach at the Extraordinary Chambers in the Courts of Cambodia. *Memory Studies*, *5* (2): 165–181.

Manning, P. 2015. Reconciliation and perpetrator memories in Cambodia. *International Journal of Transitional Justice*, *9* (3): 386–406.

McEvoy, K. and McConnachie, K. 2013. Victims and transitional justice: Voice, agency and blame. *Social & Legal Studies*, *22* (4): 489–513.

Mohan, M. 2008. Reconstituting the "un-person": The Khmer Krom & the Khmer Rouge Tribunal. *SYBIL*, *12*: 43.

Mohan, M. 2009. The paradox of victim-centrism: Victim participation at the Khmer Rouge Tribunal. *International Criminal Law Review*, *9* (5): 733–775.

Morris, S. 2010. Mock trial: How America is helping to whitewash Cambodia's crimes against humanity. *New Republic*, 26 July.

Nguyen, L. and Sperfeldt, C. 2014. Victim Participation and minorities in internationalised criminal trial: Ethnic Vietnamese civil parties at the Extraordinary Chambers in the Courts of Cambodia. *Macquarie Law Journal*, *14*.

Olsen, T., Payne, L. and Reiter, A. 2010. Transitional Justice in balance. Comparing Processes, Weighing Efficacy. Washington, DC: United States Institute of Peace.

Open Society Justice Initiative. 2012. The future of Cases 003/004 at the Extraordinary Chambers in the Courts of Cambodia. Available at http://www.opensocietyfoundations.org/sites/default/files/eccc-report-cases3and4-100112_0.pdf. Last accessed 23 September 2016.

Petit, R. 2010. Lawfare and international tribunals: A question of definition: A reflection on the creation of the Khmer Rouge Tribunal. *Case W. Res. J. Int'l L.*, *43*: 189.

Pham, P., Vinck, P., Balthazard, M. and Hean, S. 2011. *After the First Trial: A Population-Based Survey on Knowledge and Perceptions of Justice and the Extraordinary Chambers in the Courts of Cambodia*. Berkeley, CA: Human Rights Center.

Sankey, D. 2016. Recognition of gendered experiences of harm at the extraordinary chambers in the courts of Cambodia: The promise and the pitfalls. *Feminist Legal Studies*, 1–21.

Sperfeldt, C. 2012a. Cambodian civil society and the Khmer Rouge tribunal. *International Journal of Transitional Justice*, *6* (1): 149–160.

Sperfeldt, C. 2012b. Collective reparations at the Extraordinary Chambers in the Courts of Cambodia. *International Criminal Law Review*, *12* (3): 457–490.

Studzinsky, S. 2013. Victims of sexual and gender-based crimes before the Extraordinary Chambers in the Courts of Cambodia: Challenges of rights to participation and protection. In *Sexual Violence as an International Crime: Interdisciplinary Approaches*. A. de Brouwer, C. Ku, R. Romkens and L. van den Herik (eds). 173–186. Cambridge: Intersentia.

Williams, S. 2015. The severance of Case 002 at the ECCC: A Radical trial management technique or a step too far? *Journal of International Criminal Justice*, *13* (4): 815–843.

Williams, S. and Palmer, E. 2016. Transformative reparations for women and girls at the Extraordinary Chambers in the Courts of Cambodia. *International Journal of Transitional Justice*, p.ijw006. *10*: 311–331.

Wilson, R. A. 2011. *Writing History in International Criminal Trials*. New York: Cambridge University Press.

Werner, A. and Rudy, D. 2009. Civil party representation at the ECCC: Sounding the retreat in international criminal law. *Nw. UJ Int'l Hum. Rts.*, *8*: 301.

5 Memory on trial

This chapter parses examples of the 'scripts' that have been put to work within the courtroom. In doing so, I hope to reflect on how trials work as a site of memory in closer detail and to identify some of the socio-political consequences that follow from the different techniques of memory that are put to work within the courtroom. Trials are not overtly exercises in memorialisation (though, notably, memorialisation is one technique that the Extraordinary Chambers in the Courts of Cambodia [ECCC] can direct as a form of redress and reparation). Yet as I argued in the previous chapter, trials – as transitional justice mechanisms – are powerfully validated and justified in the name of renewing shared histories and national memories. Moreover, memory is invoked as an object in the trial process. Memory is called upon explicitly and implicitly in varied ways and against different registers; for example, probing the reliability of individual memories, hearing and acknowledging recollections of victims' suffering, examining artefacts of memory that are thought to disclose knowledge of the past and, ultimately, rendering verdicts and sentences that make normative judgements about and over memory. These different judicial practices – which lay claim over memory in varied ways – hang together to constitute the trial as an unresolved and open process.

Three effects of such judicial practices are important to note as starting points. Firstly, these techniques work as interplays between differentiated and hierarchical subject positions, that is, the accused and their representatives, witnesses, the prosecutor(s) and judges. Such subject positions are roles that ground the prevailing 'scripts' of the courtroom – its 'enunciative modalities' (Foucault 2002: 55–56) – each furnishing particular obligations, expectations and strategies around which memory is called into being, demanded, tested, acknowledged and auscultated.[1] The scripts appended to these positions are not, of course, determinant. Indeed, as Tovares argues with reference to the South African Truth and Reconciliation Commission (2016), the scripts of transitional justice can be elided in unpredictable ways that allow the reframing of the meaning of events, a possibility we will return to. Secondly, the specific forms of objective, legal knowledge and truth – implicating, invoking and remaking *memories* – that such positions seek to locate are important. As Allo notes, while the courtroom is conceptualised, configured and authorised as a neutral 'Euclidean' space, it can act as a site of domination, constraint and subordination that is generative of conflict and resistance (2015).

For our purposes here, today, the dramatisation of such work – widely recognised and conceptualised as much a performative as normative spectacle of deliberation (Allo 2010; Cole 2010) – becomes a ritualistic crucible for the production and clarification of legal truth *as* social narrative (Falk 2008; Bilsky 2004). Thirdly, the wider effects of the trial as a spectacle are crucial. Foucault explains that judicial practices and techniques – deliberative, reasoned courtroom intercourse and judgement – have been integral to the constitution of wider formations of social order because they reproduce (changing) sets of rules that are obliged in the name of regimes of legal truths (1994). Such legal truths become self-authorising and taken for granted as a 'general knowledge'; we can see why and how trials are the preferred technique within transitional justice – the 'gold standard' within the liberal, legalist normative world-view – for 'renewing' societies and inaugurating 'rational', rule-governed and 'democratised' social worlds.

The chapter proceeds as follows. I firstly identify specific patterns, or 'scripts', evident in prosecutorial and victim statements within the courtroom, locating memory claims that are registered on the basis of their apparent reliability or their testimonial weight. I then examine how defence teams have contested these memory claims, focusing in particular on strategies of 'acquiescence', 'denial' and 'rupture'. Lastly, I examine examples of how the outcomes of the court process can be 'unscripted' and the way they can be received by stakeholders – specifically Civil Parties – in problematic ways. I aim here to examine, in closer detail, not only how trials work on, invoke and produce memory in their minutiae but also how memory work within the courtroom generates unexpected and unforeseen outcomes and resistances that elide the outcomes anticipated from the ECCC process.

The pursuit of legal truth

The central purpose of the criminal trial as a *deliberative* spectacle is the adjudication of the guilt or innocence of suspects, a process authorised as legitimate through the normative ideal of a *rational* apolitical and objective identification of knowledge about the past. The trial process can powerfully then either vindicate or denounce past actions, reframing memory under new moral terms. Two issues are notable here. On the one hand, it is important to bear in mind that the arrival at and reception of such adjudications is, however, far from neutral. Trials remain deeply political and contested processes. Yet, on the other, the search for and very possibility of legal *truth* is a constitutive premise of the trial as an authoritative exercise. The courtroom is conceptualised as a space that can locate and discern the *truth* of what happened, implicating arguments that point to trials as crucibles for the adjudication or accommodation of competing memories (see e.g. Osiel 1997). How does this process work at the level of detail? Lynch and Bogen explain that the basic discursive structure of a trial process is a 'question' and 'answer' format; this is necessarily contested according to adversarial positioning of accusatory and defendant subjects and their various accounts of past events (1996: 130). In this sense, we can see one characteristic of the way memory is reconstructed within the courtroom: competing claims over the past that are located on factual registers of legal truth. These are, of course, delimited by and contained within the mandate of the ECCC.

There are several useful examples from the ECCC proceedings that illustrate this. The prosecutorial strategy against Duch in Case 001, running through 2009 and 2010, located his role as a 'most responsible' figure within the perpetration of atrocity at the S-21 site, utilising documentary evidence such as confessions extracted from prisoners and the testimony of his subordinates and the survivors of the centre. The interplays between prosecution and defence during Case 002 have been characterised by attempts to *prove* or *refute* – specific genres of memory claim – the roles of 'senior leaders' on the basis of their position and authority within the Communist Party of Kampuchea command structure. For example, substantive hearings against Nuon Chea and Khieu Samphan have seen the prosecution attempting to corroborate and 'triangulate' proof between documents such as Civil Party testimony on 'self-criticism'[2] (as a mode of 'confession' encouraged by the leadership); reports from lower-level Khmer Rouge to the leadership outlining the 'situation of internal enemy'[3]; and communications between districts and *Angkar* (command) on the policy of 'smashing enemies' (members of the former regime)[4]. Together, these submissions were intended to evidence eliminatory intent and/or complicity on the behalf of the accused. As such, they characterise a central genre of memory claim at work at tribunals: that knowledge of the past, as a set of memories and artefacts, can be objectively reproduced as a set of unequivocal facts. This is pivotal to the way trials seek to authorise a renewed memory of past political violence because of the premise that the past *can* be disinterred objectively, definitively stated and placed on record.

Victim hearings

A second genre of memory claim visible within the trial process is victim testimony. As noted in the previous chapter, the promise of victim participation at the ECCC has a mixed record, with opportunities to address and participate curtailed to expedite proceedings following Case 001, before being reconfigured as substantive 'Victim Impact Hearings' and through 'Statements of Suffering' during Case 002/01. As the ECCC Public Affairs Office declared in June 2013, "over the last two weeks of trial hearings, 15 victims [out of 3,866] who are participating in Case 002 as Civil Parties provided emotional testimonies about the harm they suffered personally during and in the aftermath of the Khmer Rouge regime."[5] Case 002/02 will include victim impact hearings and statements that are drawn from a representative sample of the Civil Parties admitted, with the aim of furnishing 'representative' accounts of harm and suffering (Ciorciari and Heindel 2016). Crucially, these types of memory claim and performance are endowed with their authority on the basis of an emotive as much as a factual register. In this sense, their participation and role within the process is authorised by emphasising the severity of the harm they have suffered as an expressive and performative gesture, ritualising grief as a dramatic spectacle (Elander 2013). This works in contrast to interchanges over the *authenticity* or factual truth of particular documents or testimonies, which have been frequently curtailed on the basis of evidential relevance, that is, the extent to which they conform to registers of proof.[6]

Under the terms of Civil Party participation, victims are *obliged* to evidence the harm they have suffered in order to qualify for admission as a Civil Party. On the one hand, victim testimony has been crucial for the presentation of the ECCC as a retributive mechanism that is more sensitive towards the needs of its constituents. Yet, on the other, there have been occasions where testimony has appeared to exceed the limits of the scripts afforded to victims at that time. On one occasion, a speaker had their microphone silenced, and on another, a Civil Party was explicitly told to 'keep grief concise'.[7] Silencing victim testimony appears at odds with the restorative ambit of the ECCC and further points to the way in which proceedings in the courtroom are 'contained' or encouraged in accordance with preferred scripts at different points. The initial internal rules provided no provisions for victim impact hearings or statements of suffering, which have been authored into the trial process as trials have progressed. In Case 002/01, when offered the opportunity to disclose a statement of suffering, early Civil Parties were unprepared (Ciorciari and Heindel 2016: 66–67). As victim impact hearings and statements of suffering became a standardised and anticipated point of procedure – rather than a provisional opportunity – victim testimony has started to take on specific temporal structures and formats that include (and move through) general descriptions of routine suffering, specific instances of loss, enduring effects and harms and appeals for redress. In this sense, the process of remembering – of pressing a memory claim – has a particular linear format. An example from the hearings on October 22nd 2012 is useful in illustrating this point. Yim Sovann's testimony opens by locating itself as an 'expression of suffering':[8]

> I thank you very much Mr President and Your Honours, for allowing me this opportunity to read out my expression of suffering. From 1975 to 1976, I was mistreated. I was accused of being a 17 of April Person. Although I was falling sick, I was still forced to work. I was very young at that time. I worked at cooperatives; the cooperatives that I had been working after I had been evacuated by Phnom Penh... As one of the 17 People (sic), I was accused by the Base People as an enemy. I did not have enough to eat. I started to pick some grains of corns, and with that I was accused of being an enemy... When I was at home, I was accused of being too liberal. And every now and – every time I recall the moment, I am traumatized, and I am always shocked to recollect the events, the times when I were forced to work days and nights. I am a good person; I was forcing myself to commit some petty crimes by stealing to survive.
>
> ...They gave me only very little food. And at one point, before the second phase of evacuation, I said to myself, if I was not allowed to go and see my parents, I would die anyway. And I lost everything. I lost my properties, cattle, and the farmland.

The opening of Yim's statement offers a general portrayal of hunger and exclusion. Memory, here, operates in a way that furnishes a broad and contextual depiction of injustice; Yim's sense of shock and mistreatment at the hands of the Khmer Rouge is bound to her categorisation as an 'enemy' and 'criminal'. Moreover, the enduring impact of suffering is invoked specifically through the vocabulary of trauma. Yim's testimony here, in the act of remembering, establishes a specific relation between memories of loss and suffering in the present. Memory is thus visible in three ways: as a performative act of remembrance, or recollection and retelling from the subject; as a spectacle of the trial process, as the subject's grief is presented as the object of the audience and site of renewal (see Elander 2013 on expressivism at the ECCC); and, through the invocation of trauma, as a set of references, frames and descriptors for the state of memory itself as an object of knowledge. Yim follows this by detailing a particular incident of loss:

> When I saw my father being arrested and his hands being tied up by the Khmer Rouge militia, I was shocked and traumatized and I could feel the pain.

The specific incident detailed emphasises the personal dimensions of loss and suffering (as distinct from the broader references to the systemic and generalised suffering of the period), a key criteria for recognition by the ECCC as a Civil Party. Yim's testimony then shifts to the present, where broader societal maladies today are linked to the Khmer Rouge period:

> I have been living in the society where I have had a lot of suffering. I have not been well educated. I have faced difficulties and all of the bad things that happened to me. I have been deprived of all my education, the dreams that I would like to be highly educated. But these dreams were destroyed by the darkest period of the Khmer Rouge.

Lastly, an appeal is made for the ECCC to rectify this past:

> And before my appearance before this Court, I did not ever imagine that I would be given such opportunity… I am grateful to this Court and I hope that you find justice both for me and for the Cambodian people – that is, those victims and Civil Parties.

Here we can see that a vital connection is established between past suffering, present suffering and the ECCC as a remedial mechanism through a specific, linear sequence of memory claims: there are memories of past suffering bound to present states of malady; these can be rectified by the ECCC as the appropriate moral agent for their amelioration. This is an important sequence because it shows how agents within the courtroom conform to and reproduce the overarching progressive schemas that validate the ECCC as an intervention that "moves forward through justice." Moreover, the consequences of such sequencing are important because they artificially locate the maladies of the present in a singular relationship to one episode of violence. Yim's references to a 'lack of education' and losing her 'dreams' are important examples here. Of course, experiences of the Khmer Rouge will have had a profound impact on education and aspiration. Yet locating such problems in a singular relationship to the Khmer Rouge further obscures and elides those inequalities, conflicts and problems that have been endemic within Cambodia's social and political order in the intervening years, notwithstanding the international ostracism of Cambodia in the 1980s that so hampered reconstruction efforts.

Strategies of the accused

The defence teams at the ECCC have – as convention – sought to undermine the prosecution on the basis of the credibility of its evidence. This is, of course, a necessary feature within the criminal legal process, but it has consequences when considered as a technique of memory with particular epistemological implications, and it holds particular analytic value in relief of other forms of claim over memory, such as testimonial or confessional disclosures. For example, archival documents held by DC-Cam have been called into question on the basis of the partiality of the stewards of the repository; defence lawyers specifically probed DC-Cam director Youk Chhang on whether the organisation was acting in the capacity of human-rights advocacy or of 'neutral' documentation,[9] illustrating the way in which artefacts of memory (as *evidence*) are themselves bound to specific histories of conservation and preservation. This again further implicates the way in which frames of representation, or 'knowing', tend to be inseparable from advocacy within the production of knowledge on human-rights problems (Moon 2012a). In a similar vein, the testimony and research of expert witnesses such as Philip Shaw[10] (Pol Pot's biographer) or David Chandler[11] (a historian of Cambodia) have been attacked on the basis of their academic credibility, or their 'poetic license', attempting to undermine their 'validity'. Moreover, memory is further invoked in the way that acts of remembrance are 'tested'. For example, the memory of witness Sao Sarun was specifically challenged as unreliable.[12] Again, this implicates the way that the trial process is presented as a means of stabilising an objective and unequivocal account of the past. By contesting the credibility of the prosecution's claims, the defence attempts to refute the substance – or 'story' – of prosecutors' attempts to stabilise a narrative of political violence. At the same time, it is important to note that it does so exactly on the terms offered by the trial, that is, through refuting or corroborating proof and evidence. As a form of memory work, this constitutes the trial as deliberative exercise, which anchors the performative role of the trial within broader progressive schemas underpinning the ECCC as an exercise that is meant to establish the rule of law and promote democratisation.

Two further, more complex strategies are afforded to defence teams in the way that memory is contested: firstly, again on the terms offered by the trial, by acquiescing to or *denying* the memory claims of the prosecution; and secondly, by contesting the legitimacy of the trial as an adjudicative exercise or through strategies of 'rupture'. The substantive hearing against Duch in Case 001 and Nuon Chea and Khieu Samphan in Case 002/01 provide useful, mixed examples in these regards.

The case against Duch principally focused on his role at the S-21 interrogation centre. Duch's contribution to the proceedings was characterised by public displays of remorse, admittance and inculpation. At the same time, Duch's gestures of contrition tended to be balanced against his accounts of hierarchy and blame within the Khmer Rouge apparatus, locating responsibility firmly at the hands of senior leaders:

> One, I would like to give analysis on the crimes across the country from the 17th of April 1975 to 6th of January 1979. After the 17th of April 1975, Pol Pot was wild... Mainly, Pol Pot had thousands of candidates in his hands. The crimes in that period was huge. In addition, the loss of life of the people is calculated as equal to one million people, and as a member of the CPK [Communist Party of Kampuchea] I recognise that I am responsible mentally for the crimes committed by the CPK in those periods of time. I would like to express my regret and my heartfelt sorrow and loss for all the crimes committed by the CPK from 1975 to 1979. I would like to express separately about the crimes at S-21. I would like to acknowledge my responsibility through legal means, legally. I mean, I would like to emphasize that I am responsible for the crimes committed at S-21, especially the tortures and execution of the people there.[13]

This statement is important. Firstly, it is an example of one of a range of Duch's statements compiled by the ECCC as a form of 'moral and symbolic' reparation for victims.[14] Secondly, it acquiesces neatly to the terms of the ECCC law: Duch accepts his role and responsibility for the killings perpetrated at S-21 yet locates blame for nationwide atrocities to the 'wild' Pol Pot (or leadership). In this sense, thirdly, we can see that Duch's bid to reframe memories of his role during the Khmer Rouge involve claims that both inculpate *and* downplay his actions. This ambivalence is important as a form of memory work because it was deployed as a bid to cooperate with the ECCC in anticipation of sentencing. As a caveat, it is important to note that Duch reneged on the key tenets of his admissions – that he was a 'most responsible figure' – during his closing statement, and I return to Duch's change of strategy as an example of the unanticipated outcomes of the ECCC in the final section of this chapter.

In situating his own role as a 'subordinate' within the Khmer Rouge hierarchy, aspects of Duch's memory claims can be read as an example of 'denial' at work.[15] Cohen has suggested that the 'discourse of official denial' is characterised by three tendencies (2001): 'literal' denial (i.e. that something didn't actually happen); 'interpretive' denial, where the significance of events are downplayed or modulated; and lastly, 'implicatory' denial, which entails the minimisation or displacement of the moral implications of the events in question (2001: 7–9).

Duch's statement, in this sense, can be seen as an attempt to displace his own moral agency on the basis that, firstly, his actions were one part of a national pattern of abuses; and secondly, he was following the directives of malign, more responsible senior leaders. The 'upward' displacement of moral agency by Duch's defence team is mirrored by the 'downward' denials of responsibility by the defence teams of the senior leaders. For example, in his opening statement, Nuon Chea remarked that:

> Some people were wearing black shirts and were disguised as the resistance group in order to liberate the country, but actually they were arresting, they were killing people. It was very, very complicated at that time. So it was very hard for us to understand, everything is chaotic.[16]

Nuon Chea is here suggesting that there was no state-directed policy of internal purges, emphasising the 'chaos' of the period. Nuon Chea is therefore denying the *ability* of the authorities to direct such policies. Moreover, on this basis, Nuon Chea's suggestion is that any atrocities must have been perpetrated by rogue elements in 'disguise' and were therefore solely the fault of lower-level perpetrators. Nuon Chea continued to advance more elaborate denials of responsibility, whilst acknowledging the occurrence of crimes in the period:

> So these crimes – war crimes and crimes against humanity – were not – and genocide – were not for Cambodian people. It was Vietnam who killed Cambodians.... I don't want to misunderstand that the Khmer Rouge are bad people, are criminals. Nothing is true about that. There were nationalists who wished to protect the country, to liberate the country from Vietnam.[17]

Here we can see Nuon Chea advancing the claim that the Khmer Rouge could not have been responsible for the perpetration of atrocities because of their patriotic loyalties. Nuon Chea is in this instance relying on popular claims about Cambodian national identity and memory that are defined against, and constituted by, racialised difference with Vietnam. This is an important example of both interpretive and implicatory 'denial' because, as a memory claim, Nuon Chea is suggesting that *something happened* but is recasting the protagonists involved. Furthermore, Nuon Chea is claiming here, secondly, that the Khmer Rouge could not be responsible because they were *moral agents* operating in contradistinction to the Vietnamese.

In a similar vein, Khieu Samphan has utilised several scripts that seek to displace the moral implications of the suffering that occurred under Democratic Kampuchea. In one instance, Khieu Samphan appealed to the popular support enjoyed by the Khmer Rouge in their ascent to power as a bid to exculpate and justify his role within the Khmer Rouge leadership:

> Regardless [if] you like or dislike it, majority of Cambodian people gave their support to us for our opposition against the Lon Nol regime...[18]

In further comments, the key 'paradox' of denial scripts is visible in the way Khieu Samphan both knows and disavows the occurrence of atrocities:

> You also stated that I must have been aware of the conditions endured by Cambodians during the period and the examination because I visited the dam work sites. But do you really think, Mr. Co-Prosecutor, that, when I visited these work sites alone or accompanied by the King, workers were being murdered in front of us with hoes or bullets in the back of the neck?[19]

As Stan Cohen notes, perpetrators can only 'deny' what they have been made already aware of (1993). In this example, Khieu Samphan is promoting his apparent ignorance of atrocities that he simultaneously depicts in detail. As a memory claim, the statement works to deny his knowledge of atrocities of the period by appealing to the gravity and exceptionality of the crimes at hand, implying that such actions could not have been 'routine'.

Rupture

A final technique that has been employed by Nuon Chea and Khieu Samphan more explicitly resists the legitimacy of the court as an adjudicative process. Strategies of 'rupture' represent challenges to the legitimacy of the court that are not reducible to its terms (Christodoulidis 2009). These strategies, most famously invoked by Jacques Verges, essentially pivot on a '*tu quoque*' question (or '*who are you to judge*?'). Strategies of rupture seek to outflank the normative authority of law by focusing on inconsistencies in the application of the moral imperative to punish. Several examples from the ECCC are illuminating on these terms:

> Mr. Co-Prosecutor, you seem to forget that, between January 1970 and August 1973, that is the period of two and a half years, the United States carpeted the small Kampuchean territory with bombs [that] outnumbered those numbers of bombs the alliance used during the Second World War everywhere, including the two big bombs dropped on Hiroshima and Nagasaki. Could you imagine what my country faced after such a bloody killing and war? You may assist in thinking what the future is and what's like for Cambodian people and the country as a whole during such carpet bombing. No, I can see you cannot make such an imagination.[20]

Here Khieu Samphan again employs a form of 'implicatory' denial by suggesting that the destruction wrought through carpet bombing both determined and constrained the range of options available to the Khmer Rouge on taking power. At the same time, by pointing to patterns of political violence that are unexamined by the ECCC, Khieu Samphan is probing an inconsistency in the way that punishments for perpetrators of human-rights abuses are applied. As Koskenniemi suggests, such strategies of 'rupture' haunt international tribunals because, as purportedly deliberative exercises that seek to adjudicate over massive political violence, tribunals inevitably implicate historical contexts that defence teams can reach for in order to exploit and equivocate the reconstruction of 'historical truth' (2002: 33). A strategy of rupture that calls attention to perceived double standards is again visible in the way Khieu Samphan questions why other individuals that occupied roles in the Democratic Kampuchea hierarchy are not being prosecuted. In this controversial instance, Khieu Samphan is speaking of the late King Sihanouk:

> Mr. Co-Prosecutor, you will also say that the fact that I was appointed the President of the State Presidium of the Democratic Kampuchea committed me to a joint criminal enterprise; in which case, why are you not prosecuting King Norodom Sihanouk?[21]

The strategies of rupture employed by defence teams have met notable resistance by judicial staff. On one occasion, the defence team sought to question Nuon Chea on the role of members of the current government who may have occupied positions of authority under the Khmer Rouge:

> BY MR. PESTMAN:
> I have almost finished. One last question: Do you know what Heng Samrin's [current Chairman of the National Assembly] other position was? He was your messenger, he was your guide; but what was his official function within the Party? And I'm talking about the period shortly before 1975 – April 1975, the liberation of Phnom Penh.
>
> MR. NUON CHEA:
> A. (Microphone not activated)
>
> MR. PRESIDENT:
> Nuon Chea, you are instructed not to respond to the question, since it is irrelevant to the historical background of the Democratic Kampuchea.[22]

Again, this example begins with a strategy of 'rupture' seeking to outflank and destabilise the ECCC jurisdiction over "senior leaders" that is, in effect, silenced here. This is important because it shows that, as a site of memory work, the ECCC judges maintain an active involvement in containing the scope of concealment and disclosure of the past at the same time as the defence teams seek to contest it.

Resistance to the ECCC and its memory work is therefore typified by two tendencies. Firstly, defence teams resist engagement with the ECCC account of past political violence *on* the terms authorised by the ECCC; that is, they attempt to refute the 'veracity' of evidence presented by the prosecution or employ codes of 'denial' to disavow, or work to minimise, their responsibility for the crimes in question. The second tendency works *against* the terms authorised by the ECCC through strategies of 'rupture' that call into question the legitimacy of the court as a neutral arbiter over competing memory claims. In the first instance, it seems that the performance of resistance is necessary for the legitimacy of the court because it constitutes a process of contested deliberation and that resistance therefore mutually constitutes the power of the court. The second form of memory work is far more ambivalent in its relation to the ECCC. It challenges the terms and moral authority of the court by calling attention to competing accounts of violence and perpetration, and yet it can be subsumed within seemingly trivial strategies of shutdown, such as the silencing of microphones within the courtroom.

Unanticipated outcomes

The trial process plays out through competing attempts to stabilise, contain, refute and rupture different claims over past political violence. This process is framed by and occurs between the mandates of the court (as determined by the ECCC law) to the minutiae interplays of the courtroom (through *active* processes of disclosure and concealment by victims, perpetrators and the arbiters of the court). Yet it remains important to consider examples of how the ECCC remains unresolved and unpredictable. As noted with respect to victim impact hearings and statements of suffering, new avenues and enunciative positions are authored into the ECCC process even as others are shut down. The ECCC continues to produce unanticipated and uneven outcomes beyond the 'scripts' identified, which appear to follow particular discursive regularities.

One useful example of such unpredictability – and an example that destabilises the ECCC in authorising a coherent, comprehensive and 'resolved' account of past political violence – was visible in the closing statements to Case 001 and the responses they generated. As noted, the trial of Duch was characterised by the defendant's admissions of responsibility and remorse, though these were mixed alongside more subtle forms of 'upward' denial, as identified. During the closing statements, Duch's defence team split tack, with his international defence lawyer pleading for recognition of his cooperation, and his national defence counsel embarking on a change of direction, requesting release for Duch and hardening his stance in relation to Duch's role as a subordinate rather than a "most responsible" figure at S-21. This raises open questions about processed of memory work that operates according to 'scripts': why self-incriminate and then deny one's role in within the perpetration of atrocity?

> I clearly understand that any theory or ideology which mentions love for the people in a class-based concept and class struggle is definitely driving us into endless tragedy and misery… I still maintain that a decision to choose which path to walk is made in a matter of seconds. However, its repercussions, if it is a wrong choice, will result in lifelong remorse.
>
> All santebal offices were equal before the party. Each prison used the same torture, the same murder, under the same order from Angkar.[23]

Duch here attempts to downplay both his own moral agency by the 'accidence' of path before denying the significance of his role at S-21 and drawing equivalences with other sites of killing. This is notable because it is so at odds with his earlier acquiescence to the preferred tack of the prosecution. Moreover, it challenges the prosecutions preferred reading of violence under Democratic Kampuchea that centred S-21 and the evacuation of Phnom Penh (the focus of Case 002/01) as synecdochal to a national experience of violence and suffering under the Khmer Rouge.

Duch was initially sentenced to 19 years' imprisonment, based on a 16-year reduction for time already served, cooperation and violations of rights related to his unlawful pre-trial detention. Research by the Documentation Centre of Cambodia (DC-Cam) at the time documented the 'confusion' and 'disappointment' of victim organisations. One audience member queried "The sentencing was unclear, so just how many years will Duch serve in prison?"[24] Another suggested that "If I were the judge, I would torture Duch in the same way he tortured others."[25] The dissatisfaction of these responses is illuminating for two reasons. Firstly, the reception of interventions that are designed to satisfy memories of political violence is uneven and can sometimes disappoint and anger those invested in processes meant to correct past violence (see e.g. Moon 2012b on initiatives to materially compensate families of the disappeared in Argentina). Secondly, as a form of memory work, the adjudication of guilt or innocence operates to stabilise a 'story' of past political violence and, inseparably, to recast the moral meaning of those events through the technique of sentencing as a form of denunciation. In this sense, even when parties are in agreement of the events under question, the efficacy of the techniques of memory that denounce those events can themselves be contested as appropriate responses to memory.

Both the prosecution and defence appealed against the initial 2010 sentencing and, two years later, Duch's term was increased to life imprisonment. The recalibration of Duch's sentence to reflect "the gravity of the crimes at hand"[26] cannot be traced directly to be a consequence of the disappointment felt towards the initial term. But at the same time, it illuminates an imminent tension in the work of the court between satisfying due legal process and the popular demands of its key constituents.

Conclusion

This chapter has examined how the ECCC works on memory at the level of detail through specific 'scripts' that advance competing memory claims, as well as the unanticipated outcomes and responses to ECCC memory work. The ECCC is notable as an exercise in *disclosure* and *concealment*, but it works on differing planes. While the wider project is validated as an intervention in the name of a wounded nation, renewing a national population and social order, the techniques and interplays of memory within the courtroom are important to note as they are enacted, negotiated and resisted by differentiated defence, accusing, victim, perpetrator and adjudicative positions. As I have argued, there are two tendencies that characterise the way in which the ECCC involves memory work in the minutiae of these procedures. The first tendency occurs on the terms afforded by the court in accordance with the mandated jurisdictions the ECCC examines. The trial is legitimated on the presumption that a definitive and resolute *truth* is possible. Prosecution and defence teams contest memory claims against criteria of accuracy, reliability and validity. Indeed, the performative and rational deliberation of an exercise that is seen to include open outcomes – and the very possibility of acquittal – is the lynchpin of the trial as a 'democratising' exercise. This works even as we recognise that the jurisdictions of the court service the containment of a politically preferred account of the Khmer Rouge (blaming senior leaders only and obscuring violence before and after Democratic Kampuchea). The production of *truth* on registers of 'objectivity' is complemented by the testimony of (some) victims that tend to accede to scripts that allow expressions of suffering, emphasising the gravity of the memories at hand. These moments are highly performative gestures of memory claims making, but we might query the political effects of such statements. As I have argued, they tend to present singular linkages between episodes of violence and present-day suffering, reflective of the wider 'grammar' of transitional justice, when there may be intervening factors, experiences and problems that are obscured and yet worthy of scrutiny themselves.

In turn, defence teams can employ more elaborate codes of 'denial' that work to disavow or to minimise their responsibility for the crimes in question. As I have suggested, these strategies further have the effect of constituting the legitimacy and power of the trial as a deliberative spectacle. Yet a second tendency works *against* the terms authorised by the ECCC through strategies of 'rupture'. These strategies attack the legitimacy of the court as an arbiter over competing memory claims, probing double standards and relying on attempts to equivocate between different episodes of atrocity. This second form of memory work is far more ambivalent in its relation to the ECCC. It challenges the terms and moral authority of the court by calling attention to competing accounts of violence and perpetration. As Foucault argues in *Society Must be Defended*, official histories tend to obviate their own omissions and overstatements, inviting their own points of resistance, destabilising the possibility of singular accounts of the past (1994). Such gaps remain politically significant because they correspond to memory claims that circulate beyond the courtroom, as I explore in Chapter 7.

Notes

1 I use this term with some interpretive license here. To auscultate is a form of diagnostic medical practice – itself obeying specific routine and regularities – that involves *listening* to a patient to ascertain the presence and extent of malady. As I discuss in the section on Civil Party testimony, 'Victim Impact Hearings' and 'Statements of Suffering' are specifically deployed diagnostic mechanisms to *hear* and ascertain the weight and gravity of harms suffered.

2 Transcript of Trial Proceedings Case File N° 002/19-09-2007-ECCC/TC 26 June 2013 p. 72.

3 Transcript of Trial Proceedings Case File N° 002/19-09-2007-ECCC/TC 26 June 2013 p. 17.

4 Transcript of Trial Proceedings Case File N° 002/19-09-2007-ECCC/TC 26 June 2013 p. 8.

5 ECCC Blog, 'The purpose of hearing victims' suffering', 7 June 2013. Available at http://www.eccc.gov.kh/en/blog/2013/06/07/purpose-hearing-victims-suffering. Last accessed 21 September 2016.

6 There was confusion and anger from defence teams when it became apparent in Case 002/01 that the statements were being used as material evidence (see Ciorciari and Heindel 2016: 65).

7 See "Khmer Rouge court Civil Parties told to keep grief concise." Phnom Penh Post, October 23rd 2012. Available at http://www.phnompenhpost.com/national/khmer-rouge-court-civil-parties-told-keep-grief-concise. Last accessed 23 September 2016.

8 Transcript of Trial Proceedings, Case File N° 002/19-09-2007-ECCC/TC, 22 October 2012 (pp. 18–22).

9 Transcript of Trial Proceedings Case File N° 002/19-09-2007-ECCC/TC, 2 February 2012 (p. 83).

10 See, for example, pp. 3–4 of the transcript of Trial Proceedings Case File N° 002/19-09-2007-ECCC/TC, 8 May 2013.

11 Transcript of Trial Proceedings Case File N° 002/19-09-2007-ECCC/TC, 23 July 2012 (pp. 139–140).

12 Transcript of Trial Proceedings Case File N° 002/19-09-2007-ECCC/TC, 6 June 2012 (pp. 35–36).

13 Transcript of Trial Proceedings 'The Duch Trial' Case File N° 001/18-07-2007-ECCC/TC31, March 2009 0903H (p. 67).

14 'Compilation of statements of apology made by Kaing Guek Eav alias Duch during the proceedings' available at http://www.eccc.gov.kh/sites/default/files/publications/Case001Apology_En_low_res.pdf. Last accessed 21 September 2016.

15 Two caveats concerning the use of Cohen's denial framework should be noted here. Firstly, as Cohen himself argues, an analysis of various forms of 'denial' is not about verification against criteria of truth or falsehood but should proceed in circumstances where knowledge of the past is contested and ambiguous (2001: 4–5). Moreover, and on this basis, in treating 'denial' as a set of discursive repertoires, we eschew analysis of the internal or psychoanalytic machinations of knowing and not knowing memory. For the purposes of this chapter, 'denial' operates allegorically to signify types of 'script' adopted in the process of reconstructing the past.

16 Transcript of Trial Proceedings Case File N° 002/19-09-2007-ECCC/TC, 5 December 2011 (p. 51).

17 Transcript of Trial Proceedings Case File N° 002/19-09-2007-ECCC/TC, 5 December 2011 (p. 52).

18 Transcript of Trial Proceedings Case File N° 002/19-09-2007-ECCC/TC, 23 November 2011 (p. 12).

19 Transcript of Trial Proceedings Case File N° 002/19-09-2007-ECCC/TC, 23 November 2011 (p. 16).

20 Transcript of Trial Proceedings Case File N° 002/19-09-2007-ECCC/TC, 23 November 2011 (p. 12).

21 Transcript of Trial Proceedings Case File N° 002/19-09-2007-ECCC/TC, 23 November 2011 (p. 16).

22 Transcript of Trial Proceedings Case File N° 002/19-09-2007-ECCC/TC 9 February 2012 (pp. 48–49).

23 Transcript of Trial Proceedings 'Duch Trial' Case File N° 001/18-07-2007-ECCC/TC 25 November 2009, 0901H (p. 68).

24 See Keo, D. 2010. Disarray and disappointment after the Duch Verdict, DC-Cam Report, Phnom Penh. Available at http://www.d.dccam.org/Projects/ECCC_Trial_Observation/pdf/Disarray_and_Disappointment_after_the_Duch_Verdict--Dacil_Keo.pdf. Last accessed 23 September 2016.

25 See Keo, D. 2010. "Disarray and disappointment after the Duch Verdict", DC-Cam Report, Phnom Penh. Available at http://www.d.dccam.org/Projects/ECCC_Trial_Observation/pdf/Disarray_and_Disappointment_after_the_Duch_Verdict--Dacil_Keo.pdf. Last accessed 23 September 2016.

26 See the ECCC 'Case 001' summary. Available at http://www.eccc.gov.kh/en/case/topic/1. Last accessed 21 September 2016.

References

Allo, A. 2010. Show in the show trial: Contextualising the politicization of the courtroom, The. *Barry L. Rev.*, *15*: 41.

Allo, A. (ed.) 2015. *The Courtroom as a Space of Resistance: Reflections on the Legacy of the Rivonia Trial.* Surrey: Ashgate Publishing, Ltd.

Bilsky, L. 2004. *Transformative Justice: Israeli Identity on Trial.* Ann Arbour: University of Michigan Press.

Christodoulidis, E. 2009. Strategies of rupture. *Law and Critique*, *20* (1): 3–26.

Ciorciari, J. D. and Heindel, A. 2016. Victim testimony in international and hybrid criminal courts: Narrative opportunities, challenges, and fair trial demands. (Forthcoming) *Virginia Journal of International Law*, *56* (2).

Cohen, S. 1993. Human rights and crimes of the state: The culture of denial. *Australian & New Zealand Journal of Criminology*, *26* (2): 97–115.

Cohen, S. 2001. *States of Denial: Knowing about Atrocities and Suffering.* Cambridge, UK: Polity/Malden, MA: Blackwell.

Cole, C. 2010. *Performing South Africa's Truth Commissions: Stages of Transition.* Bloomington, IN: Indiana University Press.

Elander, M. 2013. The victim's address: Expressivism and the victim at the extraordinary chambers in the courts of Cambodia. *International Journal of Transitional Justice*, *7* (1): 9–115.

Falk, B. J. 2008. *Making Sense of Political Trials: Causes and Categories.* Ontario, CA: Munk Centre for International Studies, University of Toronto.

Foucault, M. 1994. Truth and juridical forms. In *Power: Essential Works of Michel Foucault 1954–1984. Vol. 3.* J. D. Faubian (ed). London: Penguin.

Foucault, M. 2002. *Archaeology of Knowledge.* London, New York: Routledge.

Koskenniemi, M. 2002. Between impunity and show trials. *Max Planck Yearbook of United Nations Law*, *6* (1): 1–32.

Lynch, M. and Bogen, D. 1996. *The Spectacle of History: Speech, Text, and Memory at the Iran-Contra Hearings.* Durham: Duke University Press.

Moon, C. 2012a. What one sees and how one files seeing: Human rights reporting, representation and action. *Sociology*, *46* (5): 876–890.

Moon, C. 2012b. 'Who'll pay reparations on my soul?' Compensation, social control and social suffering. *Social & Legal Studies*, *21* (2): 187–199.

Osiel, M. 1997. *Mass Atrocity, Collective Memory, and the Law.* New Brunswick, NJ: Transaction Publishers.

Tovares, A. V. 2016. Going off-script and reframing the frame: The dialogic intertwining of the centripetal and centrifugal voices in the Truth and Reconciliation Commission hearings. *Discourse & Society*, *27* (5): 554–573.

6 Complementary knowledge

One striking feature of the transitional justice process in Cambodia over the past decade has been the prominent role of civil society and non-governmental organisations (NGOs)[1] in facilitating, supporting, arbitrating and supplementing 'transitional justice'. These efforts are oriented to a diverse range of legal, therapeutic and civic outcomes in the name of ameliorating Cambodia's experiences of violence and atrocity, and they have worked, to varying degrees, to complement (and occasionally in conflict) with both the Extraordinary Chambers in the Courts of Cambodia (ECCC) and the Cambodian government. While negotiations over the establishment of the ECCC were unfolding in the early 2000s, NGOs such as the Centre for Social Development and the Khmer Institute for Democracy were gauging the public appetite for Khmer Rouge accountability and attitudes to reconciliation (see Vannath 2002). As the ECCC prosecutions have proceeded, NGOs such as the Documentation Centre of Cambodia (DC-Cam) – a longstanding advocate of 'genocide justice' – have played a key role in publicising and promoting the work of the court. Others, such as the Open Society Justice Initiative, have led efforts monitoring and reporting on due process and legal standards at the ECCC. NGOs have also directed their work with one eye on the future legacy of the ECCC, offering input on the shape of reparations projects and looking towards issues beyond the immediate orbit of the court: Youth for Peace, for example, are now actively liaising with Cambodian communities about the erection of new local memorial sites, educational centres and 'peace libraries'. NGOs are therefore a crucial part of a story that troubles a tendency to conceptualise transitional justice as a set of 'cases' that are inaugurated and authored through one site or mechanism, one means of justice or one process of reconciliation. Indeed, one aim of this chapter is to illustrate, via two cases, how the terms 'justice' and 'reconciliation' can operate as free-floating signifiers that become meaningful in the varying forms of practice that invoke them. Moreover, for our immediate purposes here, different NGOs have invoked, implicitly and explicitly, questions of memory and remembering in the focus and aims of their work.

The increasingly prominent role of NGOs within Cambodian public life is a result of a specific political history. As Caroline Hughes has pointed out, the United Nations Transitional Authority UNTAC (1992–1993) was unprecedented as a form of international intervention in the scope and extent of how it sought to redefine the Cambodian state and political order. One consequence of UNTAC was the inauguration of an era of routine international involvement and presence in the Cambodian polity, principally realised through aid programmes during the 1990s that sponsored civil society organisations to *do* 'development', 'nation-building' and 'democratisation' (C. Hughes 2003, 2009). Importantly, the role of such NGOs, the scope and scale of their work and their relationship to existing Cambodian political institutions was never neutral, because the funding for such projects was conditional and contingently anchored to specific international expectations and assumptions about how post-conflict spaces should be managed, the problems that attend them and the ends to which their work must be directed (C. Hughes 2007). Moreover, the centrality of NGOs within Cambodia's experiences of peace building, development and democratisation entrenched aid relationships as a key resource within civic administration; it also embedded the supervisory and managerial tendencies international actors have adopted regarding Cambodia's trajectory since, either as in situ organisational arbiters of Cambodian civil society or as sponsors and benefactors of Cambodian-led organisations. It is therefore unsurprising that both international and local NGOs – and that distinction must be understood as both porous and often mutually constitutive – have played an integral role in arbitrating the efficacy and direction of Cambodia's transitional justice efforts (see also Dosch 2012).

The place of memory within NGO work varies. A broad range of NGO organisations have supported and partnered the ECCC Public Affairs Office, leading ECCC outreach and public education work, screening verdicts and soliciting complaints and applications for recognition as Civil Parties at the ECCC (see Sperfeldt 2012). The role of NGOs here increased following criticism of the ECCC's failure to provide comprehensive public education on its work. In 2009, a nationwide Berkley Human Rights Centre study, 'So We Will Never Forget', found that 85 per cent of Cambodians had little or no knowledge of the ECCC, recommending improved 'outreach' to maximise the domestic acceptance of the court (Pham *et al.* 2009: 5). During key phases of its work, the ECCC came to rely on outsourcing civil society 'partner' groups to supply its outreach, given limits for the budget for the Public Affairs Office (Ciorciari and Heindel 2014: 240). As I will discuss in the next chapter, these initiatives often seek recourse to pre-existing memorial spaces and sites of memory such as the Tuol Sleng Museum of Genocide Crimes and Cheong Ek Killing Field as contexts within which the *truth* of the atrocities of the Democratic Kampuchea regime are evidenced, furnishing a specific history of Democratic Kampuchea; and the *need* for the ECCC as the appropriate ameliorative agent is obviated and naturalised. In these contexts, memory plays a role in the justification of the ECCC as a specific form of political intervention in the present, implicitly, in the name of renewing a national history.

NGOs can and often do invoke memory explicitly as an object of transformation and as the locus of efforts of redress in its own right. Memory is present in appeals for the promotion of intergenerational remembrance and the attendant dignification of survivor memory, for example. Moreover, several Cambodian NGOs draw explicitly on psycho-therapeutic frameworks to lead efforts to educate Cambodian communities about trauma and attendant techniques for knowing and coping with post-traumatic stress disorder (PTSD) therein. In particular, previous work by the Center for Social Development (CSD) and the Center for Cambodian Civic Education (CIVICUS) and ongoing work by the Transcultural Psychosocial Organisation (TPO) have led nationwide efforts to promote strategies for recognising symptoms of PTSD and encouraging the integration of trauma frameworks and guides within Cambodian higher education institutions, as well as offering instructions on coping strategies for mental health and distress. In particular, these NGOs encourage testimonial techniques to disclose experiences of the Khmer Rouge years and have – variedly – encouraged participation and investment within the ECCC process as a wider cathartic referent.

We might return here to Foucault briefly. As memory is situated as an object of intervention – a civic, technical and medical problem that can be transformed or corrected in the name of managing the vitality or life of the population – techniques of memory are deployed that carry important socio-political consequences. The critique I aim to develop here, then, especially in regard to the two cases I focus on – efforts to engender civic renewal and reconciliation through genocide education, firstly; and then therapeutic and trauma-based strategies for coping with memories of suffering – is not rooted in a straightforward objection to the goals that they are intended to provide. The premise of my argument is exactly that these strategies appear self-evidently necessary, unproblematic and incontestable. Cambodia's education system is desperately underfunded, and the Khmer Rouge, as a topic, has been broadly absent from the curriculum until recent years. Given the perceived lack of transparency within the public education system and expectations from donors to *see* value for money, an audited and nationally standardised program for genocide education is entirely understandable and desirable. Given the absence of affordable, publicly provided psychiatric support and the widespread problems of mental health in Cambodia, initiatives to ameliorate and reintegrate traumatic memory are requisite and urgent. The embarkation point of my argument here, though, is that each of these fields of intervention are themselves contingent means of knowing and acting on populations afflicted by massive political violence. They have specific socio-political implications and consequences – depoliticising memories of the Khmer Rouge with, contrarily, acutely political consequences – that foreclose some ways of remembering the Khmer Rouge just as they open up others. Moreover, as I hope to show through the following discussion, they embody both institutional and epistemic assumptions that can allow us to further reflect on the basic conceptual 'grammar' of transitional justice as a field of knowledge and practice.

The Documentation Center of Cambodia

DC-Cam was established in Phnom Penh in 1995 as part of Yale University's Cambodian Genocide Program (CGP). The Yale CGP was launched following the award of a grant from the United States (US) Department of State, enabled by the passing of the 1994 Cambodian Genocide Justice Act, in order to document and preserve evidence of the atrocities of the Democratic Kampuchea regime in anticipation of future prosecutions of Khmer Rouge leaders. DC-Cam became an independent NGO entity in 1997, enjoying funding from a broad range of international benefactors to continue its work, and it is currently establishing the Sleuk Rith Institute, a permanent documentation and research site. The Sleuk Rith Institute will also host a new memorial museum devoted to the Democratic Kampuchea period.

The early work DC-Cam undertook was principally focused on documenting the primary evidence of Khmer Rouge atrocities: mapping mass grave and prison sites across the country; and the preservation, organising and archiving of the extensive records created by the Democratic Kampuchea state. The records of interrogations, 'confessions' and portrait photographs of those interred and murdered at the S-21 Tuol Sleng site in Phnom Penh were particularly significant within this process. These objects continue to carry huge significance as artefacts of memory. The S-21 documentation and other records of the *Santebal*, the Khmer Rouge security police, have been pivotal throughout the ECCC prosecutions in evidencing a nationwide and hierarchically coordinated network of murder operating under a chain of leadership. Moreover, the portrait photographs of those detained at S-21 have been appropriated, circulated and displayed across a range of global (and local) contexts, propelled by the currency and power of internationalised discourses of humanitarian intervention and witnessing and acting as an 'ex-locus memorial' of the Khmer Rouge atrocities (R. Hughes 2003: 24). The archived materials were catalogued and assembled for access in an online database, as well as substantively constituting a material record that remains under the custody of DC-Cam itself. In 2010, DC-Cam had catalogued some 150,000 documents, with a further 400,000 pages still yet to process (Caswell 2010: 29). These documents and images – and the principal site at S-21 that they are associated with – are thought to be central to the constitution of a 'collective' memory; indeed, Caswell has claimed that DC-Cam itself is synonymous with the public memory of the Democratic Kampuchea years (2010: 38).

The principal rationale for the formation of DC-Cam was the collation of evidence that would precipitate and buttress prosecutions of Khmer Rouge leaders. In other words, DC-Cam's mandate was the construction of inculpatory evidence. The role and mandate of DC-Cam would therefore inevitably be scrutinised within the ECCC process according to the purportedly (apolitical) neutrality demanded by the courtroom. It is unsurprising that defence teams at the ECCC have sought to trouble the admissibility and validity of evidence and documentation drawn from the DC-Cam archives.[2] In the first instance, over 15 years lapsed between the fall of the Khmer Rouge and the start of the cataloguing process. But perhaps more significantly, the role of DC-Cam as custodian of an independent evidential archive as well as an advocacy group for genocide justice appears to present a tension in the registers of how and why memories and artefacts of political violence are coded, known and understood for what they are. This goes to the heart of the 'grammar' of transitional justice and human-rights advocacy, which treats the relationship between *knowing* atrocity and *doing* something about it as self-evidently connected and sequenced (Moon 2012). Moreover, it invites further questions about the agents who are authorised to steward, curate and then direct memories (and artefacts of memory).

The story of DC-Cam as an arbiter of memory in Cambodia cannot be explained without attention to the role and thinking of Youk Chhang, a survivor of Democratic Kampuchea who lost several relatives under the regime. Chhang was a leading figure in the early work of DC-Cam, becoming Executive Director in 1997, and he has since played a pivotal role in expanding the scope and range of DC-Cam's activities beyond documentation and archival work. From 2000, Chhang led the initiation of a quarterly DC-Cam publication, *Searching for the Truth*, which included a range of features, such as testimony of survivors, family tracing and testimonial accounts of different aspects of life under the Khmer Rouge, as well as legal discussion and debate on potential prosecutions (and obstacles to them). Since 2004 and the agreement to establish the ECCC, Chhang has also overseen more expansive outreach and public education efforts about the Khmer Rouge period and prosecutions, including the "Living Documents" project (bringing representatives from Cambodia's provinces to the court), organising provincial film screenings that are intended to educate the communities about the atrocities of the regime and eliciting public testimony from survivors (Ly 2008: 24–27). The sheer range and scope of DC-Cam and Youk Chhang's work over the past two decades has been remarkable in its own right.

Youk Chhang is also discernibly able to *speak* transitional justice. Chhang powerfully describes and explains his vision of Cambodia through the language of healing, reconciliation and accountability. He is, in this sense, a 'moral entrepreneur' in the way he has been able to amplify and attract international attention to a social problem through the currency of specific human-rights tropes (Cohen 2011),[3] that is, remembering and prosecuting genocide. In 2007, Chhang was named one of *Time* magazine's top 100 heroes and pioneers in recognition of those "whose power, talent or moral example is transforming the world." In an accompanying interview, Chhang remarked that "Cambodia is like broken glass… Without justice, we cannot put the pieces together."[4] The metaphor of fragility, breakage and reconstruction is powerfully evocative of the prevailing assumptions of the role of memory within transitional justice. Writing in the *Phnom Penh Post* in 2010, Chhang downplayed his past desires for revenge against the Khmer Rouge; instead, he emphasises the need for answers and *truth*, under the headline claim that "a society cannot know itself if it does not have an accurate memory of its own history."[5] Here we see the distinction between the 'local' and 'international' that holds traction in human-rights thinking come unstuck. Invoking the conceptual frameworks and key terminology at play within transitional justice advocacy and scholarship authorises Chhang's role as an arbiter of Cambodia's management of its histories of past political violence. Conversely, as a Cambodian survivor, his claim for justice and memory also serves to naturalise and obviate the need for specific templates of intervention – truth and accountability – that are bound to internationalised discourses of human rights and transitional justice. The 'local' and 'international' are mutually constituted precisely at these moments.

The longstanding place of DC-Cam as an organisation within Cambodia's civil society and political landscape is illuminating. Youk Chhang and DC-Cam have seemingly navigated a pathway that directly attends to the most sensitive political history in Cambodia's past, while carving out a relatively productive relationship with the Cambodian government (who must approve NGO initiatives at local, provincial and especially national level), as well as with those international benefactors that gravitate toward and fertilise the language of 'truth', 'healing' and 'justice' (and tend to be hostile toward the Cambodian government). Such a balancing act is no small feat. During a personal interview in 2009, I had asked Chhang about DC-Cam's approach and understanding of reconciliation processes, a sensitive area given the Cambodian government's opposition to broader based prosecutions of Khmer Rouge leaders.

> In the last thirty years Cambodia has not had a final judgement. We believe in the tribunal, it will help provide a foundation. The tribunal will not bring a closure, but it is a foundation... as a nation, as individuals. But the second process is restoring belief in education… This is why we are launching the genocide education program, which is nationwide. Almost 1 million children we are working with… It took us several years to reach this process, recently approved by the government. We believe that the best way of healing is at home… When a child asks a question of their parent there are varied responses. One is providing a long history and storytelling. These tend to be the most effective healing. The third process that we strongly believe in is the long term study and research for the living. People hardly visit museums or memorial sites. That's why we want to build a permanent institution alongside the smaller processes, like forums, exhibitions. In the past a lot has been done. We have to remember the efforts of the past – the effort by the victims and the government. A lot has been done in the past… It is another process of healing.[6]

Chhang's comments are important for several reasons. Suggesting that the tribunal is a foundation for processes of reconciliation is a frequent iteration across those invested in the ECCC process, from the government and the United Nations to NGO groups, albeit in varied forms; indeed, the fact that the aims of transitional justice – reconciliation, accountability, truth – have proved so difficult to define is partly a consequence of the variety of epistemic frameworks through which they are furnished. Acknowledging the role of past government efforts in promoting either reconciliation or healing is a far less common claim among Cambodian NGO leaders, who have tended to adopt hostile and sceptical positions regarding state-led commemorative practices. Perhaps most importantly, Chhang's conceptualisation of reconciliation through genocide education as a formally driven process within schools, in tandem with the state, shows how transitional justice and memory projects can be appended to and between the work of the ECCC and the state as a symbiotic exercise. This further shows how the outcomes of transitional justice efforts can be renegotiated and authored on new terms (see the International Center for Transitional Justice [ICTJ] guidance report, Ramírez-Barat 2012: 19).

Genocide education

The work of DC-Cam in actively promoting the education of younger Cambodians about the Khmer Rouge years, attempting to further enhance youth engagement with the ECCC and 'dignifying' the experiences of Democratic Kampuchea survivors on this basis, has been twinned with further projects including the erection of 'anti-genocide' memorials, often in former Khmer Rouge strongholds like Anlong Veng or Phnom Malai on Cambodia's northern and western borders, respectively. The assumptions at work here are important. For DC-Cam, the aim of promoting inter-generational remembering pivots on the expectation that remembrance enables specific socio-political outcomes: public genocide education is reconciliatory to the extent that it is 'anti-genocidal', is believed to prevent the recurrence of violence and helps young Cambodians understand the experiences of their elders.[7] The DC-Cam strategy is striking because the structure of its deterrent claim raises important questions about who should be reconciled and to what – and how – especially given that school-age Cambodians were not party to the Cambodian conflict. Reconciliation, envisaged here, appears as a broad concept that is defined around and enabled by the stabilisation of a 'national memory' and national history, principally supported through the delivery of civic education.

One crucial technique within the DC-Cam genocide education programs is the dissemination of a new school textbook to support teaching within Cambodian public schools about the Khmer Rouge years. The book, *A History of Democratic Kampuchea 1975–1979* (2007), was written by Khamboly Dy, a senior researcher at DC-Cam and coordinator of the DC-Cam Genocide Education Project, who drew on a range of existing historical writings and expertise to assemble the text. The book is broad in its 42-page treatment of Democratic Kamphucea. It develops an account of who the Khmer Rouge were; their rise to power; the Democratic Kampuchea state apparatus; experiences and testimony of life under the regime, including reflections on violations of children's rights and gender-based violence; and the *Santebal* security system. One chapter is devoted to the role of S-21, before a final set of chapters offer an evaluation of the fall of the regime. The book is largely descriptive and minimalist in tone, as might be expected of any high-school history textbook, but it does not shy away from highly sensitive and contentious areas within Cambodia's political history: a figure of 300,000 deaths are attributed to the US bombing campaigns of the 1970s as a key causal factor in the Khmer Rouge rise to power, and Chinese and Thai patronage of the Khmer Rouge during and after the regime are noted. At the same time, the text broadly does not diverge from the Cambodian government's preferred account of blame for the atrocities of Democratic Kampuchea – mirrored at the ECCC prosecutions today – eliding the role of lower-level perpetrators in killing while emphasising the hierarchical structures of the regime and therefore the responsibility of the Khmer Rouge leadership.

A History of Democratic Kampuchea 1975–1979 is a careful and detailed treatment of the Khmer Rouge years. But the way that responsibility is depicted narrowly to the leadership of Democratic Kampuchea, with a more austere tone vis-à-vis historical responsibility adopted, can be read to reflect the political sensitivity of the task at hand. After all, public education is a central avenue for the construction and consolidation of national identities, memories and myths[8] but also a specific technique within peace building and transitional justice (Bekerman and Zembylas 2011; Cole 2007). As Youk Chhang remarked, the publication and adoption of the text required approval from the Cambodian state; there is a note in bibliographic detail that permission was granted from the government that "the text can be used as supplementary discussion material [for teachers] and as a base to write a history lesson for high school students" (Dy 2007: n. p.). At the same time, it is noted that the text was also supported by the Soros Foundation's Open Society Institute and the National Endowment for Democracy. The attraction of the project is visible in Chhang's foreword, which again powerfully situates Cambodia as a site in need of mnemonic intervention and management:

> Writing about this bleak period of history for a new generation may run the risk of re-opening old wounds for the survivors of Democratic Kampuchea. Many Cambodians have tried to put their memories of the regime behind them and move on. But we cannot progress – much less reconcile with ourselves and others – until we have confronted the past and understand both what happened and why it happened. Only with this understanding can we truly begin to heal.
>
> (2007: n.p.)

The co-presence, on the one hand, of the (conditional) approval of the Cambodian state, alongside, on the other, the material and ideological support of international benefactors in shaping a specific technique of memory – that is, learning and teaching from a history textbook deployed to effect memory work within the public education system – is important to note. Specific interests have been brought to bear in the production and shaping of this text. Yet it also reflective of a wider dispersal, fragmentation and devolvement of memory work to non-state agents and further appropriation of a freighted normative language for seeing and acting on the world that is embodied and sustained by the wider vocabulary of transitional justice scholarship and practice. Chhang's foreword is appealing because it renders visible a set of clear sequences about how and why we must remember atrocity, presenting a linear process of knowing, integrating and then ameliorating the present.

Alongside the production and publication of *A History of Democratic Kampuchea 1975–1979*, DC-Cam has worked with the Cambodian Ministry of Education to produce a teaching guidebook to support the delivery of genocide education across Cambodia. The text, *Teacher's Guidebook: The Teaching of "A History of Democratic Kampuchea (1975–1979)"* (Dearing and Chea 2009) includes specific directions around the 'goals', 'aims', 'materials' and lesson procedures for individual classes, as well as a list of 21 overall course objectives, including outcomes such as students' developing empathy and valuing the knowledge of survivors, as well as considering "the counterproductive effects of revenge upon Cambodian society and understand the need for reconciliation." (2009: 6). In the preface to the guidebook, it is noted that 300,000 copies of Khamboly Dy's original text had been distributed, with the aim to distribute a further 700,000 to ensure that every student from grades 9–12 would be equipped with a copy (2009: i). For so long, the topic of the Khmer Rouge had been absent from the Cambodian school curricula; today, plans are in place to allow the standardisation and management of content and delivery on an unprecedented scale.

As part of the Genocide Education Project, DC-Cam has also initiated frameworks for the monitoring and evaluation of the delivery of genocide education to ensure 'Quality Control'.[9] A field observation report in Kompong Thom in 2011, conducted jointly by DC-Cam and the Ministry for Education, mapped out quality-control project objectives, a series of evaluation measures, before reflecting on the progress and efficacy of student-led learning in the delivery of genocide education through some examples from the classroom initiatives prescribed in the *Teacher's Guidebook* (comparing the examples of Hitler and Mussolini as distinct from Pol Pot, who killed his own people as opposed to other races). The language and expectations presented here are striking. Quality control, enhancement and assurance are benchmarking, calculative practices that embody a specific form of 'audit culture' and pedagogy within education, deriving legitimacy from its transparency and accountability, which, in starkly different contexts, has attracted criticism because it seems to engender excessive managerialism and individualism, objectifying both students and teachers and risking the suppression of creativity and autonomy (see Shore 2008 on United Kingdom [UK] higher education).

The grievances of UK academics about the vagaries of audit culture in higher education are, obviously, removed from the vexed and important questions of genocide education and memory in Cambodia. We might, however, pause for thought here to reflect on some of the challenges and issues the DC-Cam team noted in their 2011 report from the Kampong Thom teaching staff that might sound familiar to others working education – which ranged from problems of basic pay, a heavy workload and schedule, the distractions students succumb to, and the efficacy of student-led learning – to ask questions in light of standardisation and audit in regard to genocide education and memory.[10] Some teachers in Kampong Thom who had lived through and survived the regime felt that the 2007 textbooks did not adequately convey the brutality of the regime, making specific remarks about executions that took place; some teachers disagreed about how to best introduce the Khmer Rouge years into the school year, either by designating its own special period in the curricula, by integrating it sequentially into a continuing account of modern Cambodian history or by devoting a whole disciplinary category to the topic; while younger teachers, unable to speak from experiences of the regime, tended to be resistant to teaching the topic at all. What light might these few remarks shed on the potential implications of standardising genocide education in Cambodia more broadly?

First and foremost, the delivery of a standardised account of Democratic Kampuchea, intended to promote memory, reconciliation and the 'dignification' of survivors, raises the immediate challenge of flattening or simplifying inevitably complex and often conflicted experiences of the Khmer Rouge years. While the hope among DC-Cam staff is that the text acts as a cue from which conversations might begin at home – a further devolvement of memory work – how certain can we be that those conversations would be happy or harmonious? What frictions might they generate? As above, the memories of different teachers who had survived the Khmer Rouge years did not necessarily map neatly onto either the content of the historical narrative propagated in the textbook or the extent to which it could capture the gravity of their experiences. These questions are fraught because, conversely, a risk emerges that those who do not remember the years of Democratic Kampuchea on the terms propagated by the textbook are excluded on veridictional registers as either 'wrong', 'in denial' or as 'deniers' themselves. The space for different memories and readings of serious political violence to coincide is fairly narrow in this context. Attending here, the reproduction of more vernacular memory claims is potentially rendered less authoritative against the place of an officially certified record. This is a problem that invariably follows from any attempt – in Cambodia and beyond – to stabilise a particular reading of past suffering, because the past will always be contested and open to multiple interpretations and memory claims. This gestures towards a more urgent problem. Memories of the Khmer Rouge years – and violence before and after – are inherently political even as they are personal. It is unsurprising that the teachers disagreed on the place, framing or sequencing of Democratic Kampuchea within the history curriculum precisely because many Cambodians do not agree on the place, framing, and sequencing of the Democratic Kampuchea period within Cambodian history.

The trauma paradigm

This chapter has so far sought to show how the landscape of transitional justice efforts and interventions in Cambodia extends beyond – but can complement – the remit and work of the ECCC. I have also sought to show how analyses of the Cambodian case that situate or conceptualise transitional justice in Cambodia, centred at the ECCC in opposition to, against or to transform the Cambodian state and its interests, tend to underestimate the complexity and diversity of practices at work in the name of transitional justice and memory now, as important still as the role of the Royal Government of Cambodia (RGC) remains. Moreover, I have tried to show how NGO organisations, in particular, rely on specific epistemic assumptions and expertise about the problems facing societies that have experienced massive political violence and what must be done thereupon. In the case of DC-Cam, this was framed around a set of civic claims about the value of history and memory and the way these could be harnessed through learning and intergenerational memory to enable truth, reconciliation and deterrence in the present. I want to now turn to examples of NGO activity rooted in a different, yet equally powerful set of claims for understanding and explicitly acting upon memories, namely, the trauma paradigm.

Trauma and mental health are now dominant frameworks through which states and other actors think about and act on societies that have experienced political violence (see Moon 2009). In Chapter 2, I argued that the linear sequence of memory disclosure, confrontation and abreaction – trauma recovery and healing – is embedded as part of the conceptual 'grammar' of transitional justice itself. The effects of the trauma paradigm are felt in several important ways. Post-atrocity societies – Cambodia included – are represented and implicitly known through a set of pathologising tropes of traumatic memory: they suffer amnesia, denial and dysfunction as a result of their inability (or prevention) from properly engaging the past (see e.g. Chandler 2008 on 'induced amnesia'), implying and obviating the need for external supervision, intervention and management (Hughes and Pupavac 2005). This follows from the increasing influence of international psychological and therapeutic assumptions about the nature and role of memory that now govern transitional justice strategies: that memory is *the* site of renewal and malady if 'untreated' (Moon 2009: 76). Trauma, here, as a condition afflicting national memories, implicates the biopolitical life of populations, whom the state and other legitimated bodies are obliged to govern in the name of ameliorating the very vitality and health of the living. Foucault's latter work on 'biopower' (1998) – as distinct from the self-interested and coercive violence of 'sovereign' power – illuminates the way that fields of scientific truth, especially the 'psy' sciences, enable and imply programs that are devised for the health and vitality of whole social groups and populations. These are often self-effected through specific techniques of health and self-betterment that individuals encounter that invite themselves into new relationships with memory. In Cambodia, NGO groups have drawn on expertise (and experts) in psychiatric health, PTSD, psychotherapy and counselling to research and operationalise a range of programs that explicitly seek to encourage Cambodians to locate, disclose and integrate traumatic memory. I turn now to discuss some examples of these interventions.

The Transcultural Psychosocial Organisation (TPO) has initiated a broad range of community mental health programs in Cambodia, especially in regard to the way mental health is gendered and implicated in violence against women and children, trafficking and the need to provide adequate mental health support accordingly around issues of domestic abuse (see TPO's 2013 annual report for a summary of these activities).[11] The wider range of services and support for mental health TPO offers in Cambodia is unprecedented, given the broad absence of publicly funded mental health capacity, and the organisation specifically seeks to embed expertise within existing and new networks of Cambodian staff able to work on and deliver mental health support. TPO has also been involved in the ECCC process, offering immediate support to Civil Parties as they testify. More broadly, as with other civil society groups, TPO partners ECCC outreach to raise awareness about trauma. In particular, TPO has actively promoted testimonial techniques in order to document and recover memories of Democratic Kampuchea, whilst positioning participation in and observation of the ECCC as one means of empowering victims in overcoming trauma (TPO 2013: 7). Memory, here, is explicitly situated as an object of medical treatment and transformation.

One hallmark of therapeutic thinking within transitional justice, Moon suggests, is that "*trauma has come to be understood not only as a consequence of war but a possible factor in its perpetuation*" (2009: 75, author's italics). Such assumptions bleed into the way that TPO depicts Cambodia, under its "Truth, Reconciliation and Healing – Toward a Shared Future" program, as threatened *and yet* defined by "Latent conflict":

> The history of Cambodia is marked by decades of civil war, and subsequent post-war recovery. Even today, this violent past continues to affect every sphere of people's lives and remains a subject of latent conflict – dehumanization, deep distrust, stereotypes and diverging collective memories persist. Many victim-survivors and former KR, many of which live side by side in the same communities – still hold grievances such as feelings of having been dehumanized by the KR regime, of sadness and loss (personal, physical and economic) and the lack of recognition of their identities as victims. A lack of communication continues to foster anger, hatred and misunderstanding. As a result, human rights abuses still occur, social capital lacks, trauma persists and economic progress is very limited.[12]

An aetiological connection is made here between 'diverging' memories of violence (implying the corollary that their convergence is benign), the absence of formal recognition of victimhood, the persistence of trauma and both personal and wider social problems of today. This passage medicalises memory with both depoliticising and re-politicising effects, because trauma is broadly situated within the wider history of Cambodia's experience of war and violence (obscuring any periodisation of atrocities within the envelope of the Khmer Rouge years), and both economic and human-rights problems of today are located as consequences of collective trauma, displacing attendant questions of responsibility that arise thereupon. I will return to the potential for the trauma paradigm to dislodge questions of agency and responsibility shortly.

TPO strongly promotes testimonial therapy, truth telling and dialogue as techniques through which 'grassroots' reconciliation might be enabled, claiming that restorative justice techniques can be deployed to complement the ongoing prosecutions at the ECCC. In partnership with Youth for Peace, a program of dialogue between former Khmer Rouge and 'victim-survivors', involving visits to sites of atrocity, truth-telling sessions and 'Truth Telling Ceremonies', is intended to enable education and 'repair relationships'.[13] Moreover, truth and testimonial therapy are advocated as techniques to be deployed within designated public forum contexts:

> Testimonial Therapy is an internationally recognized, pragmatic trauma treatment method that was specifically developed for the treatment of

> post-traumatic stress resulting from organized violence. It was first described by Lira and Weinstein in Chile and has since been tested in different socio-cultural settings. TPO has been adapting this testimonial method by integrating traditional and religious practices in cooperation with local pagodas and Buddhist monks, reflecting the significance of traditional coping mechanisms in Cambodia's spirit-based culture. In testimonial therapy as applied by TPO, Civil Parties, all trauma survivors of the Khmer Rouge, are invited to talk about their traumatic experiences. With a counselor they restore their painful memories and convert them into a written testimony, which, in turn, is read aloud and delivered to the survivors by monks from a local pagoda in a Buddhist ceremony (or equivalent person in the local mosque, church, or temple depending on the client's religious orientation) in presence of other survivors, relatives, community members, local authorities, government officials, NGO representatives, youth and others. This promotes the acknowledgement of suffering, the de-stigmatization of survivors and restores their dignity. It also allows the survivors to ease the suffering of the spirits of ancestors and pay respect to deceased relatives.[14]

TPO's epistemic claims here are important. TPO invokes 'internationally' recognised techniques for the disclosure of traumatic memory as means of treating PTSD, enabling 'acknowledgement', 'de-stigmatization' and catharsis therein. How should we treat these claims? In the first instance, testimony is not a necessarily cathartic experience. Brounéus has shown how women testifying in the Gaccaca Courts in Rwanda have found the experience 'retraumatizing' (2008), while Ross has shown how victim testimonies at the South African Truth and Reconciliation Commission circulated and proliferated beyond the control of their authors, contrary to their apparent empowerment and acknowledgement (2003). In the second instance, we must ask if participants within such programs do so on the terms that are formally expected. As colleagues at other groups would remark of other outreach contexts, NGOs often have to nurture and cultivate interest within public education initiatives, and part of the appeal for Cambodian constituents is the conferment of status and reputation through formal participation as much as therapeutic benefit. This is not to suggest that the work of TPO has encountered or generated either problem but to simply point out that testimonial and truth-telling techniques *can* have iatrogenic and harmful effects or can be attractive to constituents on terms contrary to the benefits they are meant to deliver.

The questions we are obliged to ask of the trauma paradigm and its claim over memory go further. Summerfield has argued that PTSD, as a diagnostic category, is bound to a specific socio-political history that relies on the assumption that there is 'one' automated and necessary medical effect of experiencing or witnessing violence and conflict – mass traumatisation – and that it therefore legitimates the universal applicability and expertise of Western psychiatric frameworks as authoritative, requisite and urgent responses to atrocities (Summerfield 1999). For Summerfield, the problem with the universal currency of the trauma paradigm – universality is precisely its appeal for international donors – is that it can displace and subordinate potentially appropriate pre-existing and embedded responses to suffering and violence, while flattening the agency of victims suffering PTSD as passive in their relationships to memories of atrocities. Yet the TPO approach seems to reflect efforts to 'localise' or 'vernacularise' its work, attempting to integrate 'traditional' *Cambodian* coping mechanisms and delivering forums within spaces of that can be mediated by purportedly more legitimate cultural agents, such as religious leaders within pagodas. The TPO efforts to embed testimonial therapies and interventions within pre-existing cultural frameworks and institutions is reflective of wider trends to 'localise' transitional justice, as if international and local ideas and agents are neatly separable rather than mutually constituting. On the one hand, Summerfield's critique implies that therapeutic interventions are *done* to post-conflict spaces, seeming to neglect the extent to which it is Cambodian agents that have studied, appropriated and mobilised techniques derived from the trauma paradigm. On the other, this should not discount the contingent presence of testimonial and therapeutic techniques at play within the Cambodian context and the need to interrogate the specific socio-political consequences that follow from them therein.

TPO is not alone in initiating trauma-based outreach and awareness raising programs. In 2008, I worked at the CSD during their public forum series on issues of "Justice and Reconciliation." CSD has subsequently undergone significant organisational change, and many of the staff, resources and projects have migrated to other organisations. Several key CSD staff moved to the Center for Cambodian Civic Education (CIVICUS), which continued to work on trauma awareness for some time. Like TPO, CSD and CIVICUS have organised public forums that have drawn heavily on a therapeutic conception of memory rooted in the trauma paradigm, deployed in the name of fostering reconciliation. Again, this is an example of the way that 'headline' concepts at work in transitional justice, namely here 'reconciliation', are made meaningful through the conceptual and expert knowledge that their proponents draw on. For TPO, CSD and CIVICUS, reconciliation in Cambodia pivots on a therapeutic transformation: that reconciliation begins with individual 'healing', understanding personal and community trauma (a reconciliation of 'self' to 'self' and 'self' to others) and, by virtue of this, the generation of broader catharsis for Cambodia's social 'wounds'.

Understanding trauma in Cambodia

It is worth briefly considering two documentary examples of the way that CSD provided information about mental health and trauma, because it is not neutral in its communication or effects. As noted, the trauma paradigm risks pathologising post-conflict communities, whilst the 'medicalisation' of memory can have implications for the construction of categories of victims. The two examples are central features of the *Understanding Trauma in Cambodia Handbook*, which was funded by the then German Development Service (DED), co-written in both English and Khmer and distributed across Cambodia at provincial public forums (CSD 2008). One item within the handbook is an image of the 'Trauma Tree' (2008: 54).

It provides a pictorial 'map' of the way that trauma is 'rooted' (invisible and hidden) in a specific set of events or experiences. The patterning of (observable) behaviours through the 'branches' illustrates the "physical," "emotional," "rational" and "behavioural" symptoms and effects of being traumatised. People encountering the image are invited to 'decode' their own ongoing 'symptoms', for example, "muscle tension," "hopelessness" or "emotional outbursts"; these are presented as potential consequences of traumatic events, though crucially, they can equally be read as their inevitable effects. As Summerfield has argued, the sequencing of such communication – the necessary translation of experiences of suffering into traumatic states – serves to situate trauma as biologically automated, objectively locatable (across cultural contexts) and amenable to 'technical' intervention (1999: 1452). The pictorial presentation of trauma as a tree, and its association with nature and naturally ordered systems, reflects the way that trauma has become naturalised as a concept that risks confusing a diagnostic category with a psycho-pathology (Summerfield 2001).

A second item in the *Understanding Trauma Handbook* is a diagnostic self-checklist, addressed to those that lived through the "dangerous Khmer Rouge years," asking the question (CSD 2008: 78): "Does this sound like you?" It invites readers to tick boxes next to sequence of "problems you still have":

> sometimes I feel like it's happening all over again; sometimes I have nightmares about the past; I stay away from places that remind me of the event; I am easily surprised and feel very upset when something happens without warning; I have a hard time trusting or feeling close to other people; I get mad very easily; I feel guilty because others died and I lived; I have trouble sleeping and my muscles are tense.

The checklist concludes that if you ticked "all or most of these boxes," "you may have Post Traumatic Stress Disorder." Part of the problem here is, as Summerfield notes, the popular conflation of distress with "trauma" as such (2001: 96). The checklist includes items that do not, themselves, mutually imply a relationship with past experiences of atrocities and conflict, yet their presentation is a powerful invitation to self-identify in accordance with the PTSD classificatory schema for understanding such memories.

Both the 'Trauma Tree' and the diagnostic checklist are important examples of techniques that act as means of self-identification as traumatised. They are, in this sense, examples of techniques of memory that are 'self-subjectifying' (Foucault and Rabinow 1997; Foucault 1998). Individuals encounter and 'know' themselves as traumatised through specific templates and categories of self-understanding. In post-conflict settings, this can have important consequences. As Moon suggests, the trauma paradigm has an influential role to play in transitional justice because it is powerfully exculpatory – dislodging 'retributive' moral orders – and opens up space for subjects' self-understanding as victims of conflict and atrocity (2009: 80–81). Summerfield points out how PTSD is bound to a socio-political recognition of victimhood; victimhood and its attendant politics and entitlements may hold more weight than, for example, simply self-identifying as a survivor or perhaps even as an unwilling perpetrator (2001). PTSD furnishes a space for perpetrators of mass atrocity to, themselves, also identify as victims. In this sense, we can begin to see how these examples of medicalised, therapeutic claims over memory and reconciliation – of 'self' to 'self' or 'self' to 'past' – are compatible with the ongoing ECCC prosecutions that have more broadly represented the national community as a wounded victim that suffered at the hands of a handful of malign Khmer Rouge leaders.

Several socio-political issues are pertinent and urgent following the above. Firstly, the work of TPO, CSD and CIVICUS is directed broadly across former Khmer Rouge and non-Khmer Rouge communities; all are prospective victims of trauma. The diagnostic self-checklist works by inviting subjects to locate their 'symptoms' of PTSD in the broad period of 'events during the Khmer Rouge years', a timeframe that obfuscates the specific origin of trauma or traumatic events (as arising from 1975–1979 specifically or the decades-long war more generally); the work of TPO is also addressed loosely to trauma arising from the Khmer Rouge years encompassing wider experiences of war and conflict. Crucially, questions of blame and responsibility – especially for lower-level Khmer Rouge – are glaringly absent from the TPO and CSD initiatives (in line with Moon's suggestion that a therapeutic ethos undermines retributive moral orders). On this basis, we see crucial and telling convergences and divergences between the work of the ECCC and NGOs in these instances. These therapeutic interventions are engaged in memory work that specifically exculpates lower-level Khmer Rouge in a way that complements the ECCC because they are omitted from its mandate; they also embrace and enfold a much wider history of political violence than the ECCC can attend to.

Conclusion

Transitional justice needs to pay greater attention to the work that goes on beyond 'headline' mechanisms. This is not the same as – or to advocate for – more holistic and broadly based 'models'. Rather, analytically, we can see that appeals for justice and reconciliation are authored in different ways, nourished by different expertise and invite different relationships between constituents and memory. We must recognise, then, that justice and reconciliation can mean multiple things, even within the same contexts and milieus. Justice and reconciliation, in these respects, can operate as free-floating signifiers for medical and socio-political work that seeks to advance and better social orders in the wake of political violence.

My argument here is premised on the point that such claims are not neutral in their work. Cambodia desperately needs financial and political investment in education and mental health. Yet, simultaneously, we must recognise that discourses of genocide education and trauma carry political consequences and implications. Exactly as these fields of knowledge are presented as technical, rather than political or ethical, enterprises, they promise to depoliticise fields of sensitive memory with, contrarily, acutely political effects. Genocide education, delivered to effect remembrance, reconciliation and deterrence, embodies the difficulties of standardising any account of atrocities, especially against the background of a strong and persistent state-sponsored narrative of blame and responsibility. Trauma awareness, as a lens and technique for knowing memories of violence, equally complements the ECCC, partly because it obliges *engagements* with memory, but equally because it services the wider articulation of *all* Cambodians as victims, the envelope of the victim-perpetrator and the exculpation of lower-level Khmer Rouge.

Notes

1 It is beyond the scope of my argument here to disinter or scrutinise the voluminous literature on NGOs and civil society more broadly. For a comprehensive review of literature on NGOs and civil society, see Mercer (2002).It is worth noting, however, that my approach here departs from conceptions of civil society as a neat 'counterweight' to the state, or as a neutral space that is only constitutive of open political terrain, that is, promoting 'democratisation' and the 'rule of law'. Rather, my interest here is specifically directed to the epistemological resources nourishing the work of NGOs that lay claim over memory. These carry political consequences.

2 See Case No. 002/19-09-2007-ECCC/TC 16/01/2012 Transcript, 16 January 2012, Trial Day 15.

3 Stan Cohen's work on 'moral panics' – periods of enhanced and sensationalised media coverage and public scrutiny of particular social problems and groups – has tended to be read to situate moral entrepreneurs, who lead the 'amplification' of attention to social problems, as a pejorative categorisation. As Cohen has argued (2011), though, we must be attentive to the normative ambivalence of this tag and open to the way 'moral entrepreneurs' work to draw attention to social problems that have been 'denied' and therefore deserve and warrant indignation, as well as those 'classic' moral panics that are fed by sensationalism.

4 Youk Chang's TIME 100 profile is available at http://content.time.com/time/specials/2007/time100/article/0,28804,1595326_1615754_1615879,00.html. Last accessed 21 September 2016.

5 See Youk Chang's commentary in the Phnom Penh Post, September 29th 2010. Available at http://www.phnompenhpost.com/lift/society-cannot-know-itself-if-it-does-not-have-accurate-memory-its-own-history. Last accessed 21 September 2016.

6 Personal interview, 22 May 2009.

7 See, for example, the report from the erection of a genocide memorial in Phnom Malai in May 2013. Available at http://www.d.dccam.org/Projects/Genocide/pdf/Genocide_Education_in_Cambodia_May_10_2013.pdf. Last accessed 21 September 2016.

8 See Wang 2008, on China, for a recent example; public education was also central to seminal theories of nationalism such as Gelner and Brouilly, 2008.

9 See 'Genocide Education: Quality Control of the Teaching of "A History of Democratic Kampuchea 1975–1969"' by Kamboly Dy. Available at http://www.d.dccam.org/Projects/Genocide/pdf/Genocide_Education_Project--Quality_Control.pdf. Last accessed 21 September 2016.

10 See, for example, the DC-Cam 'Quality Control on Teaching "A History of Democratic Kampuchea 1975–1969" Report from Kompong Thom, 2011'. Available at http://www.d.dccam.org/Projects/Genocide/pdf/Quality_Control--Report_from_Kampong_Thom.pdf. Last accessed 30 September 2016.

11 TPO 2013 *Annual Report*, available at http://tpocambodia.org/wp-content/uploads/2015/08/TPO-annual-report-2013-part1.pdf. Last accessed 21 September 2016.

12 See the TPO website programme summary, available at http://tpocambodia.org/towards-a-shared-future-partner/. Last accessed 21 September 2016.

13 See the TPO website programme summary, available at http://tpocambodia.org/towards-a-shared-future-partner/ . Last accessed 21 September 2016.
14 See TPO website, http://tpocambodia.org/justice-and-relief-for-survivors-of-the-khmer-rouge/. Last accessed 23 September 2016.

References

Bekerman, Z. and Zembylas, M. 2011. *Teaching Contested Narratives: Identity, Memory and Reconciliation in Peace Education and Beyond*. Cambridge, UK: Cambridge University Press.

Brounéus, K. 2008. Truth-telling as talking cure? Insecurity and retraumatization in the Rwandan Gacaca courts. *Security Dialogue*, *39* (1): 55–76.

Caswell, M. 2010. Khmer Rouge archives: Accountability, truth, and memory in Cambodia. *Archival Science*, *10* (1): 25–44.

Center for Social Development (CSD). 2008. *Understanding Trauma in Cambodia Handbook*. Phnom Penh, Cambodia: Civicus. Available at http://www.civicus-cambodia.org/trauma-handbook/. Last accessed 23 September 2016.

Chandler, D. 2008. Cambodia deals with its past: Collective memory, demonisation and induced amnesia. *Totalitarian Movements and Political Religions*, *9* (2): 355–369.

Ciorciari, J. D. and Heindel, A. 2014. *Hybrid Justice: The Extraordinary Chambers in the Courts of Cambodia*. Ann Arbor, MI: University of Michigan Press.

Cohen, S. 2011. Whose side were we on? The undeclared politics of moral panic theory. *Crime, Media, Culture*, *7* (3): 237–243.

Cole, E. A. 2007. Transitional justice and the reform of history education. *International Journal of Transitional Justice*, *1* (1): 115–137.

Dearing, C. and Chea, P. 2009. *Teacher's Guidebook: The Teaching of "A History of Democratic Kampuchea (1975–1979)"*. Phnom Penh: Documentation Centre of Cambodia. Available at http://www.d.dccam.org/Projects/Genocide/pdf/DC-Cam_Teacher_Guidebook_Eng_Nov_23.pdf. Last accessed 23 September 2016.

Dosch, J. 2012. The role of civil society in Cambodia's peace-building process. *Asian Survey*, *52* (6): 1067–1088.

Dy, K. 2007. *A History of Democratic Kampuchea (1975–1979)*. Phnom Penh: Documentation Center of Cambodia.

Foucault, M. 1998. *The History of Sexuality, Vol. 1: The Will to Knowledge*. London: Penguin.

Foucault, M. and Rabinow, P. 1997. *Ethics: Subjectivity and Truth*. New York: W.W. Norton.

Hughes, C. 2003. *The Political Economy of the Cambodian Transition*. London: Routledge.

Hughes, C. 2007. Transnational networks, international organizations and political participation in Cambodia: Human rights, labour rights and common rights. *Democratization*, *14* (5): 834–852.

Hughes, C. 2009. *Dependent Communities: Aid and Politics in Cambodia and East Timor* (No. 48). Ithaca, NY: SEAP Publications.

Hughes, C. and Pupavac, V. 2005. Framing post-conflict societies: International pathologisation of Cambodia and the post-Yugoslav states. *Third World Quarterly*, *26* (6): 873–889.

Hughes, R. 2003. The abject artefacts of memory: Photographs from Cambodia's genocide. *Media, Culture & Society*, *25* (1): 23–44.

Ly, S.-K. 2008. Conveying Khmer Rouge history to young people. In *Searching for the Truth*. Phnom Penh: Documentation Centre of Cambodia, 24–27.
Moon, C. 2009. Healing past violence: Traumatic assumptions and therapeutic interventions in war and reconciliation. *Journal of Human Rights*, *8* (1): 71–91.
Moon, C. 2012. What one sees and how one files seeing: Human rights reporting, representation and action. *Sociology*, *46* (5): 876–890.
Pham, P., Vinck, P., Balthazard, M., Hean, S. and Stover, E. 2009. *So We Will Never Forget: A Population-Based Survey on Attitudes about Social Reconstruction and the Extraordinary Chambers in the Courts of Cambodia*. Berkeley, CA: Human Rights Center.
Ramírez-Barat, C. 2012. *Engaging Children and Youth in Transitional Justice Processes: Guidance for Outreach Programs*. New York: ICTJ.
Ross, F. 2003. On having voice and being heard: Some after-effects of testifying before the South African Truth and Reconciliation Commission. *Anthropological Theory*, *3* (3): 325–341.
Shore, C. 2008. Audit culture and illiberal governance: Universities and the politics of accountability. *Anthropological Theory*, *8* (3): 278–298.
Sperfeldt, C. 2012. Cambodian civil society and the Khmer Rouge Tribunal. *International Journal of Transitional Justice*, *6* (1): 149–160.
Summerfield, D. 2001. The invention of post-traumatic stress disorder and the social usefulness of a psychiatric category. *BMJ: British Medical Journal*, *322* (7278): 95.
Summerfield, D. 1999. A critique of seven assumptions behind psychological trauma programmes in war-affected areas. *Social Science & Medicine*, *48* (10): 1449–1462.
Transcultural Psychosocial Organisation. 2013. *Annual Report 2013*. Phnom Penh. Available at http://tpocambodia.org/wp-content/uploads/2015/08/TPO-annual-report-2013-part1.pdf. Last accessed 21 September 2016.
Vannath, C. 2002. Khmer Rouge and national reconciliation. *Peace Review*, *14* (3): 303–307.
Wang, Z. 2008. National humiliation, history education, and the politics of historical memory: Patriotic education campaign in China. *International Studies Quarterly*, *52* (4): 783–806.

7 Victims and perpetrators

The task of transitional justice, as Mutua presents in its idealised form (2015: 2), is the management of the competing needs and expectations of conflicted parties, stabilising societies that have experienced violence and atrocities through necessary compromises, while ensuring some accountability and challenge to states of impunity. Mutua's critical characterisation of the prevailing transitional justice doctrine implies the presence of a clear, visible and finite moral economy between guilty perpetrators and innocent victims that is bargained, mediated or redressed in the name of societal renewal. Transitional justice, as a set of decontextualised imperatives, pivots on visible, clear-cut categories and groupings of victims and perpetrators. This bifurcation has, on the one hand, been furnished by the historical gravity and authority of 'legalism' and the imperative to prosecute individuals for crimes under international law (Ainley 2011; McEvoy 2007); and, on the other, an increasing global amplification of 'victimhood' as a human rights trope, rationale and target for the work of transitional justice in its own right (Bonacker 2013; McEvoy and McConnachie 2012, 2013). Our understanding of transitional justice and memory can be enhanced by examining the ways that people negotiate, resist or elide the victim and perpetrator classifications and groupings that they encounter or are invited into.

Attempting to cleanly delineate victims and perpetrators as social cleavages in the wake of atrocities is challenging and raises important questions for transitional justice more broadly. Borer has shown that any grouping of victims or perpetrators should be treated as heterogenous and differentiated, and that often there are significant overlaps between the two, when victims become perpetrators of political violence or perpetrators become victims themselves (2003). While the fields of human rights and transitional justice have been historically constituted, in part, by a manichean liberalism and legalism that dichotomises innocence and guilt or 'good' and 'bad', different communities may renegotiate their own memories to identify themselves within exculpatory and politically entitling victim categories irrespective of their location within legal proceedings (Eldridge 2010). In Cambodia, recognising such complexities is important, given the unfolding, varied perpetration of political violence throughout the latter half of the twentieth century across the country and the propensity of the Khmer Rouge leadership to target and purge from within their own ranks during the Democratic Kampuchea period itself. We are therefore obliged to look more closely at how different memories of political violence in Cambodia are rallied and channelled into claims for victimhood, advanced and recognised on specific terms, and which are subordinated or elided. Moreover, we must attend to how the recognition of victims within transitional justice can work through discursive templates that actually serve to deny victims the very kinds of agency and empowerment that they are promised (Madlingozi 2010). These cautionary reflections are pressing because transitional justice tends to organise its subjects through different techniques of memory, affording varying hierarchical entitlements and forms of recognition. These are, in turn, partly generative of peoples' expectations, resistance, disappointments and frustration with transitional justice.

How do Cambodians of various and complex backgrounds and experiences navigate the categories and histories that they are invited to identify with? In this chapter, I draw on work at public forums[1] and events held across Cambodia to illuminate how different communities negotiate, accede to, or resist the sorts of claims made about victimhood and perpetration that emanate from the Extraordinary Chambers in the Courts of Cambodia (ECCC). My analysis does not present an exhaustive or 'representative' survey of attitudes at public forums. Rather, I aim to illustrate different tendencies and responses to public outreach that are politically significant and therefore analytically instructive in their own right. As I hope to show, claims about victimhood and perpetration in Cambodia can be varied, often unstable and ambiguous, with political implications and lessons for transitional justice and memory in Cambodia and beyond.

Tuol Sleng and victimhood

The public education work of the ECCC and its partners has made great use of the Tuol Sleng Museum of Genocide Crimes. The ECCC March 2015 Court Report, for example, boasts of twice-weekly ECCC Public Affairs 'study tours' to Tuol Sleng, the Choeung Ek memorial site and the court that each aim to bring 200–300 'villagers' from across Cambodia to Phnom Penh (2015: 11). Why would one particular memorial museum play such an important role in promoting a legal process? The answer is twofold. Tuol Sleng is mobilised as evidence or public 'proof' of the violent intentions of the Khmer Rouge, obviating the need for the ECCC as a response to violent crimes. Secondly, Tuol Sleng promotes a specific account of blame for the Khmer Rouge years – showing the hierarchical structure of the regime and the responsibility of the Khmer Rouge leadership and eliding the role of lower-level perpetrators – that corresponds neatly to the mandate and focus of ECCC prosecutions today. The representational work of the site is therefore complementary to both the rationale and mandate of the ECCC.

Tuol Sleng (along with the 'killing field' memorial at Choeung Ek) is today the principal Cambodian museum site dedicated to the atrocities of the Khmer Rouge. The museum building is a former high school in Phnom Penh, though during Democratic Kampuchea, the site was put to use as an incarceration centre, dubbed 'S-21'. At that time, it was the largest of a network of prisons operated by the Khmer Rouge security apparatus. Chandler's approximation of the numbers interred at S-21 indicates that around 14,000 people were held at the centre, the overwhelming majority of whom were killed (1999: 36). The S-21 site was discovered by the Vietnamese after the capture of Phnom Penh in January 1979 and the founding of the People's Republic of Kampuchea. The People's Republic of Kampuchea government quickly recognised the potential of the site in purchasing popular support and legitimacy on a domestic footing. The site was thus projected within Cambodia as proof of the atrocities of the Khmer Rouge and, in the context of an ongoing civil war, to legitimate the new People's Republic of Kampuchea state (Hughes 2003: 176–178).

It is the 'untouched' appearance of the artefacts on display that make Tuol Sleng both authoritative and a challenging space to visit (Hughes 2003: 176–178). The museum is organised around objects and displays that are 'primary' artefacts of atrocity (Williams 2004: 242). These include photographs of corpses found in cells when the site was first discovered; torture implements and shackles that remain in place as they were left in 1979; blood stains that marked sections of the cell blocks were only recently washed from the walls; and, in building B, displays including the iconic portrait photos taken upon entry of those interred at the centre. The supporting textual information that is available at Tuol Sleng communicates culpability for the atrocities committed at the site around the Khmer Rouge leadership.[2] The images of victims that are on display are anonymous and undifferentiated, aside from the visibly varying ages and genders of the subjects, and no mention is made of the fact that many of those displayed were themselves Khmer Rouge victims of Khmer Rouge purges. The representational challenges posed by 'complex political victims' were present before the ECCC was established (Bernath 2015: 54). Whilst the museum attributes guilt to senior Khmer Rouge leaders who were intent on genocide and is muted about the role of lower-level Khmer Rouge, it communicates suffering as nationally generalised (Ledgerwood 1997), with the entrance board noting that S-21 was the largest in a nationwide prison system. As Ledgerwood argues, the curation of Tuol Sleng cannot be understood without attention to the political and military challenges confronting the People's Republic of Kampuchea government in 1979. The People's Republic of Kampuchea government relied on the construction of a master narrative demonising the Khmer Rouge leadership and lamenting a 'glorious revolution' in 1975 that was stolen and hijacked by a small number of 'murderous criminals' (1997: 91). The narrow account of blame for Khmer Rouge atrocities was twinned with the deployment of informal reconciliatory initiatives through the 1980s that offered amnesty and exculpated lower level Khmer Rouge willing to defect (Gottesman 2003: 60–62). The historical parallels and continuities with the ECCC mandate that are at work here are striking in the way blame is principally attribute to the Khmer Rouge leadership.

Today, Tuol Sleng operates principally as a tourist attraction with non-Cambodians comprising the majority of visitors to the site (Williams 2004; Hughes 2008).[3] This raises important questions about how and why the museum is deployed for Cambodian visitors in the name of the ECCC. During an interview with Youk Chhang, director of the Documentation Centre of Cambodia (DC-Cam), I had asked how sites such as Tuol Sleng could contribute to transitional justice processes in Cambodia. His answer was illuminating in the way it cast Tuol Sleng in conflicted roles:

PM: How can the memorial sites like Tuol Sleng and Choeung Ek help in this process [reconciliation]?

YC: Actually, not now – it's for tourists... a message for the world. Cambodia has no more tears to cry... we no longer have anger. Right after the Khmer Rouge, there was anger, we thought anger would make us stronger. You see at most of those sites [provincial memorials] are transferred to the pagoda, they have transferred the skulls to a Buddhist stupa. They have transferred to a pagoda, close to home, close to culture and close to religion... They go to places like that, they don't go to Tuol Sleng. In the village, people go to the temple, this is where people see the skulls, even if one or two skulls... it is more meaningful.

PM: Does DC-Cam use Tuol Sleng or Choeung Ek in their own outreach?

YC: We use that [Tuol Sleng], like I said, because it is the most well documented and well preserved. But for people in the village, we might take them to a nearby [memorial]. Here, we use that as a need for the documentation. It speaks for itself. Cambodians use mostly oral history, but written is stronger. And written scripts, seen visually, we use them as a point of discussion, as visual evidence. But in terms of daily [life], you know, it's not like people go there.[4]

Chhang's remarks raise a number of important questions about the different roles of the Tuol Sleng Museum. Its principal audience, as Chhang suggests, is not Cambodian. Chhang implies that, for the purposes of memory and remembering, more culturally meaningful sites are available that communities might seek recourse to, a question I explore in the final chapter of the book. In locating Tuol Sleng within past 'anger' at the Khmer Rouge, Chhang implicitly references the role of the site as a key tool the People's Republic of Kampuchea utilised for political legitimacy (and a continued source of political currency and legitimation for the Cambodian government today too). Yet Chhang's remarks also reflect how significant Tuol Sleng (or S-21) has been within the ECCC process as a spectacular marker of mass violence, both legally as a site of evidence and in terms of the public presentation of the court. In the first instance, Case 001 focused on the Tuol Sleng site and its archived documentation, and it included Duch performing a 're-enactment' of his role and duties as head of the site. Tuol Sleng has also provided a significant weight of documents in the prosecution of Case 002/01 and ongoing Case 002/02, connecting the Khmer Rouge leadership to an organised and systematic set of criminal plans and structures.

Tuol Sleng is a site of memory that reflects the challenges of stabilising any single historical account of atrocities for public promotion. On the one hand, the site was curated and is presented as the heart of a nationwide network of prisons, implying a generalised and uniform experience of national violence and suffering. On the other, it is an exceptional space that is meant to depict the worst excesses and malice of the Democratic Kampuchea regime. This tension is reflected in the porous and unstable connections between the different memory claims for victimhood and responsibility that subsequent Cambodian governments, the ECCC and non-governmental organisations (NGOs) have propagated through the site: today, recognising the suffering of individual victims; connecting (and subsuming) individual experiences within a broad category of national victims; staking out the presence and possibility for perpetrators to themselves be victims; and, crucially, emphasising the guilt of a centrally omnipotent Khmer Rouge leadership. These claims are implicitly visible in the rationales that NGOs and ECCC partners provide for directing outreach exercises to the Tuol Sleng site because they tend to presume that Cambodians are unfamiliar with the S-21 site, that they have little or 'incomplete' knowledge of the regime and that their memories and experiences must be reoriented to specific readings of Democratic Kampuchea, characterised by violence and the guilt of the leadership. As one NGO outreach staff remarked, bringing Cambodians to Tuol Sleng

> is about building their schema, their existing knowledge. Even though they may have experienced those four years [of Democratic Kampuchea] they have never been to these two or three places. In their imagination Tuol Sleng is like this, or like this – they have absolutely no information... We want to activate their memory. On the road from the province to Tuol Sleng, we don't see emotion. But when they come to Tuol Sleng they start to remember whatever happened at that time.[5]

The premise of outreach, therefore, is the 'activation' of memory. The principle that witnessing and touring sites of violence activates 'memories' implies that memory is principally repository and archival (whereas we can argue that memories are constantly renegotiated in meaning, content, and form, according to the cues and contexts that call them into being). As above, Tuol Sleng performs this role in accordance to specific claims about culpability and responsibility. Another NGO staff member working on outreach specifically explained that Tuol Sleng could 'complete' or supplement existing memories of the Khmer Rouge:

> It is a place where torture and punishment was done to people during that regime. And for people that experienced the regime, some of them experienced that, others experienced hunger, they died of hunger, but they didn't see any punishment. Tuol Sleng, for people that never experienced that kind of thing, it adds to their memory. It adds another view, which makes their view of the regime more complete, it helps to fill in the picture.[6]

Here we see the challenge of consolidating and aligning public and personal accounts of experiences of the Khmer Rouge. Cambodian attendees are invited to orientate their own memories of the Khmer Rouge in relation to a specific representation of Democratic Kampuchea. This representation emphasises the systematic, organised and directed aspects of Khmer Rouge violence, conforming to past state-sponsored and present ECCC claims over memory. Moreover, remembering the Khmer Rouge *without* Tuol Sleng is implicitly presented as an 'incomplete' picture. As central as Tuol Sleng is and was to the story of Democratic Kampuchea, it is worth pausing to reflect on possibility that there are memories and experiences that are poorly accommodated in the representational work of Tuol Sleng. Indeed, as some memories and histories are foregrounded (and flattened), others are elided or muted.

ECCC partnered outreach

The ECCC 'Study Tour' visits to Tuol Sleng Museum are often followed by a seminar at the ECCC site. Similarly, NGO-led and partnered outreach events often pivot on a visit to Tuol Sleng before a tour of the ECCC court buildings, but they can extend to include a public forum featuring discussion of the tour, provide further updates and discussion of ECCC proceedings and offer an opportunity for Cambodian constituents to ask questions of ECCC staff. At one ECCC seminar I attended, notably hosting a group of residents of the former Khmer Rouge stronghold Pailin, the tone of exchanges was set early on. As Reach Sambath, the then head of ECCC Public Affairs and seminar leaders, enquired, "Those objects [at Tuol Sleng and Choeung Ek] are real, everything is real. How closely did you watch the skulls?" In response, one Pailin resident remarked "Close, very close, to ensure that they were real."[7] The premise of this exchange is veridictional, oriented to registers of authenticity and truth. Presenting the primary artefacts of atrocity – the site and instruments of torture at Tuol Sleng and the display of mass graves and human remains at Choeung Ek – as *evidence* coincides here, in the context of the ECCC, with the story of nationwide responsibility of omnipotent Khmer Rouge leaders. These initiatives tend, therefore, to be structured to show the evidence – or 'proof' – of what happened before demonstrating and obviating the ECCC as *the* appropriate response to the atrocities of the Khmer Rouge (Manning 2012: 9), though, as I argued in the previous chapter, NGO-led outreach efforts often author further initiatives and agendas within and onto these exercises, such as genocide education or trauma awareness raising.

The presentation of objects and artefacts of violence had powerful effects among visitors, who would often point out that they had not been to Tuol Sleng previously or had not witnessed killing:

> When I took the tour to PP, it was the first time. During the regime, in the Eastern zone, I did not see killing. I only learned about the killing a few days ago at Tuol Sleng. I was emotional and shocked because I never knew this happened.
>
> ("Public Forum on Justice and National Reconciliation," Sisophon, Banteay Meanchey, February 27th 2009)

Former lower-level members of the Khmer Rouge were equally attuned to the registers of truth, veracity, authenticity and evidence through which these sites were presented. As one remarked:

> The documents of the massacre I saw when I visited Phnom Penh. I saw a lot of events, true evidence which cannot be denied. I had no idea about secret killing during that period.
>
> (Center for Social Development [CSD] Public Forum on "Justice and National Reconciliation," Oddar Meanchey, February 20th 2008)

Is this a problem? After all, an absence of knowledge or familiarity with the systematic, planned evidence of the killing that occurred under Democratic Kampuchea, or the denial of such events, underwrites rationales for genocide education and the historical and truth-seeking roles that have been ascribed to the ECCC as outcomes of the prosecutions. There are still caveats that are worth bearing in mind here. The first is simply that those who did not experience the years of Democratic Kampuchea in conditions reflected at Tuol Sleng, or are today unfamiliar with S-21, are not necessarily blind to or ignorant of the wider suffering that occurred during that period. They may remember experiences, as a colleague at CSD remarked above, that did not include witnessing killing. The second caveat is, perhaps, more important. The *proof* of the violent and criminal intent of the regime depicted at Tuol Sleng is bound to a specific political history of culpability that elides lower-level responsibility and is deployed in a way that implies that the ECCC is the natural and only appropriate response to the atrocities depicted. In this sense, the orientation and fulfilment of individuals' memories through the representation of killing and blame at the hands of the Khmer Rouge leadership is, in effect, a means of disciplining already painful memories into accordance with preferred political and legal readings of the past.

Public forums on justice and reconciliation

Across the public forums I analysed, stories of suffering, sickness, loss, death and hunger under the regime were overwhelming. But they were often coincident with procedural questions about delays to proceedings, mistrust of the court and worries about the expense of the trials. At times, the forums worked as the form of space within which stories and experiences of Democratic Kampuchea could be expressed, individual suffering heard publicly, anger vented and, occasionally, contrition from lower-level Khmer Rouge volunteered. This picture corresponds to the ideal aims of 'localising' transitional justice from the 'bottom up', utilising existing cultural and political resources and authorities to enable informal or unofficial restorative justice techniques as complements of judicial exercises (Bickford 2007; Ciorciari and Ramji-Nogales 2012: 23–24). Testimony, within limits, was particularly encouraged. For example, prefiguring their recollections with a question about personal jurisdiction, one participant in Takeo recounted:

> I am very happy to participate. We have the trial for only 5 people? Why only 5 people? During [the] Khmer Rouge time we didn't have lawyers, we died without defence. I lived in Tram Kok under Ta Mok. In 1975 why was my father brought to be killed? In July 1975 I was brought to Krak Chang prison. I lived there for three years. My sister and cousin also were brought to prison. In the prison they were starving. Their body was bony, just skin. It was hard to meet my brother. He was a soldier. He was brought to jail. I was in jail three years. My children, too. My children were killed when they came free. They used sticks. You can go to Kang Chang prison. They killed. They made the loudspeakers loud so they don't hear the killing. So when I came out I was alone.
>
> (CSD "Public Forum on Justice and National Reconciliation," Takeo, August 1st 2008)

Such personal accounts of suffering, often including questions of why a relative was lost or killed and presented alongside a procedural query, were common across forums I attended. Notably, forums also sometimes featured both recognition and regret among former members of the Khmer Rouge. As one former cadre suggested, noting the role of the ECCC:

> All Cambodian people across the country suffered from regime… but to me I think, I am sorry, from my point of view, what Khmer Rouge did. It should have not been done by Khmer. Who's right and who's wrong? Now we have ECCC I support the court, of course I want to find out the reason of the genocide.
>
> (CSD "Public Forum on Justice and National Reconciliation," Oddar Meanchey, February 20th 2008)

These testimonies demonstrate and imply different forms of recognition that connect personal to public memory claims. The public forums provided a space within which individual testimony and memories are voiced and victims are seemingly *recognised* by authoritative agents – NGO institutions are held in high public esteem in Cambodia – especially given the frequent presence of ECCC staff or provincial government personnel at these events. Equally, community participants are invited to recognise their own memories and others' as embedded within national and collective experiences of suffering, furnishing connections with broader national claims for victimhood and, crucially, cementing the sense that *all* Cambodians – young and old – are therefore victims of the regime. The ECCC, in turn, is centred as the institutional site through which both personal and national memories of political violence are arbitrated redressed.

At other times, the forums seemed to foreclose and redirect voices that did not advance specific questions directly about the ECCC or offer forms of testimony that did not resemble expressions of suffering that were based on experiences of Democratic Kampuchea. A set of exchanges at a CSD public forum in Siem Reap was striking in this regard. For a group of attendees, the CSD sponsored tours of Tuol Sleng and Choeung Ek had engendered and provoked questions implicating political violence before 1975, specifically in how the war enabled the Khmer Rouge to rise to power. After speaking about the coup against Sihanouk in 1970 and the ensuing conflict, reading from some notes he had written, one participant was interrupted and asked to direct his question to the ECCC specifically:

> My impression is that the destruction of Cambodia then stemmed from what I have told you earlier. I wonder where the both sides got the weapons from to wage the war because we could not produce weapons. In my idea, there were foreign countries behind. In this regard, I would like the Khmer Rouge tribunal to think of how those countries joined war in Cambodia and the concerned countries should be sentenced or not.
>
> (CSD "Public Forum on Justice and National Reconciliation," Siem Reap, March 2nd 2007)

Another participant narrated a similar account of the overthrow of Sihanouk in 1970, explaining then how he had joined the resistance fighting against Lon Nol, referencing the killing of the 'Khmer White', a militia group of the Khmer Krom ethnic minority principally residing in the Mekong Delta in Southern Vietnam, before recounting how his allegiance to the movement had been called into question.

> I was the former National Liberation Army in 1970 [Khmer Rouge]… Khmer Rouge soldiers came to conduct [the] surveillances. After preparing the surveillance, they maltreated the people in the areas which we liberated, 70 percent of the country. Then, Khmer Rouge started to kill many people in the liberated areas, especially Khmer White. Vietnam established Khmer White. I wonder what Khmer White was established for. Fight Khmer Rouge. But I was the side of Vietnam to fight against Lon Nol at that time… They alleged that I stepped forward on two feet – one foot is on this mountain and another on that mountain. Vietnam investigated me and I felt insecure. I told the division that we must not interfere and we only fight against Lon Nol.
>
> (Facilitator: Please ask the questions, uncle).
>
> O.K. Why does the tribunal sentence the Khmer Rouge leaders from 75 to 79, not before that?
>
> (CSD "Public Forum on Justice and National Reconciliation," Siem Reap, March 2nd 2007)

Again, the forum facilitator intervenes to delineate what is relevant testimony and therefore recognised, circumscribing recollections of the personal challenges of negotiating the political flux and conflict of the years leading up to Democratic Kampuchea. Participants are redirected to questions specifically about the ECCC, narrowing what can be said – and therefore publicly remembered – into a question-and-answer format addressed to presence of ECCC staff at the forum. Attending the Siem Reap event in 2007 was the ECCC Cambodian co-prosecutor, Chea Leang. Her response to forms of testimony and questions about events beyond the

ECCC mandate that query the demarcation of the ECCC temporal jurisdiction to 1975–1979 – and therefore the categories and groupings of perpetrator responsibility animated therein – is notably circular, ahistorical and depoliticising:

> Mrs Chea Leang: I would like to thank you for many questions. First question: It is related to the neighbouring countries. You asked that "Must those countries be sentenced if being investigated to be involved?" In this regard, we must understand our principles of law as I have told you earlier that I am a technician who enforces the adopted [ECCC] law. There is not any law talking about the foreign countries involved. It is only about the trial of individuals in which there are only two groups [senior leaders and those most responsible] that are clearly written in law. This question is the same as the third person as well as the first person, so I would like answer in total. That law was clearly written about two groups-first about senior leaders and second about the people who are responsible. Through both points, we could not do beyond that. As a technician and not a writer of the law, I only analyze and enforce the law.
>
> (CSD "Public Forum on Justice and National Reconciliation," Siem Reap, March 2nd 2007)

Chea Leang is jointly responsible for investigating, preparing, and prosecuting cases at the ECCC and, here, nothing else. The ECCC law states that only specific groups can be held legally responsible. Why? Because the law says so. Here we see that questions of historical context and responsibility – and personal recollections of politically inconvenient histories – are foreclosed through the presentation of law as a technical rather than political or moral exercise. This should not come as a surprise; it reflects the need to *perform* law and politics as separate, delineated spaces. Yet it is also instructive because it illustrates again how the different organs of the ECCC will speak about, defend and delineate their work on varied terms (here as narrow retributive dispensation as against, say, the victim-centred support work of the Victims Support Section or the grander claims of the Public Affairs Office). Moreover, perhaps more importantly, in the context of the forum, peoples' memories, testimony and questions about political violence that destabilise established categories of victimhood and perpetration are not recognised or received in the same way as more politically congruent testimony of suffering under Democratic Kampuchea. This captures and throws into relief the contradiction haunting the ECCC and other *ad hoc* tribunals: they are, on the one hand, exceptional and contingent products of political agreements that recognise a narrow window of human-rights violations but, on the other, they are validated through a purportedly transcendental, universal and continuous set of human rights legal protections and obligations.

Lower-level perpetrators

Memory has the potential to disrupt the templates and scripts it is invited into. One fascinating tendency within the outreach efforts and public forums I attended was how participants would renegotiate or question the relationships with memories of violence they were asked to establish, the categories of victimhood that they were invited to co-identify with and the categories of responsible perpetrators that they are invited to blame, as above. This is important for our wider understanding of memory as a reflexive and relational process and transitional justice as a field that administers and manages competing memories. Memory claims can emerge from within or against other memory claims over the past, contesting what happened but also what should be done about it. As hinted above, questions about the scope of prosecutions were often pronounced, contesting how the ECCC has narrowly defined responsibility to a particular timespan and to a handful of individuals. In the CSD report from a forum in Ratanakiri in Cambodia's north east, it was noted that:

> There were doubts among the participants of why only the Tuol Sleng chief [Duch] has been brought to the court trial while there were 167 detention centers across the county, every one of which had the responsible chief, as expressed by participants that people still recognize the living detention chiefs and where they live now.[8]

The thorny question of lower-level responsibility remains outstanding for many Cambodians because the ECCC animates a *de facto* amnesty for lower-level Khmer Rouge by omission. As Vietnamese forces captured Phnom Penh in 1979 and Democratic Kampuchea fell, many Khmer Rouge fled to the Thai border and now populate towns on Cambodia's western and northern frontiers, like Pailin, Phnom Malai and Anlong Veng. But many lower-level perpetrators stayed within Cambodia's interior. While some were killed in revenge attacks in the aftermath of the regime and others were imprisoned under the People's Republic of Kampuchea authorities, many now live in close proximity to families and communities that suffered violence that they may have been implicated in. The narrow mandate of ECCC prosecutions invariably invites counter-claims about responsibility:

> The court is trying the senior leaders and those most responsible. What about direct perpetrators? There are communities where people were killed, and some where nobody was killed. In other places, why there was lots of killing. These killers are not the five accused today. Why are the direct perpetrators not on trial?
>
> (CSD "Public Forum on Justice and Reconciliation," Sisophon, February 27th 2009)

> What about the commune and district levels? I saw them killing people.
>
> (CSD "Public Forum on Justice and Reconciliation," Oddar Meanchey, February 20th 2008)

> There was killing, it was not the order of the top leaders. The Village Chief was killing people. It was his order not from the five persons. I have

> questions… I would like to speak about the killing. My uncle and my brothers were teachers. The three were arrested and killed… why ECCC did not bring those killers to the court? If we say it is the general court we should bring them all to the court. Is it true that there will be war again?
>
> (CSD "Public Forum on Justice and Reconciliation," Takeo, August 1st 2008)

For these participants, the importance of lower-level accountability of 'direct' perpetrators emerges in relief of the prosecution of senior leaders. The argument implicated also here, that too broadly based prosecutions in the wake of atrocities can provoke the resumption of conflict, is a hallmark of early, formative debates within transitional justice that opposed reconciliation and peace, on the one hand, with accountability on the other. It is telling that the Cambodian government has regularly reproduced exactly such arguments as they have opposed prospective prosecutions in Cases 003 and 004 at the ECCC in the name of ensuring 'national reconciliation'. While there is little likelihood of a resumption of conflict were Cases 003 and 004 to proceed, the potential for the narrow scope of those prosecutions to satisfy the above injuries is also unclear. Moreover, it is uncertain whether outstanding, proximate and often intimate grievances that persist within some Cambodian communities are straightforwardly amenable to the conventional set of alternative, non-judicial repertoires that transitional justice presents for their management. For example, a public forum held in Stung Treng in April 2009, coinciding with Case 001 and Duch's gesture of apology, invited participants to discuss the place of apologies.

P: Duch, I can accept his apology. If someone steps on our feet and says sorry we can forgive them. The court will do the legal punishment.

Facilitator: Do you want the other four [senior leaders in Case 002] to say the same thing?

P: It is unacceptable to me. I lost my father and four brothers because of starvation. Many people died, the bones are like the mountain. I can only forgive if the direct perpetrator comes and apologises.

(CSD "Public Forum on Justice and Reconciliation," Stung Treng, April 10th 2009)

The audience held mixed views towards the possibility of apologies. At the Stung Treng forum, another participant became animated about the problems of reconciliation with former Khmer Rouge, claiming the inadequacy of gestures of contrition. He identified a neighbour he believed to be responsible under the regime:

> If I go to them to seek an apology, it's crazy. He lives near me, in my community, sometimes I want to kill that person… Making an apology for everything, then there would be no law. We cannot forget about what happened even if they make an apology. We should confiscate their property and build

> reconciliation. If I wanted to do something illegal I already would have, just a little gasoline no problem, I burn the house [forum breaks out in laughter].
>
> (CSD "Public Forum on Justice and Reconciliation," Stung Treng, April 10th 2009)

The question of lower-level responsibility is vexed. On the one hand, such grievances – historically persistent, reaffirmed and pronounced *despite* the ECCC – could quickly be folded back into validations for a variety of restorative justice techniques, including genocide education or other truth-seeking exercises and PTSD coping strategies, or through techniques and forms of mediation envisaged as appropriate by stakeholders. On the other, borrowing from Holocaust survivor Jean Améry's reflections on his own feelings of resentment towards perpetrators, we might further trouble a premise that has been central to transitional justice: that such personal grievances can and should be surrendered or corrected. Writing in *At the Mind's Limits* (2009), Améry argued that resentment did not constitute petty grudge bearing or a pathology. For Amery, resentment was neither a prescription for others nor synonymous with revenge. Resentment was a specific personal response to his experience of suffering that grew and ossified exactly as it became clear to him that the past could not be resolved through an objective moral economy of redress and equivalence between victim and perpetrator. Promises that such wrongs could be righted, the past settled or society 'moved forward' – resolving the irresolvable through a hollow and politically conditioned political consensus – were the kinds of claim that animated Améry's provocative outrage in the form of resentment. Améry's argument is relevant here less because of its cross-cultural normative implications – which might suggest that there is a right to maintain grievance and object to contrition and forgiveness – but more in the fact that his resentment seemed to grow co-productively and reflexively with society's wider claims to have 'dealt with' what had been done. In other words, we can see why participants' outrage at the failure to reckon with lower-level perpetrators might be inflamed *exactly* when they are told that justice is being done at the ECCC.

The problems that arise from the presence of 'direct' or lower-level perpetrators within Cambodian communities are fundamentally not complaints that the prospective further ECCC prosecutions through Cases 003 and 004 could begin to resolve. This point is equally applicable to the initially mooted propositions by the UN Group of Experts in 1999 to prosecute 20–30 Khmer Rouge figures, which would not encompass the lower-level perpetrators implicated above. Conversely, we must also be wary of rendering the actual relationships that communities have established with memories of political violence – and those implicated in them – invisible, especially within discursive spaces such as the CSD public forums. The challenges of living alongside former perpetrators of atrocity that some Cambodian communities confront would persist without the work of the ECCC and, of course, punishment in these contexts can never meet the scale of the crimes at hand. But it is exactly as the ECCC, United Nations (UN) and

Cambodian government ask communities to accept that only "senior leaders" and "those most responsible" should be prosecuted that the contingent scope and form of redressing Cambodia's experiences of past violence is illuminated, engendering questions and counter-claims over the responsibility of perpetrator categories as above.

National subjects and national wounds

An important question that seems to trouble Cambodian communities is why Khmers would perpetrate violence against Khmers. Again, while this is an issue that could be quickly invoked in validations for ECCC outreach or genocide education, as seemingly superficial evidence of ignorance of the record and nature of the regime, or even as a form of 'denial', it also raises important questions about the frameworks that enable, inhibit and shape relationships with memories of political violence. The question of how Khmers could commit violence against other Khmers grates with conceptions of national and 'racial' solidarity – often articulated in Cambodia as synonymous – and the continuity and integrity of the national community. This tendency was reflected in questions about perpetrator responsibility that sought to externalise blame beyond Cambodia's borders:

> I have one question. What is the real ideology that was applied during the regime? Why is it more brutal than Hitler regime? Hitler killed people in war and other nationalities, Khmer Rouge killed their own people, why?
>
> ("Public Forum on Justice and Reconciliation," Stung Treng, April 10th 2009)

> During the Khmer Rouge I lost all my family members, I saw this with my own eyes. I saw people taken on trucks and then shot on the hillside. During the Pol Pot regime, why did they kill people? What was the purpose of the massacre? Who backed the massacre, which countries?
>
> (CSD "Public Forum on Justice and Reconciliation," Pailin, October 24th 2008)

> Who participated in the destruction in Cambodia? Were the KR leaders themselves the mastermind or others behind the tragedy? Was American bombarding the root of the genocide?
>
> (CSD "Public Forum on Justice and Reconciliation," Ratanakiri, March 28th 2008)

The questions raised here should not be dismissed out of hand. It is indeed important to think about the traction of those ideological and political visions that were globally circulating and appropriated in extremis by the Khmer Rouge leadership; the Democratic Kampuchea government did enjoy support and patronage from other states; and, of course, the United States (US) bombardment did play a key role in bringing the Khmer Rouge to power. Yet importantly, too, each one of these queries implicates (but displaces) the more troubling question of why Cambodians would kill other Cambodians. Today, the rhetoric of Cambodia's political landscape is defined by competing nationalisms that emphasise solidarity between Khmers, often in relief of or against 'othered' neighbouring states and 'races' (often Thailand, but principally Vietnam), or the international community in general. The idea that Khmers could kill other Khmers – especially given that the victims of Democratic Kampuchea cannot be located within conventional nationalist tropes of valour and sacrifice (Hughes 2005) – is a breach and rupture of national and racial solidarity that is difficult to integrate comfortably into the 'imagined community' of the present. The ECCC is a mechanism deployed in the name of national renewal, and yet the traction of specific nationalist tropes within Cambodia can engender memory claims that seem hesitant to subscribe to the way it has accounted for responsibility as a 'Khmer' problem.

Prevailing discourses of nation and nationalism condition and reframe Cambodians' relationships with memories of the Khmer Rouge in uneven and often contradictory ways. In the extreme, there are instances of historical revisionism and denial of the atrocities perpetrated under Democratic Kampuchea – a problem that is not confined to former Khmer Rouge members – which are principally driven by race-based nationalism and xenophobia. In particular, those critical of the current government, and thus the way that it garners legitimacy through its purported role as the 'saviour' of the nation from the Khmer Rouge, tend to subscribe to anti-Vietnamese political worldviews, seeing the Vietnamese as a historical rival and existential threat. This political premise contributes to several problems. On the one hand, it reproduces forms of anti-Vietnamese xenophobia that are not entirely indistinct from those that characterised the Democratic Kampuchea government. On the other, it is precipitant to revisionist accounts of Democratic Kampuchea that blame the Vietnamese for the rise of the Khmer Rouge or, in the extreme, suggest that atrocities perpetrated under Democratic Kampuchea have been 'fabricated'. In 2013, Kem Sokha, a leader of the opposition Cambodian National Rescue Party, claimed that the S-21 Tuol Sleng site was a Vietnamese creation: "The Vietnamese created this place with pictures [of the victims]. If this place is truly Khmer Rouge they would have knocked it down before they left. You should know that if the Khmer Rouge killed people, would they keep it to show to everyone? If they knew they killed many people, why would they keep this place?" (*Cambodia Daily* 2013). Sokha's comments were, predictably, seized on by the government, who quickly passed a law against the denial of Khmer Rouge atrocities and mobilised sympathetic survivor organisations to denounce the opposition and reaffirm the role of the government as saviour of the nation. The point here is that when prevailing political currents, defined by competing accounts of the national biography and national solidarity, contest and question responsibility for the atrocities of the Khmer Rouge, it is unsurprising that Cambodian communities can ask questions about the responsibility of 'foreigners' that appear discordant with the how the ECCC prosecutions are expected to 'set the record straight'.

Cambodian nationalism(s) and its relationships to memories of the Khmer Rouge can cut both ways here though. Among former members of the Khmer

Rouge, recollections and accounts of their involvement in the movement, at its birth or after its fall from power, invariably invoke patriotic narratives of national defence and integrity as they locate themselves within collective histories that are fuelled by a sense of existential threat at the hands of others. These are, however, often articulated in ambivalent or even supportive relationships to the ECCC, congruent with the way it animates claims for national reconciliation. As one former Khmer Rouge cadre proclaimed at a public forum:

> I strongly believe in national reconciliation in Cambodia. If you look at the situation after Khmer Rouge. Ta Mok escaped and now others have been arrested. If they are not honest they [would have] escaped to other countries. We have to ensure [there are] leaders who care are in this country. The [Khmer Rouge] policy was to give power to the farmers actually, so the poor farmers were in power. People of Oddar Meanchey, what we have to do now, is develop our living condition in the province. I'm getting a lot of training. I myself gave up everything for the development of the country. So we love our country, [the] Khmer Rouge also love their country. We gave up the war and the idea of making more war. Now we need justice for those who are leaders. I want to see if they are found guilty or not. From 1998, after the end of civil war, none of us escaped, we all stayed in the country. This is what we call reconciliation.
> (CSD "Public Forum on Justice and Reconciliation," Oddar Meanchey, February 20th 2008)

Lower and mid-level Khmer Rouge – whom the ECCC Public Affairs Office, NGO outreach efforts around trauma awareness and DC-Cam's genocide education projects articulate specifically as themselves victims of the regime – are able to renegotiate categories of victimhood, responsibility and perpetration in contradictory, uneven and ambivalent ways. Lower-level Khmer Rouge will often proclaim the benevolent intentions of their former leaders, stress the need to focus on material and economic improvement while, paradoxically, accepting the need for the ECCC and acknowledging the wrongs of the Democratic Kampuchea period. As I have argued elsewhere, they are simultaneously reconciled to the ECCC project exactly as they subscribe to memories that appear un-reconciled to the way the ECCC denounces the Khmer Rouge leadership (Manning 2015). The possibility of such ambivalence is specifically rooted in the way that conflicting memories can be subsumed within the protean and often contradictory possibilities of nationalism as a scaffold and imperative of memory (Bhabha 1990). In other words, when it comes to the national biography and national myth making, anything is congruent so long as it is servile to the integrity of the nation.

Contesting memory

The public forums held in former Khmer Rouge zones, such as Pailin or Oddar Meanchey, showed that lower-level Khmer Rouge – 'complex victims' – were often receptive to the way the ECCC articulated responsibility for the suffering of Democratic Kampuchea period to the Khmer Rouge leadership alone. This, perhaps, is not surprising given that the ECCC mandate, by omission, pivots on their reassurance of a *de facto* amnesty for their involvement in the regime. Yet this quiescence towards the ECCC was not uniform among former Khmer Rouge. More direct challenges and forms of resistance to the ECCC were voiced, reflecting how, as claims over the past are advanced, memories are called forth with uneven effects and consequences. In Pailin, both denial and appeals for exculpation were visible:

> The Khmer Rouge leaders did good things. Without the leaders there would have been no agreement in Paris. The Khmer Rouge leaders did not intend to kill people, this our belief.
>
> (CSD "Public Forum on Justice and Reconciliation," Pailin, October 24th 2008)

> I also want to ask about forgiveness. They are Khmer and they love their nation, and protect their land. Will there be any pardon for them?
>
> (CSD "Public Forum on Justice and Reconciliation," Pailin, October 24th 2008)

In Sisophon, when invited into dialogue about 'reconciliation', one participant's response was abrupt and jarring.

Facilitator: Is there any reconciliation in your community? Is there reconciliation in Cambodia?

P: Reconciliation is to stop talking about this.

("Public Forum on Justice and Reconciliation," Sisophon, February, 27th 2009)

It is not surprising that these forms of resistance to discourses of accountability and reconciliation are occasionally present. Memories of Democratic Kampuchea are diverse, and they are rallied under different banners and referent points in varied ways. Two issues are important here though. Conflicting memory – or resistance to a specific transitional justice mechanism – does not, in and of itself, self-evidently obviate the need for more 'reconciliation', 'truth', 'accountability' or otherwise. Transitional justice is a discursive field that tends to *see* the world and such phenomena as self-evident justification for their own transformation. Secondly, resistant or hostile responses to appeals for the need for reconciliation or the ECCC prosecutions are less politically significant, here, where they specifically do not contest categories of victimhood, responsibility and perpetration. Rather, the politics of memory are strained when communities reproduce and present counter-claims about victimhood and perpetration over events beyond the ECCC mandate. I now turn to examples of these to think through their socio-political implications.

Objections to the ECCC are often rooted in perceptions of double standards and hypocrisy in prosecuting some alleged crimes but not others. Within former Khmer Rouge communities, some of these reflect, even perhaps mimic, the strategies of rupture or '*tu quoque*' questions – '*who are you to judge*?' – that Khmer Rouge leaders Nuon Chea and Khieu Samphan have advanced during ECCC proceedings, as discussed in Chapter 5. These are memory claims that reach for moral equivalency and therefore equivocation, attempting to contest the moral authority of the institutions tasked with arbitrating justice. For example, in Pailin, one participant asked:

> I want to know who gave the order to kill. Was it the Khmer Rouge or someone else? I know that Pol Pot was a genocide regime. So America dropped bombs on Cambodia – was it genocide too?
>
> (CSD "Public Forum on Justice and Reconciliation," Pailin, October 24th 2008)

Posing a moral equivalency between the American bombing and the genocide of the Pol Pot regime is a political riposte and challenge to the integrity of the classification of perpetrators animated at the ECCC. My interest here, firstly, is how and why such statements are politically feasible and consequential. We might query whether such claims are advanced in genuine good faith; as contrarian responses to the work of the forum in evidencing and denouncing the malice of the Democratic leadership; as forms of 'self-defence' and denial by implication, as Cohen conceptualises (2001: 9); or because of the tendency to 'exteriorise' issues of responsibility because they grate with conceptions of national solidarity. Yet, at the same time, this does not mean, conversely, that we should read all memory claims about suffering, political violence and responsibility that occurred beyond the ECCC mandate as attempts to equivocate, and therefore not take them seriously.

> In the KR regime 1975–1979, but there were killings in 1974. Who killed people in 1974?
>
> ("Public Forum on Justice and Reconciliation," Stung Treng, April 10th 2009)

> You have already interpreted the trial of the Khmer Rouge leaders from 1975 to 1979. What if the people are killed before 1975, what kind of courts should I file a complaint to? Because you said that the national and international court could not sentence. Now, I want to sue. I want to file a complaint to the court to sentence before 1975. So, what kind of court should I file a complaint to? That's all.
>
> (CSD Public Forum on "Justice and National Reconciliation," Siem Reap, March 2nd 2007)

Memory claims over political violence and suffering before 1975 are important because, as they implicate questions of responsibility that will remain unscrutinised at the ECCC, they also imply claims for victimhood that are not formally acknowledged. As public forums are intended to promote and publicise the ECCC as a mechanism of justice and accountability, questions about political violence beyond its mandate seem incommensurable to the very language of *justice* and *accountability* that underpin them. While bids to equivocate between periods of violence can be read as political tactics made in bad faith, we see persistent appeals for memory and recognition of suffering beyond the ECCC mandate that warrant attention. These claims were fraught because the ECCC is a mechanism that is frequently presented as offering a comprehensive justice. Counter-claims against the ECCC over memories of political violence and suffering, perpetration and victimhood, accountability and recognition, are animated exactly because Cambodian communities recognise the ECCC jurisdictions as politically contingent categories. Moreover, they pose questions for wider debates in transitional justice because the ECCC is predicated on the purportedly universal imperative to punish all perpetrators of serious political violence as both an end in itself and deterrent to future conflict.

The neat periodisation of the ECCC jurisdiction around the 1975–1979 Democratic Kampuchea years can provoke claims for the recognition of violence after the Khmer Rouge were removed from power too. There is a generation of Cambodians that grew up during the 1980s under conditions of continuous conflict, suffering and violence whose experiences, memories and concerns tend to be elided or subsumed. The fact that the Khmer Rouge enjoyed international recognition and patronage throughout the 1980s and 1990s, despite evidence of atrocities perpetrated at their hands, was itself a point of issue for some. At a public forum in Sisophon, one participant specifically called for the recognition of responsibility for states supporting the Khmer Rouge:

> Does ECCC investigate only Cambodia, or other countries? We need to speed this process up. In the past I was in the army. I joined the government to fight against the Khmer Rouge. They had support from Thailand, Thailand has responsibility. I was a soldier 1985. Then I went to Russia to study tank management. Then I worked with the government to push out the Khmer Rouge. Thailand helped the Khmer Rouge with logging, to make money. They have responsibility.
>
> ("Public Forum on Justice and Reconciliation," Sisophon, February 27th 2009)

We might, as I argued above, read such grievances through the reassurance of locating responsibility beyond Cambodia's borders and as a feature of the ongoing idealisation of national integrity and solidarity (more so in light of the fact that 2008 and 2009 was a period of strain in Thai–Cambodian relations and witnessed several serious outbreaks of violence between Thai and Cambodian troops along border zones). Yet it is equally important to think through the implications and effects of these claims, connecting personal experiences and memories to public histories;

they are indicative of the ways that Cambodian communities are attuned to the political sensitivities and vast (international and domestic) impunities that characterise the recent history of the country and persist in the present day. As one participant at the Pailin forum remarked, "So you have been talking about the anger against the Khmer Rouge. Police and soldiers kill people in Poipet [today], there is no trial for them. I am hopeless with the trial [ECCC]. The bombing in front of the assembly in 1998 [attacking an opposition demonstration]. Hundreds injured, many died." When Cambodians point to contemporary patterns of human rights violations – and question the way the ECCC was mandated according to both international and domestic interests, omitting histories implicating other states or violence by members of the current government – it seems that interwoven international and domestic impunities are thrown into relief, rather than the victim and perpetrator categories being animated, at the ECCC.

Ambivalent accounts

My intention, in working through these different examples, has not been to provide an exhaustive or comprehensive disinterring of the memories of Cambodian communities as they are invited into specific relationships with memories of political violence. Rather, I hope to have illustrated tendencies and political counter-claims over memory that are significant and instructive in their own right. One final set of responses seems important to highlight in these respects. At some public forums, communities voiced ambivalent feelings towards both the ECCC and the past.

> I to want to ask you a question and share some talk about national reconciliation. I was a victim. I [was] tortured and suffered from [the] regime… To this problem we will never finish this problem. We don't want to have more war. We need more respect. I want to bury the past.
>
> (CSD "Public Forum on Justice and Reconciliation," Oddar Meanchey, February 20th 2008)

On the one hand, this appeal for forgetting, as such, corresponds to accusations of state-induced amnesia, whereby peace or development are prioritised over the apparent jeopardy posed by justice. Yet, on the other, as the enunciation of a self-identifying victim, we might caution ourselves before dismissing this claim and think through *who* is authorised to reject this claim as illegitimate. This is not to read appeals for forgetting as prescriptions; rather, we might be more sensitive to the potential place and legitimacy of claims that see this as a "problem that we will never finish."

Public forums also often encountered seemingly prosaic and practical reluctances to engage with the ECCC. Cambodian communities are well aware of how expensive the ECCC has been and, as one former outreach staff told me, the court has increasingly been seen with some exasperation among the public in this regard.[9] Indeed, a 2008 survey led by the Human Rights Center at Berkeley showed that 75 per cent of Cambodians preferred the government to focus on the "problems of their daily lives" rather than accountability for the Khmer Rouge (Pham *et al.* 2009: 2). At a public forum in Koh Kong, for example, one participant queried "Will the court spend over [a] million dollars to sentence only five people or continue searching [in] this process?"[10] Concerns over costs, which, as of September 2016, were running at over $300 million, common and understandable. On the one hand, the ECCC could certainly be better presented and explained in terms of its 'value' for money, however that might be calculated or rendered. On the other, it is worth bearing in mind that these concerns and queries over the costs of the ECCC might be driven by the clear disparities in financial support the court has received relative to other basic public services and amenities that are more immediately present within Cambodian communities.

One final point is worth pausing on here. The logic of transitional justice, embodied in the ECCC slogan "moving forward through justice," is that it is mechanisms of redress and renewal that enable and permit societies to establish 'corrected' relationships to the legacies and memories of atrocity. Transitional justice, here, is conceived as a self-authorised, linear sequence. This underpinning grammar of the field poses problems because it elides the ability of communities to develop relationships to their experiences and memories of atrocity outside of the formal parameters transitional justice. This is not to say that Cambodian communities have all done so on desirable terms, nor to advocate for *more* grassroots transitional justice. Rather, it gestures to the how transitional justice practitioners and scholars needs to learn to better *see* the different ways that communities can establish relationships to memories of violence beyond their conventional armouries, for better or worse. As one exchange at a forum in Stung Treng highlighted, these can emerge on varying terms:

P: In 1979 I was a soldier of Heng Samrin [PRK]. I met someone of the KR soldiers. In the past during war when we came to meet each other we were very violent and very brutal. Now we live together in unity.

Forum leader: Did you ever meet that other soldier, do you ever talk about your experiences?

P: We drink together. When we have a party we talk to each other and drink together. We don't talk about that past. Now we never talk about that.

("Public Forum on Justice and Reconciliation," Stung Treng, April 10th 2009)

I present this anecdote because it *can* be read as a justification for 'more' or 'better' transitional justice, locating silences over the past (and drinking) as 'symptomatic' of a failure to properly come to terms with legacies of division. My point here, simply, is that we might alternatively and equally see in this exchange a proactive relationship that accommodates and emolliates past animosity.

Conclusion

Public education and outreach is increasingly recognised as a key means through which transitional justice mechanisms broach and are mediated with their constituents. In doing so, public education and outreach are also key points of friction around which claims over memory work. In the first instance, this means that we need to pay greater attention to the kinds of memory work that occur beyond and at the nodes of transitional justice processes. As I have tried to show in this chapter, ECCC and partnered NGO outreach initiatives tend to invite their audiences into relationships with memories of the Khmer Rouge that follow from the 'juridifed' categories at work at the ECCC, animating, firstly, claims about the responsibility of the Khmer Rouge leadership while, secondly, licensing space for a wider envelope of *all* Cambodians as national victims of the regime. This work is especially supported by pre-existing memorial and museum sites such as Tuol Sleng and Choeung Ek because they carry meanings about violence that correspond to the same account of blame. At the same time, we see here that one feature of these processes is the propagation of a 'flattened' category of victimhood that works to consolidate personal experiences within a collective account of loss, violence and guilt.

As I have tried to show, memory does not neatly map such invitations. It seems that, instead, it is exactly at these points, crucibles and nodes through which the ECCC is presented that memories that elude or contest the terms of the ECCC are manifest. In particular, we have seen counter-claims emerge about the responsibility of both lower-level 'direct' perpetrators who specifically are not within the remit of the ECCC prosecutions, as well as attempts to highlight responsibility for violence perpetrated before 1975 and after 1979. Some of these appeals appear as tactical attempts to render histories of political violence equivocal, mimicking the strategies of rupture and denial deployed by the defence in the courtroom. Others appeared to be motivated, in good faith, as appeals for the recognition of suffering beyond the scope of the ECCC. It is these appeals that pose outstanding questions for the way transitional justice tends to address legacies of political violence selectively. This is notwithstanding the often ambivalent relationships that Cambodian communities can establish with memories of political violence. As I turn to in the next chapter, we need to pay closer attention to the different terms on which memories of political violence are made meaningful beyond the work of transitional justice.

Notes

1 'Public forums' are a form of public engagement widely used by NGOs in Cambodia. Each will vary in content and scope according to the organisational priorities and expertise of those leading the forum. This chapter draws principally from public forums hosted and led by the Center for Social Development between 2007 and 2009, events co-sponsored and attended by ECCC staff. The CSD forums were not the only NGO-led exercises to engage communities with the ECCC process, and my analysis here does not intend to offer a comprehensive account of all public forum events occurring in these years. Rather, I take the CSD forums as significant data because they were 'high profile', attracting media coverage and public interest, and they develop an analysis of important tendencies and possibilities within the politics of memory as significant in their own right.

2 All information at the site is in Khmer, English and French.

3 See Hughes (2008) especially on 'dutiful' and 'humanitarian practices of visitation at Tuol Sleng by non-Cambodians.

4 Personal interview, Phnom Penh, 22 May 2009.

5 Personal interview, Phnom Penh, 7 October 2008.
6 Personal interview, Phnom Penh,4 January 2009.
7 ECCC Seminar 7 October 2008.
8 CSD "Public Forum on Justice and Reconciliation" Ratanakiri, 28 March 2008.
9 Personal interview, former outreach coordinator, Phnom Penh, March 2016.
10 CSD "Public Forum on Justice and Reconciliation", Koh Kong, 6 May 2008.

References

Ainley, K. 2011. Excesses of responsibility: The limits of law and the possibilities of politics. *Ethics & International Affairs*, *25* (4): 407–431.

Améry, J. 2009. *At the Mind's Limits: Contemplations by a Survivor on Auschwitz and its Realities*. Bloomington, IN: Indiana University Press.

Bernath, J. 2015. 'Complex political victims' in the aftermath of mass atrocity: Reflections on the Khmer Rouge Tribunal in Cambodia. *International Journal of Transitional Justice*, *10* (1): 46–66.

Bhabha, H. 1990. *Nation and Narration*. London and New York: Routledge.

Bickford, L. 2007. Unofficial truth projects. *Human Rights Quarterly*, *29* (4): 994–1035.

Borer, T. A. 2003. A taxonomy of victims and perpetrators: Human rights and reconciliation in South Africa. *Human Rights Quarterly*, *25* (4): 1088–1116.

Bonacker, T. 2013. Global victimhood: On the charisma of the victim in transitional justice processes. *World Political Science*, *9* (1): 97–129.

Cambodia Daily. 2013. Kem Sokha says S-21 was Vietnamese conspiracy, 27 May. Available at https://www.cambodiadaily.com/archives/kem-sokha-says-s-21-was-vietnamese-conspiracy-26755/. Last accessed 23 September 2016.

Chandler, D. P. 1999. *Voices from S-21: Terror and History in Pol Pot's Secret Prison*. Berkeley, CA: University of California Press.

Ciorciari, J. D. and Ramji-Nogales, J. 2012. Lessons from the Cambodian experience with truth and reconciliation. *Buff. Hum. Rts. L. Rev.*, *19*: 193.

Cohen, S. 2001. *States of Denial: Knowing about Atrocities and Suffering*. Cambridge, UK. Malden, MA, Polity. Blackwell Publishers.

Extraordinary Chambers in the Courts of Cambodia (ECCC). 2015. *The Court Report: March 2015*. Phnom Penh, Cambodia.

Eldridge, C. 2010. Blurring the boundaries between perpetrators and victims: Pied-noir memories and the harki community. *Memory Studies*, *3* (2): 123–136.

Gottesman, E. R. 2003. *Cambodia after the Khmer Rouge: Inside The Politics Of Nation Building*. New Haven: Yale University Press.

Hughes, R. 2003. Nationalism and memory at the Tuol Sleng Museum of Genocide Crimes, Phnom Penh, Cambodia. In *Contested Pasts: The Politics of Memory*. K. Hodgkin and S. Radstone (eds). New York, London: Routledge. 175–192.

Hughes, R. 2005. Memory and sovereignty in post-1979 Cambodia: Choeung Ek and local genocide memorials. In *Genocide in Cambodia and Rwanda: New Perspectives*. S. Cook (ed). New Haven, CT: Yale University Center for International and Area Studies.

Hughes, R. 2008. Dutiful tourism: Encountering the Cambodian genocide. *Asia Pacific Viewpoint*, *49* (3): 318–330.

Ledgerwood, J. 1997. The Cambodian Tuol Sleng Museum of Genocidal Crimes: National Narrative. *Museum Anthropology*, *21* (1): 82–98.

Madlingozi, T. 2010. On transitional justice entrepreneurs and the production of victims. *Journal of Human Rights Practice*, *2* (2): 208–228.

Manning, P. 2012. Governing memory: Justice, reconciliation and outreach at the Extraordinary Chambers in the Courts of Cambodia. *Memory Studies*, *5* (2): 165–181.
Manning, P. 2015. Reconciliation and perpetrator memories in Cambodia. *International Journal of Transitional Justice*, *9* (3): 386–406.
McEvoy, K. 2007. Beyond legalism: Towards a thicker understanding of transitional justice. *Journal of Law and Society*, *34* (4): 411–440.
McEvoy, K. and McConnachie, K. 2012. Victimology in transitional justice: Victimhood, innocence and hierarchy. *European Journal of Criminology*, *9* (5): 527–538.
McEvoy, K. and McConnachie, K. 2013. Victims and transitional justice: Voice, agency and blame. *Social & Legal Studies*, *22* (4): 489–513.
Mutua, M. 2015. What is the future of transitional justice? *International Journal of Transitional Justice*, *9* (1): 1–9.
Pham, P., Vinck, P., Balthazard, M., Hean, S. and Stover, E. 2009. *So We Will Never Forget: A Population-Based Survey on Attitudes about Social Reconstruction and the Extraordinary Chambers in the Courts of Cambodia.* Berkeley, CA: Human Rights Center.
Williams, P. 2004. Witnessing genocide: vigilance and remembrance at Tuol Sleng and Choeung Ek. *Holocaust and Genocide Studies*, *18* (2): 234–254.

8 Beyond the tribunal

Genocide memory in Cambodia is being pulled in a diverse and often conflicted set of directions. On the one hand, as I have tried to show in the previous chapters, the Extraordinary Chambers in the Courts of Cambodia (ECCC) prosecutions have involved and catalysed a series of juridical, therapeutic and civic claims over memories of the Khmer Rouge. These claims are propagated by and enmeshed within an assemblage of organisations and networks that implicitly and explicitly address their formal expertise towards *memories*. On the other hand, beyond the immediate work of the ECCC and human-rights and civil society organisations, Cambodian communities enjoy a complicated and varied set of relationships with memories of political violence. This is not to suggest that there are clear and stable oppositions of 'local' and 'official' memories in Cambodia. Rather, a range of actors have made the Khmer Rouge years and wider civil war stand for different meanings and uses – visible often through work around memorial sites – that mean that memories of atrocity are pulled between complex private and public, sacred and profane, reverential and commercial, ethical and political and, indeed, local, national and international imperatives. This chapter examines and tries to disentangle some of the ways that sites of memory are rallied to and caught between such frameworks. I argue that a consequence of these varied practices of memory, understandably, is that many Cambodians feel ambivalences towards the pasts that are called attention to through prevailing memorial practices.

My focus in this chapter are Cambodian accounts of the Wat Thmey pagoda and genocide memorial in Siem Reap, where, in early 2009, I spent time visiting to observe the day-to-day life of the site and speaking to nearby residents and attendees. I begin the chapter by introducing Wat Thmey while trying to map the social and political role of pagodas within Cambodian communities today. The second section situates the Wat Thmey memorial within a history of Cambodian state-sanctioned memorial initiatives dedicated to the atrocities of the Khmer Rouge that started in the 1980s. In the third section, I look at the key representational technologies at work at the memorial site: the display of mass human remains and the employment of an information board that positions the site towards an international tourist audience. The fourth section tries to present a series of Cambodian accounts and perspectives about the Wat Thmey memorial to illustrate the often ambivalent views Cambodians can have towards these kinds of memorial practice.

I outline the varied and uneven way the memorial animates conflicted, resistant and uncertain memories of political violence. The final section contrasts these day-to-day accounts of Wat Thmey with a significant state-led commemorative initiative, the May 20th 'Day of Remembrance'.

The Wat Thmey genocide memorial

Wat Thmey[1] – translated simply as 'new temple' – is located roughly 3km North of Siem Reap on a small road running toward the UNESCO World Heritage Angkor temples (Cambodia's principal tourist attraction). I first visited Wat Thmey in 2005. At that time, the surrounding land around the pagoda[2] was relatively sparse, to the extent that the tourism boom in Siem Reap witnessed over the past two decades (and attendant increases in land values) had not encroached on the area through visible (and soon to follow) property development or intensive construction work. To the south of the pagoda was a major local children's hospital and, in 2005, the early signs of some building development. To the north lay a forested area protected by the Autorité pour la Protection du Site et l'Aménagement de la Région d'Angkor (APSARA) Angkor heritage authorities (the group charged with the management of the Angkor conservation area), and to the west of the compound, land use remained principally agricultural, with the only immediately proximal public amenity a small children's school.

By 2009, the area had changed dramatically. Since the end of the war in 1999, Siem Reap has sprawled from its centre outwards in all directions but particularly along arterial routes, and the area around Wat Thmey had visibly 'urbanised': much of the road from Siem Reap to the temples was itself now lined with Cambodian, Thai, Chinese and Korean-owned hotels, new residential properties and, directly opposite the Wat Thmey pagoda compound, a large development of pink condominiums with ground-floor office and retail units. Many of these apartments were vacant, with for-sale or rental signs placed in the windows, and only a few of the ground-floor units were in use. The nascent tourism and property 'booms' have been characterised by the 'pricing out' of less affluent sections of society from the property and rental markets, particularly in 'high end' developments such as condominiums and especially for those without access to established patrimonial political networks. As Springer has noted, the marketisation of Cambodia's post-conflict economy has afforded opportunities for existing elites to – often kleptocratically – consolidate, expand and acquire capital through existing patronage networks; importantly, this has conterminously afforded new forms of political control and regulation through the distribution of capital, that is, property titles or material and economic support for social, public and religious bodies (Springer 2009, 2011). Religious institutions exist alongside and within these contexts and are not exempt or immune from the political and economic interests that are bound to such patronage networks. This reality is at odds with the purported apolitical and market-exempt role that pagodas are meant to enjoy within Cambodian public life (Kent 2007). This has important implications for the wider injunction to remember atrocities and suffering that attends transitional justice and human-rights thinking, because memorials erected at religious sites not only exist within locally embedded political networks but are also subject to economic demands that can entail the 'commoditisation' of memories of violence. The politicisation and 'marketisation' of memory might grate against ethical duties to remember that are predicated on affording a sense of justice and dignity for victims of the regime, rather than through generating revenue or political capital.

As Kent has noted, the proliferation of newly constructed pagodas and the reassertion of Buddhism as central component of public life has been a hallmark of Cambodia's transition to peace and its attempts to re-establish social and moral order (Kent 2007). At the same time, because Cambodia's economic fortunes have blossomed in uneven ways – principally in favour of existing political patronage networks – pagodas are increasingly subject to the demands of their immediate and wider political and economic environments. Pagodas tend to be maintained and funded by donations from members of the local community. As a result of the uneven distribution of the fruits of economic expansion, pagodas must also seek recourse to political support and patronage – which in turn confers religious authority, making 'merit'[3] and political capital to the patron – or look for alternative means of generating revenue. As I will outline, the negotiation of a role as a 'sacred space' within both political networks and relations of economic exchange remains a vexed issue for pagodas and their perception by Cambodians.

In accordance with Buddhist practice in Cambodia, the pagoda site is comprised of and structured around a central *vihear* (temple), which is the focus of daily ritual activity (Chouléan 1988; Marston 2006). Wat Thmey also housed a community of monks and supports a school facility that teaches basic general education and *pali*[4]. Pagoda compounds also usually include a set of memorial *chedais* (stupas)[5] dedicated to and preserving the remains of deceased venerable monks and abbots. The central *vihear* is the lynchpin from which the outer perimeter boundaries of the pagoda compound are demarcated. Drawing on Mary Douglas' seminal *Purity and Danger* (1991), Kent explains how the perimeter limits of any pagoda are important for the wider community because they also designate the boundaries of a key set of distinctions and dichotomies that are crucial for the maintenance of social order: not only sacred and profane and religious and secular, but also, importantly, the designation of a purified space that is *intended* to be 'immune' from the realm of politics and economic exchange (Kent 2007: 337–338).

Pagodas are a key point of mediation between spiritual and secular realms. They are therefore the focus of exceptional religious observances and holy days. These include *Visaka Bochea* (honouring the birth, enlightenment and passing of Buddha) and *Meak Bochea* (venerating the teachings of Buddha); and, whilst the Khmer New Year is a largely secular observance, traditionally falling to mark the end of the harvest season, offerings and rites are performed at pagodas to 'make merit' for the new year ahead. One of the most important annual observances in Cambodian pagodas is *P'Chum Ben* or the 'ancestors' festival'. *P'Chum Ben* usually falls in September or October and is observed over two weeks to honour and pacify the spiritual realm of past ancestors. During *P'Chum Ben*, the monastic community and pagoda site act as the key points of mediation between the living and the dead. Cambodian communities provide offerings of rice balls, representing 'merit' transfer and thus the spiritual rejuvenation of the community. Notably, Kent has suggested that the "rapid revival of *P'Chum Ben* since the end of the war may be understood in part as an attempt to reassert the distinction between the realm of the dead and the living, and thus to mollify the country's traumatic history" (2007: 342). This is an important point to bear in mind, as the state-directed memorialisation and commemoration of the Khmer Rouge period – practices that do not originate in religious or theological tradition – have increasingly appropriated religious elements, rites and iconographies.

In the centre of the Wat Thmey pagoda compound is a memorial *stupa* to victims of the Khmer Rouge. The centrality, size and form of the *stupa* immediately set it aside as exceptional from the other *stupas* at the rear of the compound (which, notably, only memorialise individuals: revered religious leaders and abbots). The local authorities and religious leaders ordered the construction of the memorial *stupa* in 1996 in accordance with the design of Cambodia's principal national memorial site outside Phnom Penh at Choeung Ek; there is an elevated pavilion and awnings decorated according to Buddhist iconographies and a lower half devoted to the public display of human remains – 'primary artefacts' – of victims of the Khmer Rouge (see R. Hughes, 2005, for a detailed discussion of the Choeung Ek memorial). As Hughes has suggested, the deployment of pavilion structures at such memorial sites is intended to indicate a place of 'cultural learning', whilst the use of traditional Buddhist funerary colouration around the lower half of the *stupa* (white) infers meanings of death and impermanence, alongside the availability of incense sticks for prayer to those deceased. Against this, the mass display of human remains runs counter to traditional funerary practice, with the preservation of human remains usually reserved only for individuals of venerable status (Hughes 2005: 274–275). The memorial is, in this sense, conflicted in its religious and political meanings because it is laden with both 'sacred' and 'profane' associations, complicating its role as a carrier and cue of memories of atrocity. This means that the Wat Thmey *stupa* potentially stirs similar discomfort for Khmer audiences, a recurring response I encountered during fieldwork at the memorial.

Wat Thmey in context

Memorials to war, conflict and atrocities enjoy changing meanings over time, developing a biographical life of their own. The Wat Thmey memorial has its own history, which must be traced back to the state-directed nationwide practices of memorialisation conducted in the 1980s. Local authorities and religious leaders ordered the construction of the current *stupa* (in its religious form) in 1996, though the site also hosted and is haunted by earlier memorial initiatives launched under the Vietnamese backed People's Republic of Kampuchea government (1979–1989). From 1983, the People's Republic of Kampuchea established a 'Genocide Research Committee' tasked with disinterring provincial mass graves across the country. The People's Republic of Kampuchea state instructed local and district authorities to display anonymous human remains in public – often simply in wooden display boxes – in order to provide public evidence of the atrocities of the 'Pol Pot–Ieng Sary clique', cautioning the population against their return to power (R. Hughes 2005; Gottesman 2003). The association of human remains and the guilt of the Khmer Rouge leadership were – and remain – central to the preferred 'national' narrative of Khmer Rouge violence promoted by the Cambodian state, though it is also corresponds to key forensic tropes at work at the ECCC in evidencing proof of mass atrocity. Moreover, local authorities have more recently made explicit connections between the memorial and the ECCC by publicising ECCC outreach materials in display cases at Wat Thmey. In this sense, the memorial has been made to connect to wider systems of meaning about blame and accountability that implicate claims that scale up and down from community to national memories.

The Wat Thmey memorial evidences the international currency of modern *nationalist* and *nationalising* memorial practices in two senses. On the one hand, Anderson's writing on the rise of the 'Tomb of the Unknown Soldier' reminds us of the incongruity of anonymous mass memorialisation as a technique for remembering anything but the sacrifice of *national subjects*: one cannot imagine "a Tomb of the Unknown Marxist or a cenotaph of fallen liberals" (2006: 10). The very possibility of a national subject and national sacrifice are therefore mutually authorising. On the other, anonymity in memorial practices – beyond allowing the memory of "everyone but no one in particular" (Gillis 1994: 11) – emerged reflecting the arbitrariness of mass violence afflicting 'national' populations, a defining feature of 'total warfare' during World War II. This is an important bridging point for the case at hand because it begins to blur the memorialisation of combatants and civilians. In Cambodia, Rachel Hughes has noted how state-led memorial practices in the 1980s, employing anonymous human remains, represented a bid to nationally reclaim, or re-'know' victims that cannot be understood as having been 'sacrificed' (2005).

The Wat Thmey memorial was one of dozens of memorials erected across Cambodia's provinces in the wake of the Khmer Rouge in the 1980s that were meant to legitimate the new government. The People's Republic of Kampuchea intended these memorials to address Cambodians through a prevailing national account of loss and salvation from the Khmer Rouge. Provincial memorial sites also provided the foci for a key state-led commemorative activity that began in the 1983 but continues today, albeit in a differing guise: *Tivea Chang Khmaeng* or 'The Day of Maintaining Anger' (R. Hughes 2000). From 1983, local communities were encouraged by their authorities to attend mass grave sites every May 20th[6] in order to denounce the atrocities of 'Pol Pot'. 'Victim's representatives' were asked to testify about their experiences under the Khmer Rouge; prominent figures from the local authorities would offer speeches condemning the Pol Pot regime; and vigilance was urged against a return of the Khmer Rouge. Hughes has suggested that although 'The Day of Maintaining Anger' was an explicitly state choreographed commemoration, the ceremony still at least resonated with Cambodian peoples' experiences of the Khmer Rouge (2000). From then on, observance of the May 20th commemoration varied contingently on prevailing political currents and the Cambodian state's military and political strategy towards the Khmer Rouge resistance. The commemoration was observed at memorial sites through the late 1980s while the insurgency continued, but, with the advent of peace negotiations in 1991, the United Nations (UN) intervention during the United Nations Transitional Authority (UNTAC) period (1992–93) and the Royal Government of Cambodia's (RGC) explicit aim of reconciling former Khmer Rouge from 1994 onwards, 'maintaining' public 'anger' became less of a political priority. The RGC resumed the ceremonies in 1999 as negotiations with the UN for the establishment of the ECCC began, demonstrating their commitment to pursuing accountability, and 'The Day of Maintaining Anger' continues to be subject to state direction today, though it is now termed the 'Day of Remembrance'. The renaming of the commemoration can be read to reflect the transition from war and to the currency of a politics of 'regret' (Olick 2007): the Cambodian state now no longer needs to 'maintain' an active public grievance or vigilance but can still garner political legitimacy from promoting the memory of both the victims of the Khmer Rouge and their own role in defeating them. In the final section of this chapter, I discuss my attendance at this event at Wat Thmey in 2009.

Representation, blame, ownership and memory

Alongside the display of bones in the *stupa* casing at the Wat Thmey memorial was an information board written principally in English, inviting donations from tourists. The lower half of the board featured photographs of former Khmer Rouge leaders (those still under detention at the ECCC as well as the deceased Ieng Sary, Ta Mok and Pol Pot); public education materials from the ECCC (though these were absent in 2005); and, notably, images reproduced from the S-21 museum site in Phnom Penh. Williams has suggested that each memorial and museum site involves a complex organisation of objects, artefacts and displays to communicate a 'cluster' of meanings about victimhood and responsibility (2007: 25). Yet, at Wat Thmey, the effect of the information board was to flatten the category of victim. The board provided no detail, in either Khmer or English, about who died at the site, their ages or genders. Moreover, the board offered no contextual background on why victims might have died here (or any historical information about the regime) and beyond imported imagery from Tuol Sleng, there was nothing to indicate how they may have died – whether from execution, starvation, disease or otherwise – beyond the claim that they died nearby, between the years of 1975 and 1979. In this sense, the board and *stupa* operate together to maintain the anonymity of victims to be remembered, beyond the implicit representation of victims as innocent national subjects that died during the 1975–1979 period. Moreover, as with the case of Tuol Sleng, we should remind ourselves of the problems of representing victims or perpetrators as 'pure' categories (Bernath 2015); the remains on display might include victims who were themselves also once perpetrators.

The information board at Wat Thmey did make more explicit references to questions of responsibility. Authorities tasked with managing the site have included pictures of those accused at the ECCC (Nuon Chea, Khieu Samphan and the now deceased Ieng Sary) within the information board, alongside images of Pol Pot's corpse at the site of his death, and Ta Mok (formerly detained awaiting trial at the ECCC, but now deceased). Tellingly, these images are captioned in Khmer, calling Cambodian attendees to the representation of blame depicted through the board. In one of the corners of the display case is the ECCC text 'Introduction to the Khmer Rouge Trials'. In this sense, religious leaders at the site have made a direct connection between the memorial and the ECCC. The inclusion of ECCC materials raises important issues concerning the 'layering' and scaling of memory cues, specifically through the assemblage and addition of new objects, images or texts in particular sequences or orders. Representing blame through explicit connections to the work of the ECCC appears to reanimate and retrieve the historical work of the memorial in locating responsibilities for the atrocities of Democratic Kampuchea at the feet of the Khmer Rouge leadership.

A second issue that complicates the assemblage of meanings on the information board is the deployment of imagery from the Tuol Sleng 'S-21' Museum of Genocide Crimes in Phnom Penh. Images directly taken from the S-21 prison cells, portrait photographs, pictures of torture instruments used at Tuol Sleng and the paintings of S-21 survivor Vann Nath are displayed on the board as if authentic to the '*in situ*' history of violence at the Wat Thmey pagoda itself. The question of the local 'inauthenticity' of such images is, on the one hand, in tension with the authority of the site as a display of human remains or *in situ* 'primary' evidence of political violence. The mobility of such images is important. Hughes has discussed the removal of S-21 imagery from its original site in Phnom Penh in her analysis of the presence of S-21 portrait photographs internationally, specifically audienced at New York's MoMA 1997 *Photographs from S-21* exhibition (R. Hughes 2003). Hughes seeks to show how internationalised discourses of 'humanitarian management' render such images appropriable in the international construction of an 'ex-locus memorial' to the Khmer Rouge. One effect, Hughes argues, is to pathologise violence in the minds of international audiences as endemic to Cambodia (2003). The presence of S-21 imagery at Wat Thmey raises an attendant set of questions in this context. The re-circulation of the prevailing, dominant imagery of the Khmer Rouge period from Tuol Sleng – through photographs of victim portraits and torture instruments – in order to represent past suffering at Wat Thmey shows how the depiction of specific experiences of the Khmer Rouge period can be made to stand as a synecdoche for the wider whole, in a similar way to how a narrow set of prosecutions at the ECCC is made to stand for a wider public experience of generic national violence.

The English language text on the information board raises a final set of questions about the principal audiences addressed by the memorial. On the one hand, because the memorial appropriates both religious Buddhist and national iconographies, it invokes a particular repertoire of meanings for Khmer attendees. On the other, as it addresses tourists, it repositions the memorial to an international and transient audience. A box marked 'donation' was located alongside incense sticks that may be burned as offerings to the dead. The implications for a sense of 'ownership' are significant: the promotion of Cambodia's memorial sites as tourist attractions, or sites of consumption and witnessing, complicates Cambodian relationships with these sites. As Sturken has suggested, the consumption of such representations within a tourist economy seems to conflict with the role of such spaces as sights of reverence and mourning (2007). Elsewhere, commenting on a deal to 'franchise' the ticket concession at the Choeung Ek memorial site near Phnom Penh to a Japanese and Korean owned firm) Youk Chhang, head of the Documentation Centre of Cambodia (DC-Cam), remarked that "This is about the memory of a country, of a nation – and that's something important for the survivors. Memories cannot be contracted, cannot be sold, cannot be purchased – and therefore it should be in the hands of Cambodian survivors to maintain the place" (BBC 2005). But that is exactly what has happened at Choeung Ek and, in a personal interview, Chhang noted that sites like Tuol Sleng and Choeung Ek are now principally tourist attractions.

Monetising encounters with memory through ticket receipts to tour the Choeung Ek memorial near Phnom Penh implies that memory undergoes a form of commodification. The commodification of genocide memory could be argued to conflict with the central aims of a memorial: to dignify the memories of victims and to learn lessons from the past. Why is this? The commodification of memory appears to run counter to the prevailing normative imperatives of a 'politics of regret' because it implies that memories of atrocities are debased as objects of exchange, instrumental use and profit. This seems to grate against the notion of regret in two ways. Firstly, memorials are thought to protect the inherent dignity of victims. Extracting profit from genocide memory seems to conflict with the idea of dignity as an intrinsic good. Moreover, that memories are instrumentally used for profit could be read as grating with an understanding of memory that sees memories constitute who we are as social beings, for individuals as a sense of self and for collective groups through a sense of a shared past. Adopting Marx's spectacles for a moment, we might argue that the commodification, sale and profit generated from memories could, therefore, imply a form of *alienation* from memory. Secondly, harnessing memory for deployment within tourist economies represents a highly instrumental use of the past. This conflicts with the premise that there are clear and stable lessons to be had from memories of atrocity that oblige reverential observance and deter further violence.

It seems that dignity – as a normative lynchpin of transitional justice – and monetisation may stand in tension here. But the cases of Choeung Ek and Wat Thmey are not identical in these respects. What is not clear in the case of Choeung Ek is whether concerns should focus more on the principle of monetising or commodifying genocide memory itself, or whether the ticket concession of the site to a 'foreign' Japanese and Korean company drives a sense of unease. Wat Thmey is owned by the local monastic community, in an occupational sense, even as it relies on tourist donations for its maintenance and upkeep. On the one hand, the Wat Thmey memorial case appears less clear cut as an example of 'commodified' memory in the absence of a straightforward monetary transaction at the site, that is, there was no formal ticket concession. On the other, especially in light of the fact that the representational devices at play seem to have been appropriated from one of Cambodia's principal tourist attractions and presented as if authentic to the *in situ* experience of the site, the presence of the donation box implies a sequence that translates 'consuming' the memorial, obliging memory and, consequently, giving money. The fact that donations at Wat Thmey seem to contribute to the provision of a range of community functions, including religious rites and education, raises important, puzzling questions about appropriate and inappropriate memorial practices and uses. As I show in the coming sections, the monks and attendees I spoke to seemed to adopt a largely pragmatic and often ambivalent approach to these conflicts.

The lives of local memorials

I spent time around Wat Thmey in early 2009, talking to monks and occasionally more senior *achars* (religious figures who lead ceremonies and who are tasked with upkeep of the memorial), larking around with students at the pagoda and speaking to people that lived and worked in the local area. Most Cambodian visitors attended the pagoda to *make merit*, a specific set of Buddhist and animistic ceremonies that were intended to ward off inauspicious spiritual forces or interpreted and employed essentially as 'good luck' or 'good fortune' rituals. Amongst those most regularly present at Wat Thmey were students attending school or being supported through food and board by the monastic community. Others were longer-staying visitors from other provinces seeking the pagoda's provision of affordable accommodation. In this sense, whilst the memorial to the victims of the Khmer Rouge was central to the layout and composition of the pagoda, the memorial itself seemed largely secondary to Cambodians' relationships to the pagoda. Indeed, for some informants, the memorial and the history it signifies seemed separate. They preferred to talk about the history of the memorial itself, rather than the history it stood for, tending to describe the *stupa* in isolation from its representational work and context. One monk prosaically explained that:

> The bones are rotting. It's gone down [the volume/number of bones] because the bones are rotting. They are almost soil inside. They are eroded. Maybe it's leaking from the rain.

Another remarked:

> Before the monks collected the bones from the field nearby and put them in the *stupa*. Before it was full, you see [gesturing to the *stupa*] it is now not full. It is difficult to protect the bones. Now it is not full. In the past the bones were in a wooden box, before the *stupa* was built [in 1996].

The concern, here, is registered around the importance of protecting bones, assuming processes of decay, but he elided a connection to why protection might be important or to wider debates around the need for public evidence that started when the first memorials erected after Democratic Kampuchea were built.

Other attendees I asked about the memorial were quicker to address the connections between the site, a public history of atrocities and personal recollections of violence. As one local resident pointed out:

> Before [there were] no people were living here. Many people were living nearer [Siem Reap] the city, but not here. Here, you know, they just grew rice, just a few people, but I know what happened here.
>
> Peter Manning [PM]: What happened?
>
> This place, here, they stand the people in line. Many, many… [lost thread] You know Khmer Rouge? The killing field [pointing away from the compound], they take them from far away and come here and kill them near here… One day, one car would come. One by one, people from Siem Reap city, they cut, they kill many people near here.

Conversations I had around the memorial 'cue', however, seemed to furnish varying responses in this regard. Several local residents explained their experiences of the regime *in situ* of the memorial, and conversations about the memorial site were often elided or interspersed with personal reflections of life under Democratic Kampuchea. I was left with the sense that these informants assumed that this was what I *wanted* to hear about, and attendant to this, what a white European *should* be told:

> Many of my family died, my aunt and sisters. I don't know a lot about the Pol Pot time or that place [the memorial]. We found it hard to survive that time. There was no rice to eat, it was very difficult. I don't understand what happened.

The 'extractive' relationship implied here – obliging the disclosure of memory for the Western visitor – was troubling because the tendency to present personal experiences was forthcoming without my asking.[7] Of course, retelling experiences of suffering could well be understood within the imperative that others *should and must know* about them. Yet from the conversations I had – despite explaining that my research was focused on the memorial as a significant public site – local residents and attendees of the pagoda assumed that my presence at the site was to look at bones and, at times, hear stories of about experiences of the Khmer Rouge. In the first instance, discussion of the Khmer Rouge period rather than the memorial itself may have been preferable because of the overtly political history of the memorial, which is troubling in the way it implies that there is greater discomfort talking about public politics than private loss. But equally, the implication that Western visitors, assumed to be tourists, *should* be furnished with stories of suffering raises questions about the way Cambodia's sites of memory have been inserted into a tourist economy. The possibility that such inter-personal dynamics extend to furnishing Western academics with the very same recollections and narratives is even more worrying.

Over the course of the fieldwork, I frequently spoke to one group of students that had grown up in the area. They seemed to enjoy the novelty of a foreigner present and seemed to like to practice their English with me, comparing our notepads and stationery. I would often also try to ask them what they thought about the memorial site in these conversations. Yet the memorial, rather than the history it called attention to, seemed a source of discomfort for them. In particular, the presence of human remains was a problem:

> When I was young I went to play over there [pointing away, toward the east of the pagoda]. When I finished, I'd come back past. I'm afraid, you know. I was always very afraid. Because the bones are like that, there are ghosts. I'm afraid.
>
> PM: Are [other] Cambodians scared of this place?
>
> Yes they are scared of this place… before I lived here. I have seen something. The bones were on the field, behind the pagoda, near here. But behind in a small river they cut one by one and they used the gun… And also over there in the forest and on the road to Angkor Wat [pointing East again]. Many people here died because of Pol Pot. When I was young I wanted to play here. But I saw the bones. We were too small, just young boys, we just picked fruit, but near the tree I looked and I thought 'oh, many bones'.

The presence of bones within the *stupa* and the pagoda compound pose several problems. On the one hand, our conversation suggests an acceptance of the principal meaning intended by the memorial: that the Khmer Rouge leadership was responsible for mass atrocity. On the other, the recounting of knowledge of both killing sites and the remains of violence (signalling danger) is positioned against adolescent accounts of 'play' and recreation (signalling safety). Collecting the primary artefacts of violence – human remains – and displaying them within a space that is demarcated as 'sacred' and functional for the community is transgressive in this sense. For Cambodians of all ages, human remains are closely associated with notions of spirit and spirituality and, in lay terms, the topics of ghosts and spirits tends to stir fear (particularly visible in these accounts of adolescence). At the same time, the pagoda, temple and monks are considered the key agents in mediating the relationship between 'life' and 'death' or, rather, between the fields of mortality and fields of spirituality. In this sense, the memorial occupies an uncomfortable place within a site of wider spiritual importance for the community.

The students were a good source of insight into the principal visitors to the site:

> PM: So who comes here then [pointing at the memorial *stupa*]?
>
> It's only tourists here. But sometimes [Cambodian] people come for the teachers, about Buddhism and the Buddhist story. Sometimes [Cambodians come] for the ceremony, like *P'Chum Ben*. They come here to enjoy, giving offerings to the monks… They pray to their grandfather, grandmother, like that.

One of the other students added:

> After the monks got the money from the tourists the pagoda got bigger. All the pictures you see, they're from Tuol Sleng!

The students were well aware of the fact that the photographs on display were not immediately 'authentic' to the history of the site. Moreover, these comments seem to illustrate that there are dual roles at work at the site: for the memorial in attracting tourists (linked through the Tuol Sleng pictures) as well as its religious functions and support. According to these accounts, there is no immediate conflict between the two.

The students tended to be keen to shift conversation away from the topic of memorial itself. As Hughes has suggested (2005), this may stem from their discomfort in confronting human bones because of the spiritual implications of uncremated remains: there are difficult questions posed by the remains because they violate appropriate Buddhist funerary practice, which demands the urgent cremation of those who died in inauspicious circumstances, and the visibility of the remains connotes danger and the presence of 'ghosts'. The students generally preferred other conversation (about the players of different English football teams, mostly; Wayne Rooney was very popular, much to my dismay as a Tottenham Hotspur devotee). Indeed, the group of students preferred talking about their own stories of who had come to visit Wat Thmey, often skilfully evading my attempts to talk about the memorial:

> You know, Peter? Before Jackie Chan came here! You know him? He is a handsome man. He came here with the USA people.
>
> PM: What did he do here?
>
> He came to support the children that [have] got HIV. Also the parents [that have] got HIV. He came to support the pagoda, he gave the money.
>
> PM: What about the pagoda, the monks, how do they help people?
>
> The monks also help people, of course. They support the parents without the [financial] ability, without the money. If parents find it difficult to find money for studying or if they need to find a place to stay. They pay a little for rice and the room.

These exchanges show how pagodas in Cambodia play an important role as loci of the community in their various religious, pastoral and pedagogical capacities (providing schooling and accommodation). For the students, the memorial itself seemed secondary, incidental or unwelcome as a central feature of the compound otherwise. Other visitors and nearby residents showed only a reluctant interest in the memorial. "Oh that place. I don't know about that," remarked one nearby resident. Another pointed out: "What does that matter now? Look around, this place changed very fast, I don't think that is important now." These tendencies are important to note for two reasons. Firstly, they show ambivalence towards attempts to call attention to memories of the Khmer Rouge as demanded by the memorial and presence of bones. Moreover, these responses gesture to Connerton's claim that memorials are poor vehicles for anchoring memory. For Connerton, memory flourishes within the often ignored but stable features of our lives, like our homes or streets (2009: 10). In this sense, the rapid urbanisation and changes affecting the Wat Thmey area could be understood to undermine the 'continuity' of memory (Cohen 2001: 243).

Explicitly antagonist or appreciative views about the memorial were rare. Those who objected to the memorial tended to do so coextensively with critiques of the government, linking the memorial to the history of the Vietnamese occupation and the apparent undue influence of Vietnam over the current government and through appeals for Khmer solidarity in the present. Those approving of the memorial tended to slip into, or reflect, overtly politicised explanations of its role and importance. One junior monk's comments notably correspond to the government's longstanding 'script' about 'salvation' from the Khmer Rouge:

> On January 7 [liberation day, marking the fall of the KR] then people come here, because they know. It's because Khmer people are very grateful to the Prime Minister... They know from him, know that he helped them, they nearly all died [under the Khmer Rouge], but after that he helped them so much and saved Cambodia.

The explanation of 'salvation' thanks to Hun Sen reflects the official state-sanctioned narrative about Khmer Rouge violence that the memorial reflects and anchors. At the same time, that such remarks were rare seems to point to a broader 'banality' in everyday perspectives about the past that the memorial lays claim to. Many local residents and attendees did not seem to see the memorial as relevant to them or the pagoda, beyond the support it afforded through donations.

Memorials and memorialisation are increasingly incorporated into transitional justice strategies because of their purportedly pedagogical and deterrent messages. Yet pedagogical and deterrent readings of the memorial were very uneven among the Cambodians I spoke to. One exception to this tendency was provided by an older resident living in the vicinity of Wat Thmey. I asked if and how the memorial was important for the community:

> Maybe if they keep those things [bones] the young might learn what happened during the Pol Pot time.
>
> PM: Do you think it is important for younger people to learn about the Pol Pot time?
>
> Sure. Maybe they learn the history more, they understand old person[s] better, maybe [they will] listen more. But that place [points in direction of memorial] is most important for make money.

There are two distinct imperatives invoked in this response. In the first instance, the older resident appeals to the importance of younger Cambodians learning about the 'Pol Pot time' as a way of enabling a 'better' understanding of the older generation. The key implication is that learning – fashioning knowledge of the Khmer Rouge period – enables understanding or acknowledgement. This imperative corresponds neatly to the work of advocacy groups such as DC-Cam that have principally targeted the education of young Cambodians as a way of 'dignifying' the experiences of survivors of the Khmer Rouge regime. The education of the younger generation is also a key outcome purported to follow from the ECCC proceedings. At the same time, the informant invokes a second imperative here – understanding the site as a source of revenue – and suggests that this is more 'important'. Although left unelaborated, the role of the site within the tourist economy is again heavily implied. This points to important issues regarding the representation of the past and practices of witnessing or consumption at Wat Thmey. Memorials lend themselves to these purposes because they tend to work to fix a particular representation of the past; in doing so, memorials *can* treat that past as static or as an object, which, like a commodity, can be consumed.

The monks seemed to treat the role of the memorial as a source of revenue for the pagoda as unproblematic, and the conversations I had at Wat Thmey did not seem to suggest that this posed questions about the 'ownership' of memory. Monks would frequently explain that very few Cambodians visited Wat Thmey in comparison with foreign visitors, emphasising the importance of tourism as a revenue stream for the upkeep and maintenance of the pagoda as a whole. As noted above, religious leaders had addressed the memorial to an international audience, with the information board (principally captioned in English) and donation box both addressed to tourists. Over the time I spent at Wat Thmey, it was clear that these groups were not infrequent in number. On a given morning, four or five buses would arrive in the compound, with tour groups staying at nearby hotels and accompanied by pre-arranged, independent guides. The larger group visits tended to include an examination of the information board and an encirclement of the memorial itself. Occasionally, the groups would oblige the donation box next to the memorial.

The Wat Thmey memorial is a site that offers a very specific, state-sponsored representation of the Khmer Rouge period through human remains as well as the Tuol Sleng portrait photos. Alongside its insertion into a tourist economy, we are obliged to address some important questions. On the one hand, the commodification of the past as an 'object' to be consumed gestures to arguments advanced in scholarship on 'dark tourism'. These suggest that the promotion and 'reification' of sites of suffering is directed to sate the appetite of globally mobile 'impulse purchasers' (Lennon and Foley 2000), which can be read as 'objectified' memory that may become 'estranged' and 'alien' to its constituents, that is, that community members can no longer feel attachments to memories that they have experienced. On the other hand, and bearing in mind the varied interpretations of the memorial mapped above, Hughes has argued that one the key *practices* of visitation to memorials (to Tuol Sleng specifically) includes 'dutiful' or 'humanitarian' witnessing. Such dutiful tourism is in turn constitutive of the meaning of sites of suffering as globally significant spaces. The tension here reflects debates about the role of memorial spaces as sites of either pilgrimage or of tourism and consumption, an opposition purportedly in conflict. As Lloyd notes, practices of pilgrimage imply mourning, reverence and 'dignification' (Lloyd 1998: 4); to 'tour' implies consumption, transience, 'kitsch' and trivialisation (Sturken 2007). The views of the local residents and attendees discussed above seem, on the one hand, to largely elide the idea that the memorial itself obliged reverence or pilgrimage. Yet, on the other, they equally seem not to view the insertion of the site within the tourist economy as a problem or trivialisation of painful memories. Their views, if anything, seemed understandably pragmatic in their relationship towards the site.

In April 2009, I had a brief conversation with one of the then more senior monks at Wat Thmey that seems now to bring together some of the varied issues and themes outlined above.

> PM: What do Cambodian people think of this memorial?
>
> You see not many Cambodians come. Only for the ceremonies, you know *P'Chum Ben* day, or Khmer New Year day. That's just what we believe.
>
> PM: But what about the bones on display?
>
> We don't want to keep the bones like this. It's not natural. We want to burn them, so all the ghosts can go away, to the new world.
>
> PM: After the court?
>
> We're not sure about the tribunal. They [the authorities] want us to keep [the bones] here for the younger generation to see. But young people don't come here much. Only international tourists come here. But that's good – for the building and for the food. There are many people coming here every day, 100, 200, 300 – 40 people on every bus. Look [pointing at a Korean group arriving]! There are many buses.
>
> PM: Have you lived here for a long time?
>
> Yes, since the 1990s. The *stupa* is now only half full because it eroded. It's not really good for the people of Cambodia. But for the next generation, it is good for the history – so this will never happen again. You know, many young Cambodians do not believe that this happened. They cannot believe that Khmer fight Khmer like this. Maybe this [memorial] help them understand. After the trial, I wish for all these bones to be cremated.

The senior monk seemed to have a more nuanced and pragmatic appraisal of the varied, competing demands that are being placed on the memorial site than the core normative approaches and scholarship in memory studies and transitional justice seem willing to accommodate: between the religious obligation to observe appropriate funerary practice and the political demand to preserve public evidence of the Khmer Rouge atrocities; between the functional roles of the pagoda as a sacred site of learning and the demands placed upon it through its insertion into the tourist economy; and, more broadly, the peripheral role the memorial itself had in relation to other Cambodian practices of visitation to the site. The memorial, in its everyday existence, seemed not to play a significant role as a carrier of memory.

The Day of Remembrance

The May 20th commemoration – previously the 'Day of Maintaining Anger', changed to the 'Day of Remembrance' in 2001[8] – is observed at sites of atrocity and mass graves under the direction of local Cambodian People's Party (CPP) authorities across Cambodia.[9] The May 20th commemorations are distinct in that their focus is ordered around memorial *stupas* that display the remains of Khmer Rouge victims (as opposed to, for example, *P'Chum Ben*, which is an extended ceremony that involves prayer and offerings to all passed ancestors at temples (*vihear*) – beyond victims of the Khmer Rouge). The key elements of the May 20th commemoration have included public testimony from victims of the regime about their experiences of Khmer Rouge rule, the public denouncement of the 'savagery' of senior Khmer Rouge leaders and the urging of vigilance, previously against the Khmer Rouge's return to power but now towards the preservation of 'evidence' about their atrocities. From their introduction in 1983, the provincial ceremonies encouraged the public to make and present placards along these themes at mass grave sites (Hughes 2000, 2005), though as the People's Republic of Kampuchea state adopted an increasingly tolerant approach towards the public practice of religion in the latter 1980s, the commemorations have also come to appropriate and incorporate religious themes: wreath laying, chanting in *pali* and collective prayer are now also key elements in the May 20th observations. It should be also be noted that opposition political parties reject the legitimacy of the May 20th commemorations, who suggest the observance is a CPP-engineered form of propaganda.

It is worth briefly considering another observation of the Day of Remembrance before turning to discuss the proceedings I observed at Wat Thmey in Siem Reap. At the Choeung Ek 'killing field' memorial outside Phnom Penh – Cambodia's principal national memorial site – the observance of May 20th has become increasingly elaborate over recent years. In 2009, students from the Royal University of Phnom Penh School of Fine Arts staged a series of re-enacted scenes intended to represent the rise, rule and fall of the Khmer Rouge to an audience of monks, senior government officials and groups of school children as well as selectively invited members of the public. The commemoration is intended 'to honour victims' and educate on the 'inhuman acts of the regime through performance' (Sreinith 2011). The re-enactments attempted a narrative account of the Khmer Rouge's seizure of power and a depiction of life under the Khmer Rouge before, finally, liberation (as salvation) by the Kampuchean United Front for National Salvation, the vanguard of the 1979 liberating forces and successor of the People's Republic of Kampuchea and now CPP governments. The fine arts students, dressed in black Khmer Rouge uniform, recreated scenes of mass killing with Khmer Rouge cadre binding and executing men, women and children, leaving the grass in front of the Choeung Ek *stupa* littered with 'dead' bodies. Survivors were depicted searching through the dead for lost relatives. The Khmer Rouge figures were then chased from the field by the liberating green uniformed forces of the Front, to be greeted by celebration and thanks by those survivors left. The performance ended with a parade of CPP and Cambodian national flags.

The commemoration appears to be a peculiar means of aestheticising and representing genocide memory: re-enactments as a representational device tend to be reserved for the 'glorification' of memories of political violence, such as imitating famous battles (Mayo 1988). This is important to note because, as Hughes suggests, victims of the Khmer Rouge cannot be understood as having been 'sacrificed' (2005). Moreover, as Mayo has pointed out, the re-enactment of political violence within sacred spaces is often problematic because violence is considered sacrilegious, raising questions about how appropriate the depiction of mass atrocity so proximate to the Choeung Ek religious *stupa* is. In this sense, we might think about the Day of Remembrance as an example of 'invented tradition' (Hobsbawm and Ranger 1983). The explicitly political narrative in the performances – hinging upon salvation from the Khmer Rouge and obliging national gratitude to the Vietnamese and People's Republic of Kampuchea as 'saviours' – is bound to the legitimation of the present Cambodian government, heirs of the People's Republic of Kampuchea and successor regimes. Moreover, in the context of the ECCC, the revival of the commemoration can be further understood as an attempt to contest the prevailing accusation that the Cambodian government is reluctant to confront the past or offer accountability for Khmer Rouge atrocities.

At Wat Thmey in Siem Reap, proceedings were less elaborate and did not include re-enactments, though they were still similarly choreographed and led by the local CPP officials. Around 2000 people were in attendance, including schoolchildren bussed in from the surrounding districts and communes.[10] The front rows of the audience were reserved for monks, CPP officials and their uniform of bodyguards, followed by rows of nuns and community leaders. The proceedings were also being filmed for broadcast on local television.

As I arrived, the monks were leading the commemoration chanting in *Pali*, alternating between offering a dedication of merit to the dead and emphasising the 'impermanence of material existence'. One of the senior monks invited the audience to participate in the chanting:

> Please ladies and gentleman and excellences, please chant after me to dedicate the memory to the dead. Please be rid of suffering and reach nirvana. We dedicate this to our ancestors, our fathers and mothers. We wish for a peaceful world.

The co-optation of religious rituals for a secular commemoration shows again how memorial and pagoda sites can be appropriated for political purposes. Moreover, the role of the monks leading the chant – borrowing from other Buddhist rituals, specifically *P'Chum Ben* – is evidence of a political colonisation of religious spaces and themes. I asked one monk to explain to me what was happening:

> Every year it is like this, it's never been changed. More people are coming every year – counting the bowls – offering food to the monks – this is merit making. This is the time to offer rice and food to the monks. We are making offerings directly to ancestors.

The monk describes the commemoration under terms that correspond to practices at the *P'Chum Ben* ancestors festival (particularly the reference to 'counting the bowls'), rather than the Day of Remembrance. I pressed this issue, asking the monk to explain further:

> We are Buddhists. We believe that this ceremony will release spirits. 'Bonn' in K'mai means merit.
>
> PM: So how is this ceremony different from *P'Chum Ben*?
>
> Not the same as *P'Chum Ben*. *P'Chum Ben* lasts for 14 days. This is just one day. And this one is just for some dignitaries and politicians. *P'Chum Ben* doesn't have the eulogies [to the victims of the KR]. Today they were teaching… like not to kill their own race, like in Pol Pot time.

Another monk added:

> This morning they testified about the Khmer Rouge. It is public denouncement. This is the way that the dead will be in peace. When we see the bones in this place, and we do this ceremony, everyone will be happier.

The commemoration in this sense hinges on two key memory techniques working in tandem. Again, this is an example of presenting what is to be known about the past and what it then obliges. In the morning, eulogy and testimonial are intended to recognise, remember and 'honour' experiences of life and loss under the Khmer Rouge. On this premise, the lesson of the commemoration, according to the monk, is a specifically national imperative: that the killing of one's *national/racial* kin is an exceptionally grave form of atrocity that must be prevented at all costs. This is essentially an appeal to national and racial solidarity.

May 20th has here harnessed religious ritual and language for the performance of an exercise in (secular) national mourning. This should not be read as a bid to conceal the political direction of the commemoration, but rather as a means of 'authenticating' and legitimising the messages and meanings that the commemoration conveys. A series of placards were embedded within wreaths of white funeral flowers (which would usually bed portraits or pictures of deceased individuals). These were clear in their political message:

> *VICTORIOUS CPP! WE ALWAYS REMEMBER THE ATROCITIES MADE BY POL POT IN CAMBODIA! LONG LIVE CAMBODIA! WE PROMISE TO PROTECT, WHATEVER IT TAKES, TO PROTECT ALL THE EVIDENCE!*

Alongside the CPP placards, more politically neutral banners were erected around the compound:

> *NATION-RELIGION-KING; HAPPINESS, PEACE AND DEVELOPMENT: THE TEACHINGS OF THE BUDDHA FOR ALL PEOPLE; NO OTHER PEACE IS BETTER THAN PEACE IN THE MIND; EARNING MERIT BRINGS YOU HAPPINESS AND PEACE*

The colonisation of the pagoda space, the appropriation of Buddhist funerary practices and the deployment of explicitly political messages through the Day of Remembrance illuminate a number of important issues. On the one hand, the Day of Remembrance can be understood as an example of an 'invented tradition' (Hobsbawm and Ranger 1983), whereby state elites reframe and operationalise the past in the service of political legitimation. Specifically here, the Buddhist framing of the performance serves to confer religious currency and authority onto the proceedings. On the one hand, recalling Ledgerwood's (1997) and Hughes' (2005) arguments, a caveat here is that, even if memory work is so overtly constructed on the terms of political interests, the past it seeks to represent may still resonate with the population to which it is directed. On the other hand, we know that opposition parties reject the legitimacy of the CPP-directed commemoration, the participation by the public on the Day of Remembrance was solicited directly from the CPP support base, and the presence of the school children as an audience was mandatory. It is clear that the Day of Remembrance is an exceptional commemoration that is unevenly received and remains a contested form of memorialisation.

As the proceedings began to conclude, monks and then figures from the local authority approached the memorial, lit incense sticks and began to pray. I spoke briefly to one senior party official about why he thought the Day of Remembrance was important:

> This ceremony was initiated by the CPP. The purpose is to dedicate merit to the ancestors. And secondly to teach the younger people about the Khmer Rouge time, the hunger the hardships and the anger.
>
> PM: I know that some Cambodians aren't sure about this place though. Perhaps they don't agree with the story that is told here. I know some people are afraid of the bones too. What would you say to them?
>
> I think they should keep the bones for historical fact. If we cremate, we'll lose the evidence and all the facts. Even after the trial, even after we find out who is responsible, we should keep the bones. To my understanding the tribunal is not about finding justice for everyone. It's about finding out about the techniques and approaches used by the Khmer Rouge.

The connection between the importance of preserving the bones, the ECCC process and ensuring that the younger generation learn about the Khmer Rouge period was surprising. The response appears to reflect the way some in the Cambodian government are committed to promoting memories of the Khmer Rouge, grating with claims by human-rights groups that the CPP's principal interest is in inducing a state of amnesia. This is, of course, an account of the past that is winnowed to suit the interests of the state; it is in this sense reflective of the ECCC prosecutions in the way that it focuses on the guilt of a handful of senior leaders while ignoring the role of lower-level perpetrators. What appears problematic about these bids to promote memory – the display of human remains, public testimony of experiences of the Khmer Rouge, the re-enactment of atrocities – is that there is very little room for more ambivalent or equivocal understandings of the past (a problem that corresponds to the rigid coding of memory as legal knowledge at the ECCC).

As the ceremony ended, a tour bus entered the compound. The tour group left the bus and proceeded to observe the (now familiar, if cursory) tour of the genocide memorial and information board, in a state of some confusion about the disembarking crowd of 2000 school children and rows of empty plastic seats.

Conclusion

The Wat Thmey pagoda and genocide memorial, its role within the community and its reception by Cambodians are haunted by a series of seemingly stark oppositions. It is first and foremost an explicitly political representation of political violence that employs the display of 'profane' human remains within a 'pure' and 'sacred' space. Moreover, Buddhist theology dictates that pagodas *should* be immune from the secular field of politics. The display of bones continues to produce uncomfortable responses among Cambodian attendees at the pagoda and, on this basis, the memorial does not necessarily produce the deterrent or pedagogical lessons it is intended to generate. Moreover, it seemed from the conversation I had around the memorial that it should not be understood specifically as a 'carrier' of collective memory. Rather, in calling attention to loss, the Wat Thmey memorial has developed a life of its own. The projection and insertion of the site within the tourist economy presents, on the one hand, an objectification of memories of political violence to be witnessed or consumed by transient tourist groups. On the other hand, the monastic community did not seem uncomfortable with this function of the memorial, and in this sense, the harnessing of the memorial for the maintenance and upkeep of the temple more broadly was a pragmatic initiative to ensure that the pagoda can continue to provide its pastoral and pedagogical roles within the community. In this sense, although the memorial itself remained a source of discomfort for some, it continues to be functionally important for the community.

The spectacular presentation of the Day of Remembrance at Wat Thmey contrasted sharply with the day-to-day meanings and appreciation of the memorial within the community. There is a reflexive point to be made about how memory works here: in interviewing, directing or focusing respondents on the memorial site, the memorial (and past) is called into being in uneven ways. Moreover, it seemed that the prevailing expectations of what a white, Western visitor would and should expect to encounter at such memorials – as a tourist or researcher – freighted conversations in ways I did not anticipate. This has serious consequences for the study of memory in the wake of past atrocity, because it shows that remembering occurs in relation to and, importantly, sometimes in resistance to the demands that are made of it. In a similar vein, the Day of Remembrance represents a reactivation and reassertion of prevailing state-sanctioned discourses of vigilance and national solidarity in the wake of atrocity that are elided in the more 'everyday' explanations of the memorial I encountered.

Notes

1 Wat Thmey is officially called *Wat Ateh Smaw Sann.*
2 I use the terms *temple* and *pagoda* interchangeably to describe the research site. Specifically though, the temple is one of – but the most important amongst – a set of buildings inside a pagoda.
3 *Making merit* refers to a specific set of Buddhist ceremonies and practices that, ideally, foster spiritual generosity and embody a denial of self. Politically, visibly 'making merit' therefore holds great currency. On a more day-to-day basis, the practice of Buddhism in Cambodia has historically been interwoven with animistic beliefs, and 'making merit', in everyday practice, is often intended to ward off inauspicious spiritual forces (or spirits). As one monk explained to me, these could be described as 'good luck' or 'good fortune' rituals.
4 *Pali* is the language through which the majority of Therrevada Buddhist scripts are written and ceremonies performed.
5 A *stupa* is a structure that contains religious artefacts or, usually, the remains of religious leaders. *Stupas* act as focal points for meditation and other rituals.
6 May 20th is observed as the anniversary of the Khmer Rouge's embracing of full-scale collectivisation of agricultural production and communal eating in 1973.
7 I had given assurances on requisite ethics checklists prior to fieldwork that I would specifically avoid asking about personal experiences of the regime, given the sensitive, invasive and potentially harmful nature of such interviewing. In the field, I felt it more a violence to shut down such conversations once started.
8 The Cambodian government has not publicly explained the change in the title of the commemoration. The change is likely reflective of previous gaps in its observance, such as during peace talks in 1991 when 'maintaining anger' was deemed incompatible with the push for a political solution to the civil war. In this sense, the change in name could be read to reflect the end of the civil war in 1999, shifting the obligation of 'maintaining anger' to one of memory.
9 Cambodian opposition groups do not recognise May 20th as a legitimate day of commemoration of Khmer Rouge atrocities.
10 A colleague accompanying me also encountered a number of friends from his commune. He was unaware that they intended to attend; he also voiced his own surprise about the scale and scope of the proceedings.

References

Anderson, B. 2006. *Imagined Communities: Reflections on the Origin and Spread of Nationalism.* London, New York: Verso.
BBC. 2005. Killing Fields deal sparks anger. Available at http://news.bbc.co.uk/1/hi/world/asia-pacific/4415873.stm. Last accessed 23 September 2016.
Bernath, J. 2015. 'Complex political victims' in the aftermath of mass atrocity: Reflections on the Khmer Rouge Tribunal in Cambodia. *International Journal of Transitional Justice, 10* (1), 46–66.
Chouléan, A. 1988. The place of animism within popular Buddhism in Cambodia: The example of the monastery. *Asian Folklore Studies, 47* (1): 35–41.
Cohen, S. 2001. *States of Denial: Knowing about Atrocities and Suffering.* Cambridge, UK: Polity. Malden, MA: Blackwell.
Connerton, P. 2009. *How Modernity Forgets.* Cambridge: Cambridge University Press.
Douglas, M. 1991. *Purity and Danger: An Analysis of the Concepts of Pollution and Taboo.* London: Routledge.

Gillis, J. R. 1994. *Commemorations: The Politics of National Identity*. Princeton, NJ: Princeton University Press.

Gottesman, E. R. 2003. *Cambodia after the Khmer Rouge: Inside The Politics Of Nation Building*. New Haven: Yale University Press.

Hobsbawm, E. J. and Ranger, T. O. 1983. *The Invention of Tradition*. Cambridge: Cambridge University Press.

Hughes, R. 2000. Remembering May 20 Day of Anger. *Searching for the Truth*. 12. The Documentation Center of Cambodia.

Hughes, R. 2003. The abject artefacts of memory: Photographs from Cambodia's genocide. *Media, Culture & Society*, *25* (1): 23–44.

Hughes, R. 2005. Memory and sovereignty in post-1979 Cambodia: Choeung Ek and local genocide memorials. In *Genocide in Cambodia and Rwanda: New Perspectives*. S. Cook (ed). New Haven, CT: Yale University Center for International and Area Studies.

Kent, A. 2007. Purchasing power and pagodas: The Sīma monastic boundary and consumer politics in Cambodia. *Journal of Southeast Asian Studies*, *38* (2): 335–354.

Ledgerwood, J. 1997. The Cambodian Tuol Sleng Museum of Genocidal Crimes: National Narrative. *Museum Anthropology*, *21* (1): 82–98.

Lennon, J. and Foley, M. 2000. *Dark Tourism*. London: Continuum.

Lloyd, D. W. 1998. *Battlefield Tourism: Pilgrimage and the Commemoration of the Great War in Britain, Australia and Canada, 1919–1939*. Oxford, New York: Berg.

Marston, J. 2006. Death, memory and building: The non-cremation of a Cambodian monk. *Journal of Southeast Asian Studies*, *37* (3): 491.

Mayo, J. M. 1988. War memorials as political memory. *Geographical Review*, *78* (1): 62–75.

Olick, J. K. 2007. *The Politics of Regret: On Collective Memory and Historical Responsibility*. New York, London: Routledge.

Sreinith, T. 2011. Day of commemoration and education. *Phnom Penh Post*. Phnom Penh, Cambodia, Wednesday, 25 May.

Springer, S. 2009. Culture of violence or violent Orientalism? Neoliberalisation and imagining the 'savage other' in post-transitional Cambodia. *Transactions of the Institute of British Geographers*, *34* (3): 305–319.

Springer, S. 2011. Articulated neoliberalism: the specificity of patronage, kleptocracy, and violence in Cambodia's neoliberalization. *Environment and Planning*, *43* (11): 2554.

Sturken, M. 2007. *Tourists of History: Memory, Kitsch, and Consumerism from Oklahoma City to Ground Zero*. Durham, NC: Duke University Press.

Williams, P. H. 2007. *Memorial Museums: The Global Rush to Commemorate Atrocities*. Oxford, New York: Berg.

9 Remembering the Khmer Rouge Tribunal

Public statements and commentary about the Extraordinary Chambers in the Courts of Cambodia (ECCC) have tended to be polarised. On the one hand, government spokesmen and UN staff have – publicly – heralded the ECCC as a success. On the other, the ECCC has been written off in many quarters before it has finished. In 2014, *TIME* magazine labelled the process a "shocking failure," citing overall costs, corruption and the relatively limited scope of prosecutions.[1] In 2012, Theary Seng, a long-serving human-rights activist, lawyer and, for a period, Civil Party member, condemned the court as a "manipulation of victims" and "exploitation of suffering," suggesting that Duch had been made a scapegoat for the Khmer Rouge years, noting the "imbroglio" of Cases 003 and 004 and claiming that the ECCC would undermine any benefits to the "rule of law" that the wider donor community sought to inculcate.[2] Brad Adams, Asia director of Human Rights Watch, has suggested that Hun Sen has used the court in a way that "appears that he is covering up for his own actions in the Khmer Rouge or those of senior colleagues in his party."[3] Even in 2006, academic writers such as Bowman had suggested that the tribunal was "not worth the wait," again condemning the "troubling" ability of Hun Sen to protect "former Khmer Rouge serving in his government" (2006: 80). These are all undoubtedly appeals made in good faith for 'more' and 'better' justice. But they also pose important and outstanding questions. Given that specific victim constituencies have invested expectations in the ECCC process – while others have, of course, been disappointed by its outcomes to date – it remains that the tone of some of the criticism that unconditionally denounces the court, or situates it as 'second rate', could be articulated with greater care. In the wider life cycle of the ECCC, for constituent groups to be solicited into a process, promised 'justice' and then told that their participation was part of a flawed or 'sham' tribunal is troubling. It is unclear whether critics have considered what the language of these condemnations mean to those people that genuinely believe in the outcomes of the process so far.

I am not here suggesting that the ECCC has not been procedurally flawed. Ciorciari and Heindel, for example, offering a more measured critique and qualifying the importance of the headline verdicts, have suggested that the ECCC hybrid make up, being exposed to domestic interference – but also technically inefficient in structure – is not a model for repeating. Neither am I suggesting that political interference has not shaped the work of the court. There is no doubt that critics are right when they point to Cambodian People's Party (CPP) influence over the judicial process. But one strand of the argument that I have tried to develop in this book is that this is a narrow and – if contextualised properly – peculiar ledger against which to judge the court, given the raft of questions and challenges that transitional justice efforts in Cambodia might present. This is especially so given that the *politics* of the ECCC extend far beyond the apparent debasement of legal process; the ECCC was born of a very specific political history. This is also notwithstanding that the relationships Cambodian communities are invited into with memories of political violence under the auspices of the ECCC can be mediated in varied ways, with *political* consequences, particularly in the myriad of initiatives that complement and support of the court. Indeed, I have tried to paint a picture that shows, far from exhaustively, that Cambodian communities variously stand in a more complex set of relationships to the different fields that lay claim over and reproduce memory, whether these are legal, therapeutic, religious, political, commercial or otherwise.

My goal in doing this – first and foremost – has been to show that in its current form and delivery, the ECCC should not have been presented (publicly) or conceptualised (academically) as able – on any terms – to offer a singular relationship to and resolution of Cambodia's experiences of atrocities, a tendency captured in the ECCC slogan "moving forward through justice." As McAdams suggests, this is the wider "illusion" of resolution that haunts but authorises transitional justice (2011). The ECCC would always disappoint on these terms. More importantly, far greater attention needs to be afforded to the different ways that Cambodians have negotiated the meaning of memories of political violence, whether through grief, loss, anger, resilience, ambivalence and even opportunity. These include lenses that are not indigenous to the transitional justice 'toolkit', which the field seems poorly equipped to *see* and accommodate. This is a lesson for the wider landscape of transitional justice, disentangling the heterogeneity of constituencies that are often bracketed within oversimplified and flattened categorisations that cannot capture experiences of multiple periods and forms of suffering, and I make this claim as a provocation to the field rather than on the basis of a definitive account of those experiences, meanings and relationships that stand 'outside' transitional justice. In this concluding chapter, I offer some final reflections on transitional justice and memory in Cambodia, at the ECCC and beyond, while flagging implications for the wider fields, and some potential questions around which further research could contribute beyond the confines of my limited analysis here.

The politics of transitional justice in Cambodia

The ECCC has been continuously attacked because of the risk, threat and influence from Cambodian political stakeholders. Indeed, Amnesty International and Human Rights Watch – key authorities within human rights and transitional justice – have, at different stages of the life of the ECCC, asked the United Nations (UN) to withdraw from the court based on the potential for the Cambodian government to interfere with the process. The ECCC, now reaching the end of its life cycle, is cast as a blemish on the record of the UN because it has been seen as *overtly* politically shaped. Political interference, in this sense, is implicitly cast as a taint or contaminant within an otherwise 'pure' and neutral judicial process. The architecture of these objections is instructive about transitional justice, especially its now prevailing *legalism*, and about human rights as discursive and institutional configurations more broadly. As Wendy Brown has powerfully argued, the modern human-rights project is a principally liberal in character – an order that is the normative fulcrum of transitional justice practice – and is discursively authorised as a form of "anti-politics" (2004). In other words, human-rights interventions, enveloping transitional justice as an institutional field, are legitimate in the way that they *must* deny that they have a politics at all, self-authorised as the expression of apparently transcendental and apolitical imperatives, or the technical dispensation of policy optimisation. In its birth and growth, the human-rights project was principally defined *against* states (Moyn 2010); transitional justice, in convergence here, was born as a field that was discursively oriented to the reordering, disciplining and renewal of *states* as repositories of 'interior' and international social order, and this orientation haunts the field despite increasing scrutiny of non-state actors within its remit. This thumbnail sketch is intended to flag, once again, the grammatical underpinnings of transitional justice as a field of expertise because it obviates preferences for who should and should not steward transitional justice interventions (legitimated external supervision) and to whom they are directed (the subordination of states to legal, political and social regulation in the name of human rights). It also necessitates that transitional justice interventions, especially legal ones, entail a visible distancing and delineation of fields of human rights *as law* against politics *as such*, which must be publicly and performatively distinct in the implementation of any justice initiative. The argument arising here is not that the Cambodian state should have had prerogative over processes of accountability and redress. Rather, my point is simply that the condemnations of political interference at the ECCC can be read as a predictable feature of transitional justice as such, because 'national' interests in the process were inevitably cast in opposition to the will and dispensation of apparently apolitical human-rights imperatives or the depoliticised execution of technical policy.

The risk of presenting a one-sided appraisal of the underpinning politics of transitional justice broadly or the politics of the ECCC in Cambodia is great here. It is worth noting why and how the Cambodian government have benefitted from the ECCC. In instigating and enacting the ECCC, the CPP sought Cambodia's re-inscription within an international order that affords political capital through spectacles of accountability in the name of human rights. In requesting UN assistance, the CPP were appropriating a marker of 'democratisation' and human rights that carried great currency within, then, their key donor communities. Indeed, as Loyle and Davenport point out, it is entirely possible for states to utilise the mechanisms of transitional justice with no interest in enacting the beneficial outcomes that are thought follow from them (e.g. truth, healing or democracy), noting forms of transitional 'injustice' (2016).Today, the Cambodian government are less reliant on Western donor stakeholders, but the weight of international and domestic investment in the ECCC – financial and political – ensures that its creators cast the process as a success story. One key consequence of the more sanguine presentations of the ECCC verdicts, and an effect of the ECCC process itself, is that this serves to 'maintain a status quo' that conceals Cambodia's politically pliant judiciary and distracts from a domestic landscape that is rife with basic violations of human rights (Coughlan *et al.* 2012). Indeed, I write these final reflections in the summer of 2016, which was marked by the suspected political assassination of an outspoken government critic, Kem Ley, and the increasing use of defamation laws and harassment against members of the human-rights community and political opposition. At the same time, while the ECCC has certainly not improved the human-rights situation in Cambodia (Ainley 2014), part of my argument in this book has been to query whether such problems are, self-evidently, a product of – or 'aetiologically' connected to – failures to prosecute Khmer Rouge figures faster or in greater number. Specifically, I have tried to argue that legacies of conflict do not have *one* determinant relationship to social and political orders of the present.

If we accept that the ECCC contributes to the maintenance of a political status quo domestically, what other 'status quos' might it buttress and sustain? Let us remind ourselves that accountability for the crimes of Democratic Kampuchea was animated, recognised and articulated as a principally *legal* problem within the 1990s, driven by shifts in the positions of powerful states like the United States (US) and the hard graft of organisations such as the Documentation Centre of Cambodia (DC-Cam) in collecting, archiving and mapping evidence to prefigure prosecutions. We should also be reminded that the specific framing of the problem of accountability at that time was narrowed. Demands for justice, truth and reconciliation are, in each instance, contingent appeals for memory, meaning specific things in different cases – different even within the same milieus – and derived from and furnished by differing political histories. The *possibility* of accountability and justice in Cambodia, as such, was co-extensively shaped by both the CPP's domestic insistence on narrow prosecutions focused on the Khmer Rouge leadership *and* vested international interests that sought to preclude scrutiny from the serious human-rights abuses, conflicts and alleged crimes against humanity perpetrated in Cambodia before and after the Khmer Rouge years. Those state leaders and their staff that directed, decided or sustained the perpetration of violence in Cambodia – variously before and after Democratic Kampuchea – will likely never be held accountable. In the first instance, it is therefore unsurprising that defence teams at the ECCC reach for these histories to attempt to rupture the normative coherence and moral legitimacy of the accounts of the past that the ECCC seeks to prosecute. We are reminded of Gregory Stanton's forceful reminder that *some* justice is better than no justice,[4] but we are equally obliged to acknowledge that the ECCC reflects regimes of international impunity as much as it embodies domestic ones. The point here, simply, is that when we recognise the value of moral and legal compromise over purism, the conversation should not stop, no matter which disciplinary orientation one might subscribe to.

Political constraints and influences that condition and enable different appeals for justice and accountability are not fixed and can change over time. It is to be welcomed that leading institutional actors within transitional justice such as the International Center for Transitional Justice (ICTJ) are now beginning to call for the recognition of and reparation for families of those that died as result of "US and Chinese policy actions" before, during and after Democratic Kampuchea,[5] offering a glimpse of the way that it is possible for a more critical and ambitious form of transitional justice to be reoriented to and against the most powerful states. The process of calling attention to a wider history of suffering in Cambodia before and after Democratic Kampuchea may be incremental. But I am reminded, more immediately and with some regret, of an ECCC-sponsored public forum in 2008, where an attempt by a resident to speak about the violence of US bombing raids in 1973 was silenced as too "political." Such statements and memories were unwelcome in ECCC circles at the time. This discrepancy, acknowledging suffering selectively, obliges us to rethink how we talk about – and what exactly we mean by – the politics of the ECCC.

Managing expectations

The ECCC has delivered concrete achievements. The headline verdicts against Duch in Case 001 and Khieu Samphan and Nuon Chea in Case 002/01, the anticipated recognition of genocide against minorities in Case 002/02, the opportunities for (some) Civil Parties to speak within the courtroom and the reparations directives that drew on the input of Civil Party stakeholders *are* important. I point this out more because Cambodian constituencies have been promised that they are significant as much as the intrinsic value of these verdicts and processes; they matter because people were told that they matter. At the same time, we must recognise the uneven responses to the verdicts. For some, these verdicts have been well received with satisfaction; for some, they have disappointed, frustrated, angered; and for others, they have meant little. While Cases 001 and Case 002/01 attracted widespread domestic and international media coverage, there is now a widespread recognition that, today, the ECCC has lapsed in importance within the wider public imagination. There are two issues that follow from this. Firstly, we are obliged to think through the question of expectation management over the whole life cycle of the court. Secondly, we need to pay closer consideration to the variety of meanings and responses that constituents of transitional justice attach to the mechanisms that address them.

Recent writing on the ECCC has pointed to the broad raft of outreach and public education initiatives the ECCC catalysed as one of the success stories that has followed from the court (Sperfeldt 2012; Ciorciari and Heindel 2014: 260). Outreach, as I explored in Chapters 6 and 7, was important for disseminating information about the ECCC, formally 'buying' communities into the court process through complainant and Civil Party applications while also often interweaving other techniques and strategies for thinking about the past, such as the examples of genocide education or trauma awareness that I have discussed. Yet wider patterns of outreach for the ECCC also followed a life cycle. International funding for much of the non-governmental organisation (NGO) – driven outreach began to dry up around 2010 (Ciorciari and Heindel 2014: 240); indeed, informants told me that the 'quality' of public education work decreased from the earlier phases when funding was abundant. It is not simply that less and poorer 'quality' outreach leads, necessarily, to less public engagement or failures of expectation management. As one NGO staff member pointed out, reflecting on their work in the early phases of the ECCC:

> back then there were NGO leaders who were very vocal. They had a big influence. The way they advocated, it was really powerful. It made it [the ECCC] bigger. They showed it was real. These were real judges, real prosecutors. They drew a lot of attention. They made it real.[6]

In other words, in animating and calling attention to the ECCC project, civil society leaders acted as the moral entrepreneurs of the ECCC, sustaining and accelerating the 'wax' of the life cycle of the court. Specific personalities led (and still lead) organisations that attracted substantial funding and who themselves carried gravity, charisma and authority in speaking about and calling attention to both the ECCC and the past. That the public attention the ECCC attracts has waned is not simply a result of diminished funding – in that insufficient money is available to provide *enough* information about the court. Some civil society leaders were especially skilled at presenting and animating the need for the ECCC as a public issue; for a myriad of reasons – one of which is international financial support for Cambodian NGOs – their places and roles within this process have changed or receded, which has coincided with (rather than determined) the diminished glow which surrounded the early work of the court.

The recognition that civil society leaders played an important role in presenting – even dramatising – the ECCC presents a converse problem. The early evangelism among some civil society leaders for the ECCC seems also to reflect the problem of over-promising outcomes the ECCC could deliver, specifically through *a language* that will invariably disappoint the people it is intended to benefit. One informant who had worked at an NGO leading outreach exercises told me a story:

> There was a man who was a member of a Civil Party association, we gave him hope. We gave him belief. He kept calling me and asking about the hearing. 'What date will the trial be? Who will be on trial?' Then he started to complain about money to travel and that sort of thing. Then, I got a call and he said 'I just heard Khieu Samphan… I want to make a bomb and kill him!' This wasn't healing or reconciliation. We gave them a lot of hope; we gave ourselves a lot of hope… And I still get calls from court staff asking for the telephone numbers of [other] applicants I first spoke to six, seven, eight years ago. We lost some people. We left them behind.[7]

Here we see the challenges of transitional justice implicated across its scales and scope. Frustrations with the legal and procedural process do not arise because the public does not understand the legal process (few, including the author, do, and possibly not even the lawyers). These mechanisms are monstrously complex, costly and slow (indeed, the informant noted how difficult it was to explain and rationalise the sheer sum of money spent on the ECCC to members of the public); people inevitably 'drop off the radar'; beneficiaries who are meant to be 'reconciled' or satisfied by transitional mechanisms can actually respond to them in ways contrary to their purpose; and the key agents who actively mediate and promote these mechanisms carry and reflexively wear the burdens of the vocabulary that they are obliged to work within. When transitional justice – as practice and scholarship – is thought through and freighted by a language of 'healing', 'reconciliation' or otherwise (truth, closure, justice, etc.), disappointment with its interventions will be endemic to rather than incidental to cases within the field.

Rethinking transitional justice and memory

One strand of my argument in this book has been an attempt to 'de-centre' and look beyond the core mechanism at play in the case at hand. Of course, as a caveat here, I have argued also that the ECCC jurisdiction offers contours that can contain and conceal specific politically inconvenient histories, and I recognise that there is a risk of presenting the ECCC as singular and determinant mechanism over memory. I have tried to remain sensitive to the heterogeneity of the institution itself, the way it is pulled in different directions by stakeholders within and beyond the court and has adapted its operations and offerings over the life of its work. Even as it 'contains' a story of past atrocity, the ECCC has been a palimpsest onto which different aims and outcomes, often nebulously framed, have been authored. What the ECCC is, what it does, why it works and for whom has been signalled in differing ways by different stakeholders, within and outside of the courtroom. Beyond the site of the ECCC – and one of the striking features of the ECCC project, which we might better examine in other cases and contexts – is the assemblage and raft of partnered and supporting organisational work that has supplemented the court, whether these be through public outreach activities – a celebrated feature of the ECCC process – and 'in-reach' consultation from stakeholders. These are not limited to the direction of legacy work or genocide education or through psychotherapeutic support and post-traumatic stress disorder (PTSD) awareness raising, but I have focused on these, firstly, because they invoke memory as a target of intervention explicitly; and secondly, because they gesture towards a landscape of work that is unfinished and unfolding that invites further analysis over the coming years. The presence and role of such assemblages implicate currents in transitional justice thinking that advocate for the implementation of 'holistic' models and approaches, whereby a deliberated mix of techniques are brought to bear on a case to deliver 'optimal' outcomes and benefits. But a different way of analysing this tendency is to think through how and why different approaches 'hang' together in the claims they make of the past, converging and diverging, while potentially opening *and* foreclosing different ways of remembering political violence.

In Chapter 6, I examined projects and techniques around trauma awareness and genocide education that explicitly invoke memory as an object of intervention and a site of transformation. My analysis here barely scratches the surface of the different projects at work in Cambodia today that have been mobilised in the name of ameliorating the present through confrontations with the past. However, two important and divergent issues are illuminated. Firstly, reconciliation is signified and called for on very different terms. Reconciliation – like other 'meta' aims of transitional justice – can mean different things even within the same milieus. Secondly, on one level, memory is always implicit in transitional justice, operating within the taken-for-granted knowledge of the field – constitutive of the generalised grammar or *savoir* of the domain (Foucault 2002: 200–202) – as a meta-language that furnishes the terminology for thinking about how and why *we must* 'confront' or 'come to terms with' past violence less it returns again to haunt us (Moon 2009). Such assumptions are taken for granted at the level of the population, whereby (principally national) collective stories are considered, confronted, redressed and purportedly renewed (Hamber and Wilson 2002; Moon 2007). Ineluctably connected to these wider assumptions, through and across institutional planes and layers, are operations at the level of granular detail, forms of work on the individual body, the psyche, and memory, be they through the textbook, testimonial or tick-box PTSD checklist. These techniques overtly rely upon and articulate memory as a site of practical expertise and knowledge, presenting memory as problem that is technical rather than political or ethical.

My argument is not oriented here to whether such programs are 'good' or 'bad', 'desirable' or not, 'optimal' or 'deficient'. The communities and constituents to whom they are addressed will respond to them in different ways, and I have deliberately eschewed an analysis oriented to 'efficacy' because the criteria of success or failure tend to be implicit within by the expertise and assumptions of each given programme at hand, and are themselves objects of my analysis, and are themselves objects of my analysis. Rather, my aim is to call cautionary attention to the way that such forms of intervention carry political consequences, even as they seemingly depoliticise fields of experience that are gravely sensitive. DC-Cam's genocide education programs oblige the memory of the Khmer Rouge in the name of reconciliation, especially elucidating the responsibility of the leadership of Democratic Kampuchea, converging at this point with the focus of the ECCC prosecutions (and coinciding with a longstanding politics of 'national reconciliation' that has been sponsored by the state). There is not a contradiction between recognising, on the one hand, that there is a need for more comprehensive genocide education and, on the other, recognising that standardised genocide education – delivered by teachers who may have survived the regime – can itself flatten and simplify complex experiences, or potentially prefigure the stigmatisation of those memories that deviate from its record. Similarly, as NGOs raise awareness about important trauma and mental-health issues, they invoke a medicalising lens through which people remember suffering and violence. Such medical frameworks have *political* consequences. As complex experiences are subsumed within the category of trauma, people are encouraged and invited to remember violence in new ways and against new registers, which might diverge from existing or accepted channels through which memory is reproduced. Moreover, as effects of medicalising memories of violence, the distinctions between different episodes of suffering are blurred, while specific moral economies of guilt and responsibility are elided as others are permitted, especially as the category of the 'lower-level' 'victim–perpetrator' is medically constituted in relief of the singular guilt of the Khmer Rouge leadership.

The point of these analytical exercises is not to provide a comprehensive account of the disparate initiatives that have been sponsored or have emerged in the context of the ECCC. I am not, of course, also arguing that they shouldn't be happening. What I do want to invite, here, is far greater attention to the way transitional justice projects, as disparate assemblages and broad rafts of techniques, *can* but don't *necessarily* work in concert with each other. In both the examples I examined, we see technical initiatives that seek to act on and shape memory that operate within a wider political regularity, that is, a moral economy that accedes to or promotes the responsibility of the Khmer Rouge leadership while eliding – or collapsing – finely poised questions of lower-level responsibility and wider historical experiences of violence. Here, reconciliation means different things: as a self-to-self integration of trauma or through the deterrent potential of education. But, fundamentally, a political exculpation of lower-level Khmer Rouge is permitted, showing that such programs are especially complementary to the work of the ECCC and the interests of the Cambodian government, even while they are not determined or driven by them. In this case, we see seemingly disparate techniques hang together in loose concert even while they seek and are justified in the name of very divergent aims. Thinking through such regularities – or their divergences – is important for appreciating how and why specific ways of acting on memory are more or less likely to happen in different contexts.

Remembering political violence

Transitional justice interventions – especially criminal trials – tend to produce accounts of the past through rigid sets of classifications. Past violence can be juridically coded and recognised within criminal categories; specifically differentiated and relational subjects are animated thereupon, especially the delineation of victims and perpetrators. Yet memory does not map or accede to neat or clean juridification. At public forums across Cambodia, I witnessed appeals for memory that are not recognised within formal accounts of past violence, anchored around the ECCC; or that present competing, counter claims about blame and responsibility. For example, calling for the prosecution of lower-level perpetrators, asking why other countries' actions are not sanctioned or even calling for *forgetting*. These are memory appeals that diverge from the principal moral and political engagement with the past at the ECCC that is *meant* to renew the polity. What are the implications of such claims?

In the first instance, memories are always reproduced in plural and varied ways. The process of rallying and inviting 'disaggregated' memories into shared social stories and histories will never be clean, especially as the repositioning of deeply felt personal memory might grate with what is being permitted or promoted collectively. These frictions are an inevitable process of the way that mechanisms such as the ECCC author and authorise specific accounts of the past that are necessarily partial. What is crucial, here, is that the reproduction and persistence of conflicting memories *can* have social and political implications for such projects. Reconciling around specific histories or accepting satisfaction from the prosecution of specific events and persons are processes that, to some degree, require an accommodation of the diversity of meanings attached to past violence. When these remain incongruous, accounts *cannot* be said to be 'settled', 'closed' or resolved. The defining teleology of transitional justice – Mutua's critical sketch of a two-step process of stabilisation and redress (2015) – is at stake here. Competing and diverse memories are not morally equivocal, but the process of acknowledging some while eliding others must be recognised as also politically encumbered. This is not an argument against transitional justice. Rather, greater recognition that consensual accounts of past violence are impossible obliges more measured language and terminology in justifying transitional interventions *in practice* and closer academic reflection on who and what is not included within every case.

A second implication is presented here that is relevant to studies of memory. If we are minded to remain shy, conceptually and empirically, of treating memories as 'pre-social', archival or as immutably inscribed within the repository of the psyche, we should note that it was at the points and nodes propagating the work of the ECCC that resistant and counter memories seemed to be foregrounded. We might, here, better appreciate how memory operates reflexively. In other words, memory claims are shaped in relation to one another and must be understood as constituted within the specific contexts and pressures within which they emerge. As Foucault's often-cited observation follows, where there is power there is resistance (1980); in this context, when the agents, technicians and moral entrepreneurs of transitional justice – and memorial sites that they seek recourse to – make demands to remember on specific terms, memory is called into being contingently and co-productively, and it is unlikely to correspond in completely neat acquiescence to those demands.

Beyond the tribunal

Beyond the ECCC, memories of political violence circulate and are reproduced through varied frameworks and within differentiated contexts. These are often detached from or ambivalent towards the forms of memorial cue – whether at memorial sites themselves or through invitations into different transitional justice initiative – that we would expect to anchor or nurture them. What this shows, I have argued, is that Cambodian communities continue to renegotiate varying relationships to memories of atrocity, often ambivalently or on registers that elide, jar with or are dislocated from the prevailing language of transitional justice and the normative injunction to remember at its heart.

Transitional justice has a tendency to rely on a specific set of representational tropes that locate its subjects as passive in their relationships to memories of violence, the political legacies of atrocity and, in some variations, the means through which redress can be delivered. As Cambodia has been variously cast as a beleaguered population[8] and a traumatised nation,[9] we see representational tropes – absolutely made in good faith – that powerfully buttress arguments for 'more' or 'better' transitional justice, but they do so at the expense of recognising the political agency of the people that they depict.

I have tried to argue that Cambodian communities stand in a more varied, complex and often ambivalent set of relationships to memories of political violence, especially as they encounter and respond to transitional justice techniques that seek to discipline particular ideas or means of thinking about legacies of atrocity. Transitional justice needs greater sensitivity to the variety of relationships people might and can establish with relationships of violence, recognising that *needs* are uneven and changing, and may not conform to the frameworks and assumptions of advocacy and, indeed, scholarship.

In Cambodia, as a sense grows that the ECCC life cycle is waning, we cannot know yet what the future legacy of the ECCC will be, how its place in Cambodian society will be authored and who by. We might persevere, still, and look further beyond the tribunal, with an open mind, to better understand the relationships with memories of war, atrocity and suffering that Cambodian communities actively shape in order to gauge this.

Notes

1 See "Cambodia's Khmer Rouge Trials are a Shocking Failure", *TIME*, 13 February 2014. Available at http://time.com/6997/cambodias-khmer-rouge-trials-are-a-shocking-failure/. Last accessed 23 September 2016.

2 See "KRT Sidesteps Victims' Rights", *Phnom Penh Post*, 9 February 2012. Available at http://www.phnompenhpost.com/national/krt-sidesteps-victims-rights. Last accessed 23 September 2016.

3 See "The World's Indifference Empowers Cambodia's Ruthless Despot", *Human Rights Watch*, January, 2014. Available at https://www.hrw.org/news/2015/01/14/worlds-indifference-empowers-cambodias-ruthless-despot. Last accessed 23 September 2016.

4 See Gregory Stanton's argument "Perfection is the Enemy of Justice". Available at http://www.genocidewatch.org/images/AboutGenPerfectionIsTheEnemyofJustice.pdf. Last accessed 23 September 2016.

5 See "After Guilty Verdicts in Khmer Rouge Tribunal, Wider Struggle for Accountability in Cambodia Continues". Available at https://www.ictj.org/news/verdict-khmer-rouge-tribunal-struggle-accountability-cambodia. Last accessed 23 September 2016.

6 Personal interview, Phnom Penh, March 2016.

7 Personal interview, Phnom Penh, March 2016.

8 Picken, M. "The Beleaguered Cambodians", *New York Review of Books*, 13 January 2011. Available at http://www.nybooks.com/articles/2011/01/13/beleaguered-cambodians/. Last accessed 23 September 2016.

9 "Second Trial May be Too Little Too Late for Traumatised Nation." The *Times*, 21 September 2010. Available at http://www.thetimes.co.uk/tto/news/world/agenda/article2734395.ece. Last accessed 23 September 2016.

References

Ainley, K. 2014. Justifying justice: Verdicts at the ECCC. *Justice in Conflict* (16 Sep 2014). Blog entry.

Bowman, H. D., 2006. Not worth the wait: Hun Sen, the UN, and the Khmer Rouge Tribunal. *UCLA Pacific Basin Law Journal*, 24: 51.

Brown, W. 2004. "The most we can hope for…": Human rights and the politics of fatalism. *The South Atlantic Quarterly*, *103* (2): 451–463.

Ciorciari, J. D. and Heindel, A. 2014. *Hybrid Justice: The Extraordinary Chambers in the Courts of Cambodia*. Ann Arbor, MI: University of Michigan Press.

Coughlan, J., Ghouse, S. and Smith, R. 2012. The legacy of the Khmer Rouge Tribunal: Maintaining the status quo of Cambodia's legal and judicial system. *Amsterdam LF*, *4*: 16.

Foucault, M. and Gordon, C. 1980. *Power-Knowledge: Selected Interviews and Other Writings, 1972–1977*. Brighton: Harvester Press.

Foucault, M. 2002. *Archaeology of Knowledge*. London, New York: Routledge.

Hamber, B. and Wilson R. A. 2002. Symbolic closure through memory, reparation and revenge in post-conflict societies. *Journal of Human Rights*, *1* (1): 35–53.

Loyle, C. E. and Davenport, C. 2016. Transitional injustice: Subverting justice in transition and postconflict societies. *Journal of Human Rights*, *15* (1): 126–149.

McAdams, A. J. 2011. Transitional justice: The issue that won't go away. *International Journal of Transitional Justice*, *5* (2): 304–312.

Moon, C. 2007. States of acknowledgement: The politics of memory, apology, and therapy. In *Crime, Social Control and Human Rights: From Moral Panics to States of Denial, Essays in Honour of Stanley Cohen*. P. Downes, C. Rock, C. Chinkin, C. Gearty (eds). Devon, UK: Willan Publishing.

Moon, C. 2009. Healing past violence: Traumatic assumptions and therapeutic interventions in war and reconciliation. *Journal of Human Rights*, *8* (1): 71–91.

Moyn, S. 2010. *The Last Utopia*. Cambridge: Harvard University Press.

Mutua, M. 2015. What is the future of transitional justice? *International Journal of Transitional Justice*, *9* (1): 1–9.

Sperfeldt, C. 2012. Cambodian civil society and the Khmer Rouge Tribunal. *International Journal of Transitional Justice*, *6* (1): 149–160.

Index

For Product Safety Concerns and Information please contact our EU
representative GPSR@taylorandfrancis.com
Taylor & Francis Verlag GmbH, Kaufingerstraße 24, 80331 München, Germany

www.ingramcontent.com/pod-product-compliance
Ingram Content Group UK Ltd.
Pitfield, Milton Keynes, MK11 3LW, UK
UKHW022124190926
475702UK00013B/1635